CASES
IN
MARKETING

RICHARD R. STILL

Professor of Marketing and Business Policy
College of Business Administration
University of Georgia

CLYDE E. HARRIS, JR.

Associate Professor of Marketing
College of Business Administration
University of Georgia

CASES
IN
MARKETING

Decisions, Policies, Strategies

PRENTICE-HALL, INC., Englewood Cliffs, New Jersey

ISBN: 0-13-118877-1

Library of Congress Catalog Card Number: 75-38411

Printed in the United States of America

10 9 8 7 6 5 4 3 2

PRENTICE-HALL INTERNATIONAL, INC., *London*
PRENTICE-HALL OF AUSTRALIA, PTY. LTD., *Sydney*
PRENTICE-HALL OF CANADA, LTD., *Toronto*
PRENTICE-HALL OF INDIA PRIVATE LIMITED, *New Delhi*
PRENTICE-HALL OF JAPAN, INC., *Tokyo*

DEDICATION

In token recognition of significant contributions made to its development, we dedicate this collection of cases to the following former students:

James M. Allen	Michael J. Kaplan
Brian P. Asher	Jerome Keave
Robert R. Baldwin	Larry Knox
Norman Baumer	Junichi Kobe
Edward M. Blackmer	Thomas D. Kohr
Joe J. Breedlove	Robert W. Krueger
John H. Breedlove	Howard Litrack
Michael V. Brisko	Chao-mu Liu
Jack R. Byrd	R. B. Melikian
Christopher B. Chapman	Patrick Monaco
J. Trevor Davies	Jaime A. Mosqubea
James J. Davis	William L. Moss, II
Clyde B. Dobson, Jr.	Harold Motes
Lawrence Dolin	James Pruitt
John M. Donnelly	Sheilah Ragan
Rowan Evans	Brad Redd
James H. Gash	Bengt Rosendahl
Lawrence J. Geary	Richard J. Rozanc
Joseph B. Gellert	Kenneth Saitz
Gary P. Gibson	Gerald H. Saltman
Michael Goldman	Robert Stell
Jonathan N. Goodrich	Floyd T. Taylor, III
Britton L. Gordon, Jr.	John Tracy
Michael Graziade	Kenneth R. West
Thomas L. Havill	Terry Williamson
Henry B. Helin	John H. Wimberly
Roger R. Hinchliffe	Robert M. Woodard
John R. Hulse	Ernest Young
	Jimmy Young

CONTENTS

4   *MARKETING CHANNELS*

5   *PROMOTION*

6 PRICING

7 MARKETING RESEARCH

8 LEGISLATION

PREFACE

Increasing sophistication in marketing instruction sharpens the need for materials capable of bridging the gap between generalized textual explanations and the specific problems confronting today's businessmen. While basic marketing concepts change rather slowly — some hardly at all — marketing situations requiring managerial analysis and decision in the "real world" exhibit endless change, even though certain fundamental problems persist. The case method provides a highly appropriate way to tie theory to practice, forcing the student to apply what he has learned in the classroom to practical problem-solving situations. Some years ago, Professor Charles I. Gragg of the Harvard Business School, used the following limerick to describe what might happen to business students without the benefit of cases:

> A student of business with tact
> Absorbed many answers he lacked.
> But acquiring a job,
> He said with a sob,
> "How *does* one fit answer to fact?"[1]

None of the 77 cases in this collection has previously been published. However, mimeographed versions of them all have been classroom-tested at the University of Georgia. The major features of this collection are:

1. The eleven sections into which the cases have been organized represent the main areas of marketing, as implied by the coverage of most marketing texts.
2. The total collection contains 47 consumer marketing cases, 24 industrial marketing cases, 4 involving the marketing of services,

---

[1] See "Because Wisdom Can't Be Told," in M. P. McNair, ed., *The Case Method at the Harvard Business School* (New York: McGraw-Hill Book Company, Inc., 1954), p. 11.

and two concerned with agribusiness situations. While U.S. cases predominate, five cases involve international marketing and domestic marketing overseas.

3. Most of the cases are concise and clear-cut, emphasizing some particular type of marketing decision, but a few longer and more complex cases require students to evaluate and/or formulate overall marketing strategy.

4. Some cases relate to the "newer" areas of marketing concern, such as those involving marketing to minority groups and franchised distribution.

5. Each case provides students with opportunities to apply what they have learned, or are learning, elsewhere to a "real world" situation.

Numerous people made important contributions to this book. We greatly appreciate the cooperation of the many executives who provided raw material for the cases. We especially thank our graduate students, not only at the University of Georgia but at Syracuse and Cornell Universities, who helped us collect and write these cases; explicit, though admittedly inadequate, recognition of this group's assistance is contained in this book's dedication. Particular acknowledgement also goes to Dr. Robert E. Tritt of the University of Georgia who helped in the early development of the manuscript. Dr. H. Lee Mathews of Pennsylvania State University provided helpful criticism and advice on the entire manuscript.

Especially helpful in preparing the manuscript for publication were Ernest W. Smith, assistant director, University of Georgia, Division of Research, and Mrs. Helen Freeman, Mrs. Beverly Swofford, and Miss Shaune Kelly, who did all the typing.

Among the many Prentice-Hall personnel who provided help, encouragement, and advice were: Chester C. Lucido, Jr., Marketing Editor, and Shirley Covington of the College Book Editorial-Production Department. Our wives, Mary C. Still and Billie Harris, as always, provided sympathetic understanding and encouragement. For all this assistance — both that acknowledged above, as well as that received from other colleagues, past and present students, and friends — we express our sincere thanks.

RICHARD R. STILL
CLYDE E. HARRIS, JR.

SECTION 1

NATURE AND SCOPE

STEUBEN GLASS DIVISION, CORNING GLASS WORKS

Producer of Artistic Glass— Marketing Program

Steuben Glass was one of eight operating divisions contributing to Corning Glass Works' 1966 consolidated sales of $444 million. Steuben's product line was aimed toward the consumer market and consisted of (1) art glass, that is, decorative nonfunctional exhibition crystal, and (2) stock glass with a utilitarian function, for example, bowls, stemware, and ashtrays. Steuben focused its marketing efforts on the population segment that constituted the top 1 percent in terms of disposable income. All Steubenware was handmade by 182 artisans at the Corning Glass Center Steuben Factory in Corning, New York. Because of the limited production capabilities of the artisans, management faced the problem of reducing the number of sales outlets. The artisans used basically the identical "offhand" process as set forth by the twelfth-century monk Theophilus. Management desired to increase dollar sales without increasing unit sales, both by emphasizing the "top of the line" and by aiming at the "in-between" markets. Items intended for sale to the in-between markets generally retailed for around six hundred dollars.

In 1903 Frederick Carder, an English glassmaker, established the Steuben Glass Works at Corning. His plan was to produce art glass in a broad variety of shapes and colors for universal consumption. In 1918 World War I produced additional demands for technical glass, and this caused Corning Glass Works to acquire the company and to rename it the "Steuben Division." In 1933, plagued by Steuben's poor financial record and its inept attempt at producing art glass, Arthur A. Houghton, Jr., grandson of Corning's founder, assumed leadership of the division. Inspired by a newly developed formula that yielded crystal glass of matchless purity, Houghton embarked on a venture to produce crystal glass conforming to the highest standards of design, quality, and workmanship. From that time on, the name Steuben became synonymous with high-quality materials, craftsmanship, and design in glass.

Steuben accounted for an estimated 25 percent of the market for artistic glass and outsold all other art glasses. Ninety percent of its sales were purchases intended for gifts (50 percent wedding gifts, 25 percent Christmas gifts, and 25 percent miscellaneous). Steuben competed with other domestic manufacturers of gift media, such as silverware, jewelry, and artcrafts, and with high-quality imported artistic glass items produced by Baccarat, Lalique, and Daum (all of France) and by Orrefors (of Sweden). Specialty items created as gifts for heads of state were still another facet of Steuben operations.

Retail prices of Steuben products ranged from $17.50 for an ashtray to $28,500 for "The Myth of Adonis" (an oval casket composed of panels of engraved crystal mounted in an elaborately ornamented frame of gold, with a jewel-cut crystal finial). Because of limited production capacity, prices had risen 25 percent since 1964. Product gross margin varied from negative amounts on some utilitarian items to substantial amounts on many artistic items. Management followed an "open stock" policy; therefore, negative margin items continued to be produced, though on a limited basis. Increasing handicraft costs were offset by management's shift away from stock glass pieces through strategic changes in pricing and advertising and through frequent stockouts of low or negative margin items.

James A. Thurston, vice-president of sales for the Steuben Division, directed an organization of some fifty people including a manager of regional shops, a manager of the New York shop, a manager of sales services, a manager of the glass center shop, a manager of exhibition glass, a secretary, and from one to three sales personnel situated in each of twenty strategically located regional shops. (See Exhibit 1.) Divisional sales headquarters were in New York City, as was the company-owned and largest retail salesroom (employing eighteen salespeople).

Steuben salesrooms (Exhibit 2) were located in selected department stores and specialty shops. Specialty shops were defined as those handling a limited variety of high-quality gift items. Salesrooms were wholly owned by the local sponsoring store and were operated under a program designed by Steuben. Stores purchased stock glass outright but carried art glass items on a consignment arrangement.

EXHIBIT 1

Steuben Division Sales Organization — 1966

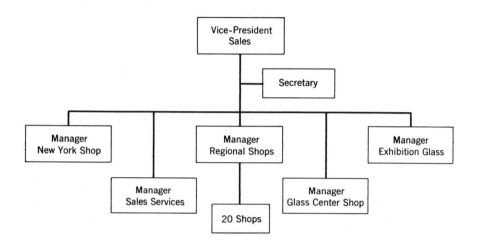

EXHIBIT 2

Steuben Glass Salesrooms

Store	*City*
Coleman E. Adler	New Orleans
Bullock's Wilshire	Los Angeles
J.E. Caldwell & Co.	Philadelphia
Marshall Field & Co.	Chicago
Frederick & Nelson	Seattle
Julius Garfinckel & Co.	Washington, D.C.
Gump's	San Francisco
The Halle Bros. Co.	Cleveland
Halls, Inc.	Kansas City
J.L. Hudson Co.	Minneapolis
Jaccard's	Clayton, Missouri
Jaccard's	St. Louis
Kaufmann's	Pittsburgh
ms, inc.	Providence
Neiman-Marcus	Dallas
Neiman-Marcus	Houston
Rich's	Atlanta
Shreve, Crump, & Low	Boston
Charles Warren Co.	Detroit
George Watts & Son	Milwaukee

The basis of selection for salesroom locations was a weighted quality index using per capita sales in the New York City salesroom as a base. The quality index was composed of inputs such as the number of people with incomes over one hundred thousand dollars, quality magazine circulations (e.g., *Harper's Bazaar* and *National Geographic*), and *Sales Management's* Index of Quality.[1] For example, the calculation for Cleveland, Ohio, would appear as follows:

$$\frac{\text{New York quality index}}{\text{Cleveland quality index}} = \frac{\text{New York per capita sales}}{X}$$

Solving for X yielded the Cleveland per capita sales. This dollar figure was multiplied by the Cleveland population and was then reduced by one-third (to compensate for the diversified line of products).

Sales personnel in Steuben Glass salesrooms were employed by the sponsoring stores but were subject to the approval of Steuben. Sponsoring stores were keenly aware of the Steuben image and sought to select sales personnel who would display the desired presence, poise, imagination, and appreciation for the mystique of Steuben as well as for the prospective customer's background. All new sales personnel went through a training period consisting of six weeks in a regional salesroom to acquire a feel for the merchandise, plus a seventh week divided between the Corning and the New York City salesrooms. In addition, each year all sales personnel attended a short but intensive sales retraining program at Corning.

Salesroom personnel were compensated according to one of two plans. About half were paid straight salaries, ranging from $3,025 to $9,300 according to the length of service. The other half received base salaries plus commissions averaging 2 percent of total "room sales." Room sales were the total sales of Steuben resulting from the combined efforts of each room's sales personnel. It was felt that the second plan helped to foster a spirit of teamwork and cooperation among room sales personnel.

Steuben capitalized on the Corning Glass Center's reputation as a national tourist attraction in promoting the display and sale of its products. In 1965, 851,349 visitors observed the making of Steuben products. Regional advertising was undertaken solely at the sponsoring store's expense. However, Steuben offered professional assistance in preparing advertising layouts and copy. Furthermore, Thurston personally kept in touch with all the salesrooms and worked on a first-name basis with the sponsoring stores' presidents.

The Steuben Division closely coordinated design, production, and pricing functions. Key personnel evaluated each design emanating from the design department to assure that it properly projected the Steuben image. Then

[1] A relative index contained in *Sales Management,* June 10, 1966.

production determined if it could make the item and, if so, at what cost. Pricing, however, was largely a subjective matter, one in which eye appeal strongly influenced the price finally determined. For example, if an item resembled one already in existence, management considered its "price relationship" as to size, workmanship, and eye appeal in setting the price. For art glass, salesrooms secured a 50 percent markup on the selling price, compared with an average 45 percent markup on art glass produced by other makers. For Steuben's "major ornamental" glass, salesrooms secured 40 percent markups, and for "exhibition" glass, 33 1/3 percent markups. However, because of the relatively small sales of the latter two types, the retail markup averaged 48 to 49 percent of selling price.

As sales vice-president, Thurston allocated 20 percent of his time to salesroom work and 40 percent to acting as manager of the New York City salesroom. Administrative responsibilities took up the other 40 percent of his time. In 1967 the sales forecast for the division included a 10 percent increase over the preceding year's sales, a matter of considerable concern to Thurston. With the limited number of artisans available to produce Steuben, he felt that the problem he faced was basically one of reducing the number of Steuben salesrooms without jeopardizing achievement of the sales goal.

Questions

1. Evaluate the appropriateness of Steuben's overall marketing strategy.

2. Should the number of sales outlets have been reduced?

3. What other alternatives should have been explored by Thurston?

1-2

MANHATTAN HANDBAGS, INC.

Handbag Manufacturer—Reorganizing Marketing after Merger

In 1957 Robert Jones and Jim Gallagher founded Manhattan Handbags, Inc., in New York to manufacture better-quality ladies' handbags. Initially, Gallagher managed the manufacturing operation, Jones handled sales and served as president, and the two men designed the products jointly. Later on, as the company grew, design and sales personnel were added. In 1967 the company faced several organizational problems tracing to its recent acquisition of the Ideal Handbag Company.

At its inception Manhattan made approximately 1,250 handbags per week, but by 1966 its production reached 2,000 per week. Dollar sales were $1.1 million in 1966, and management estimated a 1968 sales volume of $1.7 million. (See Exhibit 1.)

Manhattan sold its branded products direct to prestigious retail stores. When competitive accounts in cities where Manhattan already had distributors indicated an interest in handling the line, Manhattan sold them private labels. For example, in Chicago, Josette sold the Manhattan brand, whereas Carson Pirie Scott sold Manhattan-produced handbags under its own label. Seventeen large customers accounted for approximately 97 percent of Manhattan's 1966 sales. (See Exhibit 2.)

EXHIBIT 1

Manhattan Handbags Company Sales 1957-68

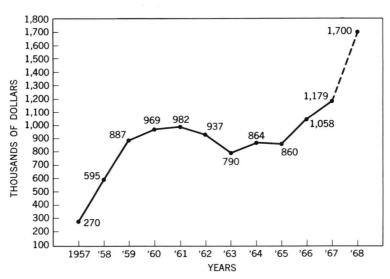

Notes:
1967 includes ideal sales.
1968 estimated sales forecast.
1963 decrease was mostly from one account.

Jones began expansion of his marketing organization in 1963 when he hired Barbara Smith, a young designer of handbags. Up until that time Manhattan was known primarily as an evening bag house with elegant taste. Customers were demanding additional bag styles, and Miss Smith worked toward expanding the product line to include the more fashionable bags. Before joining Manhattan, Miss Smith had attended a design school and had then served as an assistant designer for a competitor. Her duties at Manhattan included designing four major lines a year and style-and-color coordination. By 1967 she had become one of the industry's leading designers, providing Manhattan handbags with a high-fashion image.

Jones recognized that his duties and responsibilities as president kept him from providing the company with adequate sales coverage. He showed

EXHIBIT 2

Manhattan's Major Accounts 1966

Customer	Number of Stores	Location	Type of Buying	Approxi- mate Dollar Volume
Bullock's	6	Los Angeles and Suburbs	Decentralized	$ 330,000
Saks Fifth Avenue	22	New York and Nationwide	Centralized	180,000
Josette	7	Chicago and suburbs	Centralized	176,000
B. Altman & Co.	6	New York and suburbs	Centralized	72,000
Neiman-Marcus	6	Texas	Centralized	72,000
Label's	2	San Francisco and Seattle	Centralized	45,000
Samuel's		New York	Centralized	30,000
Joske's		Houston	Centralized	26,000
Jaffee's		Minneapolis	Centralized	22,000
Milgrim, Inc.	3	Cleveland and Detroit	Centralized	21,000
Sakowitz		Houston	Centralized	18,000
Garfinckel & Co.		Washington, D.C.	Centralized	13,000
Josette (Oak Brook)		Oak Brook, Ill.	Centralized	11,000
Carson Pirie Scott & Co.		Chicago	Centralized	11,000
Smith's		Philadelphia	Centralized	11,000
Gidding-Jenny		Cincinnati	Centralized	10,000
R.H. Stearn Co.		Boston	Centralized	10,000
Total				$1,058,000

particular concern for service and sales coverage in the West and Southwest, areas with great potential, and with this in mind, he hired Thomas Berle in February 1965.

Berle, age 28, was a graduate of a junior college. His previous experience included three years as an assistant handbag buyer in a major department store and five years as a handbag salesman on the West Coast. He was married, had no children, and enjoyed traveling. Jones hired Berle on the recommendation of buyers at Bullock's stores in Pasadena and San Fernando, both of whom knew him as a salesman.

Berle received a 10 percent commission on his sales plus a 5 percent commission on house accounts in his territory. Jones personally serviced *all* Manhattan house accounts, but some, such as Saks Fifth Avenue, operated stores in Berle's territory. Berle paid his own traveling expenses except for three trips a year to New York and one to the National Ladies Handbag Show in Chicago. Jones assigned Berle eleven accounts with an estimated 1965 sales potential totaling $265,000. (See Exhibit 3.)

EXHIBIT 3

Thomas Berle's Accounts 1965

1. Bullock's — San Fernando	6. Nordstrom Best — Seattle,
2. Bullock's — Pasadena	Nordstrom Best — Portland
3. Bullock's — Westwood	7. Joske's — Houston
4. Bullock's — Santa Ana	8. Krupp & Tuffly — Houston
5. Label's — San Francisco,	9. May — D & F — Denver
	10. Paul's — Fresno
	11. Hull's — Pasadena

THE ACQUISITION   By late 1966 Manhattan could produce two thousand handbags weekly at full capacity. At that time the company took over the Ideal Handbag Company and increased the production capability to four thousand bags weekly. With the expanded productive capacity, management's attention shifted increasingly to the sales organization.

Jerald Hametzstein had organized the Ideal Handbag Company with home offices and manufacturing facilities in Philadelphia in 1936. Ideal produced high-grade handbags; sales peaked at $2.5 million in 1950, and its seventy-five accounts were among the industry's best. However, after 1950 Ideal's sales gradually declined and at the time Manhattan acquired the company (April 1967) only twelve accounts remained. (See Exhibit 4.)

Management felt that the Ideal purchase strengthened its production capabilities, added a popular brand, extended its distribution, and provided several additional prestige accounts, such as Lord and Taylor and Bonwit Teller.

John Grant, a salesman for Ideal for twenty years, was asked to stay on by the new owners. Although Grant would retire in three years, he knew Ideal's accounts intimately, and Manhattan wished to retain as many of them as possible. Grant called upon all of Ideal's accounts except Lord and Taylor, which Jones classified as a house account. Grant visited his accounts four times a year and saw them twice a year at handbag shows. He received a $250 weekly salary and full reimbursement of expenses.

EXHIBIT 4

Ideal's Accounts at Acquisition

Account	Location	Sales Volume – 1966
1. Lord & Taylor	New York	300,000
2. J.W. Robinson	Los Angeles	92,000
3. Bonwit Teller	Philadelphia	53,000
4. Marshall Field	Chicago	38,000
5. J.L. Hudson	Detroit	20,000
6. Halle Bros. Co.	Cleveland	15,000
7. Frederick & Nelson	Seattle	15,000
8. Woodward & Lothrop	Washington, D.C.	14,000
9. Joske's	San Antonio	12,000
10. Joseph Horne	Pittsburgh	11,000
11. Titche-Goettinger	Dallas	12,000
12. Foley's	Houston	7,000

EXHIBIT 5

Thomas Berle's Performance Chart with Manhattan

Account	$ Volume Given to Berle 1964	Sales 1965	Sales 1966	Sales 1967
Bullock's				
San Fernando	33,739	84,300	75,480	65,940
Pasadena	43,421	70,350	68,010	47,475
Westwood	34,320	47,340	53,805	47,325
Santa Ana	7,680	41,550	58,935	26,370
Lakewood[a]		53,760	38,865	35,025
Del Amo[a]			33,285	26,370
Downtown[a]				26,280
Hull's	5,220	3,315	2,295	1,665
Joske's	16,785	11,430	23,070	15,645
Krupp & Tuffly	6,240	2,820	6,270	6,765
Label's	56,565	67,485	45,720	35,745
Nordstrom Best	15,630	10,110		
Sakowitz[a]		6,570	16,890	
May – D & F	22,980	15,030	6,525	6,000
Paul's	22,520	4,530		
Neiman-Marcus[a]		7,980	67,650	163,245
Total $ Sales	265,100	426,570	496,800	503,850

[a]Accounts opened by Thomas Berle.

In early 1968 Berle suggested to Jones that the territories be reorganized on a geographical basis. Jones sensed a need for territorial reorganization but was hesitant to act upon Berle's suggestion. He was not certain that Manhattan and Ideal brands could reach their full potential in any territory with one man servicing both groups of accounts. Although Berle increased his sales volume by more than $230,000 in three years, he had only limited success in securing new accounts. He had started with eleven accounts in 1964 and had only sixteen in 1967. (See Exhibit 5.) Because of this, Jones doubted that Berle could handle the Ideal accounts in his territory. He also doubted that any salesman in any territory could adequately handle both brands.

Questions

1. Should Jones have reorganized the sales organization along geographical lines?
2. What other organizational changes, if any, should have been made by Manhattan?

1-3

STAR MANUFACTURING COMPANY

Textile Manufacturing Company— Transition to Marketing Orientation

In July 1968 Star Manufacturing Company's board of directors reviewed the company's progress following changes made as the result of recommendations several years earlier by a management consulting firm. Many improvements had occurred, but some unforeseen problems had arisen and by 1968 additional changes appeared necessary. Although the consultants worked only in the marketing area, the changes resulting from their recommendations had a sweeping effect on the entire company.

Founded in 1879 Star was a product-oriented textile manufacturer, largely owner managed until the late 1950s. In 1968 it produced a broad line of finished and unfinished textiles in twenty-five mills in South Carolina; with eighty-five hundred workers, it was the state's third largest employer. Its mills represented fixed assets of $105 million and, with sales of $150 million, the company ranked nineteenth in the textile industry. It manufactured high-quality products and gave excellent delivery and service.

When the consultants arrived at Star in 1960 they found the company using outdated marketing and management methods. Most executives had read or had heard of the "marketing concept," but its implementation proved difficult and slow, as older managers concerned themselves primarily with manufacturing and accounting. One manager, referring to notes taken at a national management conference, came upon a "model (See Exhibit 1) and definition" of this concept:

"The marketing concept is defined as a managerial philosophy concerned with the mobilization, utilization, and control of total corporate effort for the purpose of helping consumers solve selected problems in ways compatible with planned enhancement of the profit position of the firm."[1]

In 1960 the company had just started production of synthetic fabrics; its main emphasis was on producing cotton and wool products. The consultants were retained when management became alarmed over a sharp decline in company sales – from $85 million in 1959 to $80 million in 1960. Management gave the consulting firm free rein in the marketing area they were to appraise, but the manufacturing, finance, and accounting areas were reserved for later study.

In 1960 the company was organized into three departments: finance-accounting, production, and sales. Each department head was a substantial stockholder and had been with the company for many years. The sales department received customers' orders and forwarded them to the production department, while finance-accounting took care of billing and collections. Market analysis was meager, product planning uncoordinated, promotion inadequate, and interdepartmental communication ineffective.

At the conclusion of their 1960 study the consultants made seven recommendations:

1. The vice-president of sales should be given an early retirement.

2. The sales department should be replaced with a sales and marketing department composed of four divisions: sales, technical services, marketing planning, and product management.

3. Marketing planning should survey the market constantly, recommend innovations, and coordinate long-range planning.

4. Technical services should coordinate market innovation with production and render technical sales advice.

5. Product managers should monitor their products, looking for new uses for old products, looking for new products, and recommending deletions from the product line.

6. The sales department should concentrate on enlarging sales in present markets while coordinating with the other three divisions.

7. The flow of communications should be increased among departments with emphasis on sales and product analysis.

[1] See R. L. King, "An Interpretation of the Marketing Concept," in S. J. Shaw and G. M. Gittinger, *Marketing in Business Management* (New York: The Macmillan Company, 1963), p. 38. (Also see Exhibit 1.)

E X H I B I T 1

Model of the Marketing Concept

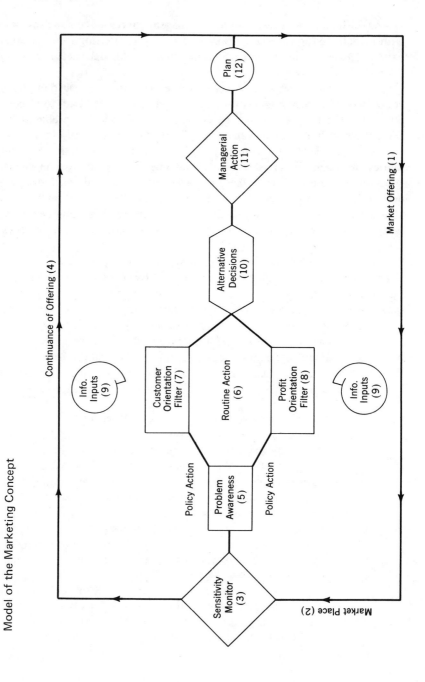

Star implemented most of these recommendations by 1964, and sales increases from 1961 to 1968 reflected improvements in technical service and market-product planning (see Exhibit 2).

EXHIBIT 2

Sales and Profits

Year	Sales (in millions)	Profit (in millions)	Profit as % of Sales
1960	$ 80	$4.8	6%
1961	74	3.7	5
1962	85	4.3	5
1963	88	4.4	5
1964	99	6.0	6
1965	104	8.3	8
1966	120	7.2	6
1967	130	4.0	3
1968	150	1.5	1

Minimal change took place in the sales organization; Star maintained six sales offices – four geographical and two located near large industrial customers. Thirty salesmen worked out of these offices; one-half of them calling upon specific customers. Star considered its salesmen among the best in the textile industry. Salesmen received annual salaries ranging from $8,000 to $14,000 and had liberal expense accounts. The sales job consisted of securing orders, servicing accounts, and proving Star's reliability and concern for the customer.

In 1960 Star sold exclusively to a small number of large retailers and manufacturers. Forty-five percent of its sales were to such retailing giants as Sears, Macy, Belk, Grant, Penney, Montgomery Ward, and Butler Brothers. Most of the remaining 55 percent were to large manufacturers, such as Goodyear and Firestone, with only a small amount going to the federal government.

Between 1960 and 1968 company sales nearly doubled as new products were put on the market. However, orders came in faster than anticipated, production lagged, and interdepartmental coordination proved inadequate. Marketing channels remained unchanged, but the sales mixture changed drastically with additions of new product lines (see Exhibit 3).

The 1960 product line had consisted of cordage and twine, semifinished cloth and fabric, sheets, pillowcases, and blankets. Little attention was paid to buyers' needs; products per se were emphasized. The product-manager concept recommended by the consulting firm resulted in the setting up

EXHIBIT 3

1968 Product Lines

Percentage of Sales	*33%* *Home Furnishings*	*27%* *Industrial Goods*

	Finished carpet yarn
	Finished scatter rug
	  yarn
	Unfinished rug yarn
	Fabric for:
	  Bedspreads
	  Upholstery
	  Drapery
	  Tablecloths
	Trimming yarn
	Mop yarn
		Tire cord
		Fabric for:
		  Belting
		  Auto upholstery
		  Auto convertible
		    tops
		  Shoe lining
		  Furniture
		  Waterproof shoes
		  Sandbags
		Cordage and twine for:
		  Fishing line and
		    nets
		  Tobacco processing
		  Post office wrapping
		Fire hose

Percentage of Sales	*13%* *Apparel*	*27%* *Consumer Products*

	Fabric for:
	  Women's skirting
	  Industrial uniforms
	Nomex—space program
	  and airlines
	  fireproof fabric
	Wool and synthetic
	  fabric
	For double knit
	  clothing
	Knitting yarn
		Sheets
		Pillowcases
		Blankets
		Bedspreads
		Carpets
		Scatter rugs

of five basic product areas: (1) floor covering, (2) rubber industry, (3) yarn, cordage, and twine, (4) cloth and fabric, and (5) consumer products. In 1968 overlapping of product lines and customers still existed; the result showed up in terms of ineffective coordination between the product managers and the sales force. While the product planning division had contributed significantly to the company's recent prosperity, other divisions of the sales and marketing department had difficulty keeping up with changing requirements.

Star management had never emphasized promotion in the company's marketing mix. In fact, Star's 1968 advertising budget of $450,000, three-tenths of one percent of sales, was the largest in its history. Most of the budget was spent on advertising in textile trade magazines directed toward retailers' and manufacturers' purchasing departments. Trade advertising themes emphasized dependability, quality, and service. A small amount of institutional advertising appeared in area newspapers.

Most orders were negotiated with purchasers as reorders and price were not a key sales factor for most Star products until late 1962. At that time the Kennedy administration lifted foreign quotas and reduced import tariffs, and American textile manufacturers met stiffer price competition. Star immediately cut some of its prices; however, so long as its prices remained within reasonable range of similar competing products, old customers continued to reorder. Rising domestic cotton prices hurt the sale of consumer items relative to their foreign competitors, but sales of the new synthetics helped somewhat to offset this. The price cuts, along with rising costs, were reflected in declining profit margins, but Star's swift pricing reaction to import competition and its continuing emphasis upon rapid delivery and good service were instrumental in keeping customers, particularly those who valued a supplier who could be relied upon to keep promises.

In some instances, rather than turn down an order from a good customer, Star filled rush orders by purchasing the items involved from other producers. Many times the company accepted small unprofitable orders from steady customers rather than have them go elsewhere. These practices irritated production executives who adhered to a policy of scheduling production in large enough quantities to minimize average unit costs. Accumulated inventory on hand at the close of 1967 had mounted to $30 million at cost. The sales and marketing vice-president was considering the possibility of using jobbers to "job out" the excess inventory at drastically reduced prices.

The board of directors believed that the company had successfully implemented the consultants' 1960 recommendations; however, the situation in 1968 indicated the need for further adjustments. Top executives believed that further changes were needed in the product management division, marketing channels, and promotional effort, as well as in the finance-accounting and production departments.

Questions

1. What kind of an organization did Star have in 1960? Why did it develop?

2. Could Star have implemented the marketing concept in 1960? How?

3. Evaluate each of the seven recommendations made by the consultants in 1960.

4. What were Star's most pressing problems in 1968?

1-4

SCIENTIFIC-ATLANTA, INC.

Electronics Firm—Problems in Growth and Diversification

Scientific-Atlanta, Inc., of Atlanta, Georgia, manufactured a wide variety of antenna test instruments, underwater sound instruments, microwave components, telemetry tracking systems, community antenna (CATV) systems, and cases, consoles and racks for electronic instruments. Sales volume totaled $12.7 million in 1967. Profits had grown each year during the company's fifteen years of operation. However, during 1968 sales declined 13 percent from the year before, and net profit fell 80 percent (Exhibit 1). This concerned top management, and it anticipated making some changes for 1969.

      Glen Robinson, president, together with a group of engineers from Georgia Tech started Scientific-Atlanta in a rented garage in 1952. The firm grew to be a world leader in its branch of electronics. Expansion and growth could be traced to innovative research and development (R & D) and to management's willingness to diversify into other fields. The company moved first to develop high frequency antennas for military applications, starting with a Navy R & D contract for a rapid scanning radar antenna. Thus, it early recognized the military's need for test equipment to measure the strength, direction, and

EXHIBIT 1

Scientific-Atlanta, Inc. Annual Operating Statement 1959-1968
(Thousands of Dollars)

Year	Net Sales	% Change	Net Profit	% Change
1959	$ 1,430	—	$ 71	—
1960	1,970	38	105	48
1961	2,247	14	130	23
1962	3,103	23	181	40
1963	4,044	17	187	3
1964	4,732	17	257	38
1965	7,720	52	376	46
1966	11,516	49	549	46
1967	12,717	10	591	8
1968	11,012	−13	118	−80

Source: Annual Report 1968.

pattern of signals transmitted or received by antennas. The company succeeded in developing an electronic instrument capable of automatically measuring and recording signal patterns transmitted from high frequency antennas.

After this initial success, Scientific-Atlanta scored further success in developing high frequency antennas and antenna test equipment and in manufacturing and selling standard items of electronic and precision mechanical test equipment, which customers used for designing and maintaining high frequency antennas. The company's high frequency antenna tracking systems were used in radar, satellite, and missile communications, and in radio astronomy, navigation, and other systems. The company also made and marketed test equipment for use in the design and maintenance of underwater sound systems for submarine detection, underwater navigation, and underseas mapping operations.

Through acquisitions, Scientific-Atlanta diversified into other product fields. In 1963 after acquiring Polyco, Inc., it began manufacturing plastic bottles for household detergents and other liquids. In 1964 having acquired Southern Tool and Machine Company, it continued Southern Tool's principal business of making precision machinery and parts for various industries. Southern's production capabilities included precision machine welding, heat treating, plating, casting, gear cutting, and assembly. In 1965 Scientific-Atlanta started to produce, on a limited basis, packaging systems for luncheon meats and similar food products. The packaging machine flushed air from semirigid, clear plastic containers, replaced it with an inert gas, and automatically sealed containers with printed lids. The machine sold for approximately ten thousand dollars. Other components in this system, sold by the company's packaging division, included both containers and lids specially designed for use with the machine. The company also made machines for packaging individual servings of jelly and similar food items (Exhibit 2).

In December 1966 Scientific-Atlanta sold Polyco, its plastic bottle manufacturing subsidiary. However, it continued serving the packaging market, introducing the Versapac packaging system in 1968. The Versapac machine incorporated several new features allowing for more efficient replacement of air with inert gases, production of a vacuum package, larger sizes and improved speeds. Scientific-Atlanta's management expected Versapac to strengthen its position in the meat-packaging field as well as enable prospective customers to utilize the system for other packaging applications.

EXHIBIT 2

Scientific-Atlanta, Inc. Dollar Sales Volume by Products (Thousands of Dollars)

Product	1965	1966	1967
Electronic and Related Products:			
Antenna & Related Test Equipment.	$3,781	$ 5,092	$ 6,962
Antennas & Tracking Pedestals . .	1,067	1,575	1,489
Others	194	751	1,138
Precision Machinery & Parts	390[a]	851	1,093
Packaging Machinery & Supplies . . .	80[b]	926	959
Plastic Bottles	1,708	2,321	1,076[c]
Total	$7,220	$11,516	$12,717

[a]Includes six months' operations following acquisition in late December, 1964.
[b]Initial development period following acquisition.
[c]Includes five months' operations prior to sale of Polyco in December, 1966.
Source: Offering Circular on Stock of Scientific-Atlanta, Inc. a pamphlet published by Robinson-Humphrey Co., Inc.

Concurrent with its acquisition program, the company began to direct more of its internal research and development effort into non-defense related areas. Projects were undertaken to add to the line of products serving the expanding CATV market. The company's telemetry tracking systems were adapted to meet the needs of the weather satellite program and the emerging satellite program for domestic and international communications. The company consolidated and expanded the manufacturing facilities for its line of OPTIMA cabinets and enclosures.

The company's electronic products and related equipment, including roughly 500 standard catalog items, were sold to approximately 700 customers by sales engineers located in eight states: California, Colorado, Georgia, Maryland, Massachusetts, New Jersey, Ohio, and Texas. Manufacturers' representatives distributed the company's electronic products and equipment in Europe, the Middle East, and the Far East. A subsidiary, set up in 1966, distributed the same products in non-United States Western Hemisphere markets, mainly to Canadian companies and government agencies. Export sales had grown steadily, and in 1964 the company had been awarded the President's "E" Award for Excellence in Export. By 1968 approximately 10 percent of the company's sales were to the export market.

Distribution strategies for the other lines were somewhat different. The packaging machinery and supplies were sold by a special sales force in the Southeastern United States and by manufacturers' representatives elsewhere. Precision machinery and parts manufactured under contract by Southern Tool were sold by the subsidiary's own general sales manager.

Either directly or indirectly, United States government agencies accounted for nearly 61 percent of Scientific-Atlanta's 1967 sales. The agencies could terminate contracts and orders at their convenience, leaving work unfinished. However, upon such terminations, the contractor normally was entitled to reimbursement for costs incurred plus "reasonable" profit allowances. The company had never experienced any significant contract terminations.

Scientific-Atlanta's business was highly competitive. It vied not only with several companies having substantially greater resources and wider product lines, but also with numerous small specialized producers. Management expected more intense competition in the future. The company pursued an extensive R & D program designed to strengthen and broaden present product lines and to develop new products compatible with existing efforts. During 1967 and 1968 the company invested about $300,000 and $400,000, respectively, in R & D. It also maintained a continuous program of trade advertising directed at its "highly skilled customers," who were engineers and scientists working on various technological frontiers, such as national defense, space exploration, and new commercial fields (Exhibit 3).

In 1968 the government sharply curtailed expenditures for the space program and for military research projects. Scientific-Atlanta's business with the government and with prime contractors was affected. The resulting sales and profit declines were the first in the company's history. In the fiscal 1968 annual report, Robinson outlined the steps the company was planning to deal with the business environment:

> *1.* A Commercial Communications Product Line has been created around the company's CATV products. Several of the company's talented microwave engineers have been assigned in order to

EXHIBIT 3

Typical Scientific-Atlanta Advertisement

make target acquisition more than a brief encounter
with a Scan-Coded Monopulse tracking system

This unique approach to automatic tracking combined with our time-proven pedestals, solid state servo, and feeds, results in a highly reliable system— the best investment for both general telemetry ranges and specialized data links.

Planning a Conversion? Send for our free Range Conversion Information Kit containing useful charts, nomographs, and engineering data. Write or call Mickey Hudspeth, Marketing Manager, Tracking Antenna Systems.

SCIENTIFIC-ATLANTA, INC.
Box 13654, Atlanta, Ga. 30324 Tel. 404-938-2930 TWX 810-766-4912
Sales and Engineering offices throughout the U.S.
Representatives in major cities throughout the world.

capture a part of the microwave communications market, which is expected to be one of the major expanding markets of the next decade.

2. The company plans to continue to make developments that will allow it to maintain its position of leadership in its areas of electronic specialization. These areas are considered basic to the expanding technological world of today. Funds for meeting the complex antenna and hydrophone research and calibration needs will only be temporarily withheld.

3. The manufacturing capability for our line of OPTIMA cabinets and enclosures has been consolidated to realize the economies and competitive advantages of high volume production.

4. The new Versapac packaging system will be pushed in the meat packaging field and for other packaging applications that can benefit from the new packaging concept.

5. The company is discontinuing its solid-state component business which had not reached a profitable level of operations.

Questions

1. What marketing problems generally are encountered by companies that deal mainly with one large customer such as the Federal Government?

2. What marketing problems should have been anticipated by Scientific-Atlanta's management when it decided to follow a diversification strategy?

SECTION 2

BUYER BEHAVIOR

BURBANKS' DEPARTMENT STORE

Retailer—Trading Up
in the Shoe Department

Burbanks' Department Store, founded in 1914, grew from a small one-store operation to an organization with twenty-one branches and gross sales of $130 million in 1968. It began in a midwestern city as a low-price retailer, dealing in unbranded apparel and catering to the lower-income market segment. In 1958 management decided to "trade up" the operation so as to appeal to middle- and high-income market segments. This move was accomplished successfully throughout the entire organization, except in the shoe department. In 1968 Burbanks' shoe offerings were still essentially a low-priced "table operation."

Shoe buying was centralized, with individual stores submitting orders to the main buying office. Shoes were purchased from three major suppliers. Consolidated orders were placed with suppliers in order to obtain maximum purchase discounts, but shipments were made direct to individual stores.

When the first attempt was made to trade up the shoe operation, a shoe merchandise manager was hired away from a large competing store. Management hoped he would move away from the table operation; however, he continued previous merchandising practices and the featuring of low-price lines. Under his direction, sales volume rose for about the first six months but then leveled off and began declining. Top management became alarmed, fired the man, and decided to make another attempt to upgrade the operation.

Executives recruited a second man, Shep Henenfeld, who had had sixteen years of retail shoe experience in New York. Top management, remaining resolute in its determination to trade up in shoes, impressed Henenfeld with this goal and made him responsible for attaining it. Henenfeld was convinced that sufficient demand existed for higher-fashion shoes and believed that it could be stimulated profitably through improved advertising, in-store displays, better salesmanship, and modern merchandising techniques.

Top department stores (such as Marshall Field, Carson Pirie Scott, and Mandel Brothers) provided keen competition in the market areas where Burbanks' had stores. Leading national shoe stores (such as McConner and Goldberg, Chandler's, Kitty Kelly, and A. S. Beck) also operated in these areas. Henenfeld soon learned that competitors carried most of the good national brands, on some of which they had exclusives.

Subsequently, Henenfeld outlined his trading-up program for shoes to top management. He made six major recommendations: (1) exclusive rights should be sought for certain national brands — as an early compromise, he suggested accepting some "dual distribution" situations (sharing a national brand with other retailers); (2) classifications and definite price lines should be established; (3) sales volume should be maintained at the present level while building up inventory in missing merchandise classifications; (4) department managers, salesmen, and buyers should be informed (or "sold") on the policy; (5) window and in-store displays should be improved through department managers' coordination with the display department; and (6) brands, fashion ideas, and product appeals should be emphasized rather than price in promotional efforts.

Questions

1. What problems does a retailer, such as Burbanks', generally encounter in "trading up"?

2. Appraise the appropriateness of Henenfeld's recommendations to top management.

ALABAMA MILLS

Textile Manufacturer—Tapping
a New Market Segment

Alabama Mills, founded in 1940 in Able, Alabama, by Roy G. Green, manufactured infants' and children's underwear. The factory's entire output was sold under the private labels of such large chains as Sears, J. C. Penney, W. T. Grant, G. C. Murphy, and F. W. Woolworth. Beginning in 1954 Alabama's sales grew at an annual rate of about 5 percent. The company's sales by 1967 accounted for roughly 13 percent of an estimated total market of $50 million. In searching for a way to expand its market share, Alabama's management contemplated marketing products under its own brand name.

Prior to World War II Alabama Mills imported silk from Italy, China, and Japan, twisting it into yarn for hosiery manufacturing. In 1941 imports of raw silk were cut off, and the company began to use nylon as a substitute for silk. Later that year the government declared nylon a critical war material and banned all civilian uses. This caused Alabama to contract with the Army Ordnance Department for the production of heads and bases for 90-pound fragmentation bombs and 40-millimeter antiaircraft shells. At the close of World War II these contracts were canceled, and the company again found itself without a product.

Shortly afterward Alabama decided to manufacture and market infants' and children's underwear. Needed raw materials were scarce and skilled workers were in short supply, thus Alabama initially experienced considerable difficulty in entering this market. However, through highly efficient production methods and by limiting the product offering (eight sizes in four colors), the company achieved low unit costs and a significant pricing advantage. Its line of underwear was comparable in quality with those of competitors, but the company's brand name failed to gain consumer acceptance, chiefly because of financial inability to provide adequate promotional support.

Private-label buyers seemed promising prospects, and Alabama executives approached several large retail chains. The success of this effort seemed assured in 1954 when the company signed a large contract with J. C. Penney. From that time on, Penney purchased about 60 percent of Alabama's total output. By 1967 private-label sales were also being made to Sears, Grant, Murphy, and Woolworth. Sales for 1955, 1958, and 1967 reflected Alabama's growth in the private-label market (see Exhibit 1).

EXHIBIT 1

Sales	1955	1958	1967
J.C. Penney	$555,000	$2,210,000	$3,900,000
Other chains	386,000	560,000	2,600,000
Total	$941,000	$2,770,000	$6,500,000
Dozen units produced	349,000	882,000	1,620,000
Employees	207	435	615

Major manufacturers (including the William Foster Company, Superior Knitting Mills, and Moss Mills) provided intense competition. William Foster, with sales of over $20 million, was the largest. It offered a broad line and had about 40 percent of the infants' and children's underwear market. Foster had its own sales force, used national advertising, and enjoyed considerable brand acceptance. However, Foster products retailed at prices 20 to 25 percent higher than the chains' private labels. Alabama's management believed that consumers would eventually recognize the similarity in product quality and buy the less-expensive underwear.

Alabama had no formally organized marketing department. Green, the president, handled the Penney account; two salesmen in New York made the rest of the sales. Salesmen received a 4 percent straight commission; they paid their own expenses and the company reimbursed them in full. The company neither advertised nor used sales promotion; salesmen carried product samples which were their only selling aids. Few ultimate consumers knew either Alabama's name or associated the company with infants' and children's underwear.

Questions

1. What problems, if any, would Alabama probably have encountered in marketing its own brand?
2. What advantages, if any, would the company have had in entering the market with its own brand?
3. Should the company have entered the underwear market with its own brand?

LENOX DEPARTMENT STORE

Department Store—Changing
a Retail Image

Located in a southeastern community of forty thousand people, including fifteen thousand university students, the Lenox Department Store was a unit of a large and highly successful national chain. The parent company, long known for its high-quality merchandise and reasonable prices, wanted to upgrade its image in order to compete in the fashion-oriented market. Store buyers purchased new stocks with an emphasis on fashion, but the company's previous image proved difficult to change. Management aggressively attempted to project the fashion image through shifts in its marketing activities but also remained concerned about serving its many old customers.

Bill Callison, with thirty years of company service, managed the Lenox store. It prospered under his leadership, becoming one of the community's largest. Sales for 1968 exceeded $2 million, an increase of 10 percent over the year before. Callison anticipated a sales increase of about $160,000 for 1969.

Lenox employed thirty-five full-time workers, many with long company service, and twelve part-timers. Employees were assigned to one of three departments:

1. Men's and boys' wear, accessories, and shoes

2. Ladies', girls', and infants' wear and accessories

3. Piece goods, work clothes, housewares, and home furnishings

The store manager deviated from normal buying procedures when he urgently needed special items not supplied to him through regular sources. He and other managers were authorized, as required, to go direct to other sources and order independently. Although Callison rarely exercised this buying option, he did find it beneficial in adjusting to the local college market, as in buying towels in school colors.

Lenox Department Store occupied a fifty-year-old building, but it was in an excellent downtown location, one block from the university campus. Nearby chain department stores and local specialty shops provided the major competition. Nearly all carried clothing and other items appealing to the college trade.

Management believed strongly in advertising, utilizing local daily papers and radio stations; local television was not available. Lenox used newspaper supplements as well as regular newspaper advertisements. The store also used direct mail promotion, sending flyers to area residents, but did not place advertising in the student newspaper. One man devoted full time to building window and store displays, using advertising kits supplied by the corporate office. Window themes were tied in with seasons and local campus events, such as football games and graduation. Management also used weekend price specials and staged special promotional events, such as fashion shows and art exhibits.

The Lenox chain emphasized customer satisfaction, providing many services, such as check cashing, exchange and refund privileges, wrapping service, and alterations. The local manager concurred with this emphasis and insisted on 100 percent customer satisfaction. Awards were made monthly to those employees regarded by management as outstanding in "customer service."

Lenox Corporation issued its own charge card, which was honored at all its stores. Store management valued credit customers as they usually were "larger buyers." Credit policy required thorough investigation of all applicants. A special "young modern" card was issued to those between the ages of eighteen and twenty-one, many of whom could not obtain credit elsewhere. Customers filling out applications were issued "courtesy charges" if they met minimum credit criteria pending arrival of permanent cards.

Questions

1. What problems are encountered by retailers such as Lenox in attempting to upgrade their "image"?

2. To what extent, if any, should such retailers make changes in their merchandising policies and practices?

3. What actions should have been taken by the Lenox Department Store to change its image? By the Lenox chain?

FINKENBERG'S FURNITURE COMPANY

Small Retailer—Marketing
in the Ghetto

Morris Segal, owner-manager of Finkenberg's Furniture Company, wondered what he should do. As a ghetto merchant, he received criticism from all sides. He constantly faced such problems as nonpaying customers, holdups, criticisms from New York's consumer affairs commissioner, and difficulties in securing insurance. He reflected upon his situation, saying, "If the ghetto is a trap, then I'm also trapped here since this is the only life I know. My family has been doing business in Harlem for 43 years."

Finkenberg's, located on Manhattan's Third Avenue, catered principally to low-income blacks and Puerto Ricans. Most of the customers had no savings with which to pay cash and could not obtain credit from downtown department stores; many were on welfare. Consequently, they shopped at Finkenberg's and similar stores where they were welcome and could obtain credit. The store had an annual sales volume of approximately $450,000.

Adapted from a report in *The Wall Street Journal,* August 28, 1970, p. 24.

Segal admitted that his prices were high; for example, an RCA 22-inch-screen television set that sold downtown at $199.99 was priced at $449.95. He said he did not buy in large lots like "the big stores" and therefore could not obtain quantity discounts. Also, his store had high operating expenses, particularly for bad debts (sometimes 10 percent of gross sales), collection work, insurance, and stock shortages. He explained, "Being in a ghetto area, we're plagued by dope addicts, burglaries, riots and thefts; my customers are plagued even more, as many times the appliance or furniture that they are paying on is stolen." Shortly after Martin Luther King's assassination in 1968, Segal spent ten thousand dollars to install iron-shutter gates across the front of his store.

An average of five customers a day patronized the store. Segal and his three salesmen tried to make sure that they did not leave without buying something, hopefully a large installment purchase. Segal admitted to stocking some shoddy merchandise, indicating the store's need to have low-priced merchandise in the windows to pull in traffic. However, he preferred to sell higher-priced items. "I put high-priced merchandise next to low-quality items since customers normally pick the best looking product." If Finkenberg's prospects showed reluctance to "switch over" to more profitable merchandise, salesmen "assisted" them. Segal believed that all consumers needed a shove; he said, "Everybody is on the brink, needs a shove, and wants it. That's a salesman's job, pushing customers over the edge." His salesmen were also taught to use "toss over" techniques on reluctant prospects — turning them over to another salesman or the manager to increase selling pressure. The Better Business Bureau condemned this practice, but Segal defended it, saying, "Some people feel that they can get a better deal from the boss. Besides it keeps them in the store longer."

At Finkenberg's, the agreement to purchase merely meant the beginning of a long relationship. After agreement came contract signing and collection. Although 40 percent of Finkenberg's customers were Spanish-speaking, contracts were printed in English. "The difference in the two languages is so minute, there's no real problem," Segal said. Customers were encouraged to buy on credit because installment buyers were viewed as repeat customers; they came into the store once a month to pay bills and would likely see another item they wanted.

Segal preferred credit customers who earned wages that could be attached, if necessary. He believed in a tough collection policy, since he felt that people who owed more than one merchant would pay the "hard-nosed" businessman first; he believed that customers stayed away from businesses where they were behind in their payments. However, he did not believe in immediate repossession, as he wanted neither to lose customers nor to take back depreciated merchandise, much of it shoddy at the time of original sale. He mailed three dunning letters — one polite, one tough, one threatening. If these did not produce results, he wrote to the customer's boss, pointing out the expenses involved in garnishment if it had to be resorted to. Next, he phoned the customer at home, and if this failed, he proceeded to garnishee the debtor's wages. Finkenberg's collected roughly 90 percent of its delinquent accounts without garnishment. Once court action became necessary, the company won virtually all cases, most by default.

Segal expressed sympathy for his customers, but he recalled his father's words — "Who is better off? The nice guys who have to close their stores, or the SOB who's still in business?" Segal admitted that he sometimes used distasteful tactics, but, he insisted, "If I were a black man, I wouldn't run this store any differently. I'm not running a charity, I'm managing a business." He reluctantly accepted his role as a ghetto merchant, but he would not accept the title of "thief" occasionally thrust upon him by politicians and consumer advocates.

Questions

1. How, if at all, should Finkenberg's have changed its *modus operandi*?

2. As a low-income consumer, how would you view Segal's operation?

2-5

ARMSTRONG CORK COMPANY

Flooring and Felt Products Manufacturer— Vendor-Rating System

The Armstrong Cork Company's vendor-rating system varied both with the types of products it purchased and with the quantities required by its individual plants. The Fulton, New York, plant, for example, used a quality inspection program for buying raw materials and fuels, and "stockless" purchasing of MRO (maintenance, repairs, operations) items by means of data-phone; the Lancaster, Pennsylvania, closure plant used a quality certification system in selecting tinplate suppliers; and the Lancaster flooring plant applied a categorical-rating system in buying corrugated cartons. The company, in other words, had no company-wide formal vendor-rating system.

Since its founding in 1860 Armstrong Cork Company had gradually expanded and diversified into four major product lines: (1) flooring products, including plastic and roto-vinyl floor coverings, asphalt rubber and cork tiles, linoleum, other resilient flooring, and installation and maintenance sundries; (2) building materials, including acoustical ceiling materials, wall coverings, and thermal roof installations; (3) industrial specialties, including friction materials of cork, felt, and synthetic rubber composition, gaskets, seals, filters, noise-damping insulation, and various adhesives (used by the automotive, textile, shoe, electrical and household appliance, air-conditioning, and furniture industries); and (4) packaging materials, including glass and plastic containers, plastic vials and prescription ware, metal and plastic caps and crowns — sold to companies marketing: (a) food items, (b) medicinal and health products, (c) household and industrial chemicals, (d) toiletries and cosmetics, (e) beer and soft drinks, and (f) wine and liquor. During 1967 the company purchased a rug manufacturing plant and added it to the flooring products operation. Armstrong emphasized both basic and applied product research and development, and of its 1967 sales volume more than half came from products introduced since 1957.

Armstrong Cork, headquartered in Lancaster, Pennsylvania, ranked among the nation's largest companies. Annual sales exceeded $370 million, and roughly nineteen thousand people worked for the company, domestically and overseas. There were eighteen United States plants and five foreign plants. Sales offices were located in trading centers across the United States. The company had affiliates in Canada, England, Australia, South Africa, Spain, Switzerland, India, and West Germany.

As a manufacturer and distributor of diversified products, Armstrong bought a wide range of raw materials, shipping and packing materials, electrical and mechanical equipment, and MRO items. The firm had a decentralized purchasing system, but centralized functional control. Armstrong's purchasing department procured major equipment, handled general contracting, and did the buying for the central engineering department. It also served as a functional control center and advisory unit for plant purchasing agents. Each plant had one or two purchasing agents of its own and a stores/inventory man. All purchasing agents handled their own expediting.

SYSTEM AT THE FULTON PLANT

The Fulton plant produced various flooring felts and fabricated industrial felt products for automotive, aircraft, air-conditioning, and similar applications. It bought three categories of items:

> *1.* Raw materials: asbestos, fillers, pigments, pulpwood, synthetic rubber, and lattices
>
> *2.* Shipping and packing materials: corrugated cartons and strapping
>
> *3.* Machinery: electrical equipment, motors, instrumentations, paper and board machinery, office equipment, and MRO supplies and services

The Fulton plant negotiated for the supply of the majority of its raw materials through twenty-five blanket order contracts; all MRO items were procured through thirty blanket order contracts.

The Fulton plant had no formal vendor-rating system. Its purchasing personnel compiled case histories when they believed a supplier's performance was approaching unacceptable levels. They collected documents, such as receiving reports, inspection reports, expediting notes, purchase orders, invoices, packing lists, and freight bills, and informally evaluated the supplier's overall performance.

According to the plant purchasing agent, this informal procedure served the plant's best interests for three main reasons. First, most large purchases (high dollar volume) came from single sources because of the need for product uniformity or because of market conditions. If Armstrong, for example, purchased a certain chemical from two different suppliers, quality differences might occur if Company X aged the chemical differently from Company Y. Market conditions (relative transportation costs for example) varied considerably for certain items, and it was generally safer policy to buy such items as rags (cloth scraps) from a single local source than from numerous distant apparel firms.

Second, Armstrong depended on technical assistance from its suppliers, expecially in the chemical field. The value of service and technical assistance was difficult to quantify; however, the plant purchasing agent believed that a vendor who was a sole supplier regarded itself as a "partner" in making Armstrong's products. Sole vendors often devoted product research and development effort to the solution of Armstrong's problems.

Third, the corporate accounting department acted as a central data bank, making all documents easily available for informal audit. This department maintained purchasing files, classified according to vendors. The files, for example, contained documents, arranged chronologically, for all company transactions with each vendor.

At the Fulton plant two aspects of purchasing were formalized. First, the plant purchasing department received inspection reports on raw materials and fuels. The raw materials test center prepared these reports (including a detailed analysis of incoming materials and the date received). The plant purchasing agent used such reports as "first indicators" of unacceptable performance. Second, a local industrial supply house stocked many MRO items and could supply the plant within twenty-four hours. The purchasing agent prepared punch cards for high-turnover MRO items and initiated needed orders by inserting the appropriate cards into a data-phone.

The Fulton purchasing agent listed two advantages of data-phone ordering: (1) reduced cost of possession (lower inventories, less physical space to maintain inventories, and fewer personnel needed to handle inventories), and (2) lower cost of acquisition (less paper work through bypassing some steps in ordering, such as supervisory checking and approving). A purchase-analysis computer print-out disclosed the number of purchases made during the past month and the cumulative six months' total. Comparisons of quantities ordered with minimum inventory levels provided evaluations of delivery performance and indicated proper inventory levels for each supplier's products. Invoice statement print-outs showed current prices, and when checked against previous invoices, permitted comparisons of prices.

SYSTEM AT LANCASTER CLOSURE PLANT

At the Lancaster closure plant, the production of packaging crowns and caps required large-volume purchases of tin-plate. The suppliers (steel companies) all quoted similar prices and offered nearly identical delivery schedules, but product quality varied from mill to mill. Therefore, management set up a weight-point rating system for ascertaining tin quality (Exhibit 1). The receiving department inspected shipments and assigned appropriate ratings. Management compiled a quarterly composite with point differentials among suppliers, thus apportioning its business for the next quarter (see Exhibit 2). For example, if Vendor C received 95.0 points and Vendor D 97.5 points, a differential of 2.5 points,

EXHIBIT 1

Vendor Rating — Crown Tinplate, Month of September, 1966

Supplier		*Vendor A*				*Vendor B*		
Base Weight		*95#*				*95#*		
Size		*20 die*		*22 die*		*20 die*		*22 die*
Finish		*matte*	*bright*	*matte*	*bright*	*matte*	*bright*	*matte*	*bright*
No. skids examined		0	23	232	0	44	0	107	0
Rating:	Points								
Net weight	10		6.8	7.9		4.6		6.4	
Dimensions	20		20.0	20.0		20.0		−40.6	
Squareness	30		30.0	29.2		30.0		30.0	
Appearance	20		20.0	20.0		20.0		20.0	
Bowing, wavy edges	10		10.0	10.0		10.0		10.0	
Sheet count	15		8.6	8.8		10.0		10.5	
Total			95.4	95.9		94.6		36.3	

	Vendor A	Vendor B
Penalty points[a]	0	−50 (150 bowed sheets)
Adjusted overall average	95.6	40.5

[a]*Production problems*: Any difficulties encountered in production, such as lamination, poor fabricating characteristics, etc., or rejectable defects as noted above but not originally detected when sampled, shall result in the following penalties:

    If one-half skid or less is involved, deduct 50 points.
    If over one-half skid is involved, deduct 100 points.

Third-quarter weighted average (July, August, September):   Vendor A = 98.3 points   Vendor B = 86.5 points

Distribution of fourth-quarter tonnage: Vendor A = 100%   Vendor B = 0

EXHIBIT 2

Basis for Distribution of Business

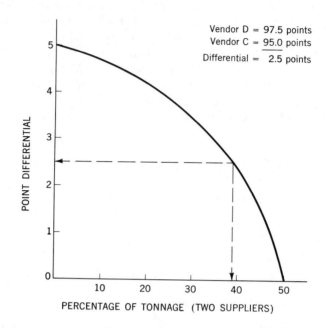

PERCENTAGE OF TONNAGE (TWO SUPPLIERS)

Armstrong would buy 39 percent from C and 61 percent from D. If a differential exceeded 5 points, the leading vendor received all the orders for the company's requirements of that particular item.

SYSTEM AT LANCASTER FLOORING PLANT

At the Lancaster flooring plant, corrugated cartons, used for packing finished products, were purchased in large volume. The plant purchasing agent applied a categorical vendor-rating system (Exhibit 3). This system incorporated the judgments of others in departments directly involved with the suppliers, thus reducing bias in the total evaluation. The plant purchasing agent used this evaluation as a basis for allocating business among vendors.

EXHIBIT 3

Flooring Plant Vendor Rating

VENDOR EVALUATION SHEET	Vendor _____ Date: _____ Code P —Purchasing E —Engineering R —Receiving & Traffic A —Accounting QC —Quality Control	ALWAYS	USUALLY	SELDOM		NEVER		PRIMARY RESPON-SIBILITY
THE ABOVE VENDOR		6	5	4	3	2	1	0	
1. Delivers per schedule									P
2. Has good quality									QC
3. Delivers per routing instructions									P&R
4. Supplies answers readily									P
5. Advises us of potential trouble									P
6. Not a chronic complainer									P
7. Helps in emergencies									P
8. Delivers without constant follow up									P
9. Free of labor problems									P
10. Replaces rejections promptly									P
11. Acts upon correction action requests									QC
12. Furnishes necessary technical data									E
13. Has a good packaging									R
14. Invoices correctly									A
15. Issues credit memos punctually									A
16. Furnishes affidavit or certifications									QC
17. Cooperates on design problems									E
18. Has adequate Engineering representation									E
19. Maintains technical service in the field									E
20. Accepts our terms without exceptions									P
21. Keeps promises									P
22. Does not ask for special consideration (Purchasing)									P
23. Prices are generally competitive									P
24. Does not ask for special financial consideration									A
Other points 25.									
26.									
TOTAL GRADE									

_____ Purchasing   _____ Engineering   _____ Quality Control   _____ Receiving   _____ Accounting

BE FAIR IN FILLING OUT THIS FORM. DO NOT BE PREJUDICED. CONSIDER ALL FACTS. MARK CODE LETTERS IN PROPER GRADE COLUMN.

Questions

1. Outline the pros and cons of the vendor-rating systems used by the three plants.
2. Under what conditions is stockless purchasing by data-phone appropriate? Inappropriate?
3. Would it have been wiser for Armstrong to centralize all purchasing activities at corporate headquarters? Should the company have used a standardized vendor-rating system?

CAB CHEMICAL COMPANY

Producer of Inorganic Chemicals—
Policy on Gifts to Buyers

In late 1961 C. A. Stringer and Robert Wilder formed the C & B Chemical Corporation, a producer and distributor of inorganic chemicals. By 1967 stiffening competition resulted in a reevaluation of the entire marketing program, particularly the approach being used to tap the market segment made up of muncipalities. Management especially wanted to develop a unique sales promotion method to use in increasing sales to this market segment.

The owners, who had earlier worked for the predecessor company (C. B. Corporation), bought it out in December 1961 and renamed it the C & B Chemical Corporation. In February 1963 the original owners of C. B. Corporation brought legal action against Stringer and Wilder for using the name C & B Chemical Corporation. Five months later the court ruled in favor of the plaintiffs. Stringer and Wilder paid the original owners a cash settlement and agreed to change the organization's name to CAB Chemical Company.

CAB Chemical made and marketed special paints, paint removers, soaps, detergents, cleaning fluids, and a variety of janitorial chemicals. The home plant at Burke, California, made most of the products. To increase paint production capacity, in 1964 the I. M. Holder Paint Company of Reno, Nevada, was purchased; management planned to shift all paint production to the Reno plant by 1968.

Net sales increased each year from 1961 to 1967, exceeding $5 million in 1967 (Exhibit 1). When additional working capital was required, accounts receivable were factored at a local bank. Funds were also borrowed on a secured basis; bank officials indicated that CAB had a satisfactory repayment record.

EXHIBIT 1

CAB Chemical Company
Net Sales — 1962-67

Year	Sales
1962	$ 179,000
1963	275,000
1964	800,000
1965	1,800,000
1966	3,700,000
1967	5,010,000

When Abraham Mitchell joined CAB as vice-president of sales in 1963, he found it selling to municipalities through widely dispersed manufacturers' representatives. Although sales had increased each year, he suspected that vast market areas were not receiving adequate coverage. Consequently, he analyzed the company's marketing system, compared it with those of competitors, and concluded that CAB should have its own sales force. The next year he developed plans for a company sales force which would operate under his direction. Top management approved his plan after reviewing the ineffectiveness of its agent system. Mitchell reported directly to Wilder, executive vice-president.

Mitchell divided the entire United States into three regions and hired a regional sales manager for each. Although he began recruiting a sales force in 1964, he continued relationships with most of the manufacturers' representatives until early 1965. By late 1965 CAB had 98 salesmen, and in early 1967, 150 salesmen were "on board." The eastern regional sales manager supervised 75 salesmen; the western manager, 50; and the southern manager, 25. (See Exhibit 2.)

EXHIBIT 2

CAB Chemical Company — Organizational Structure — 1967

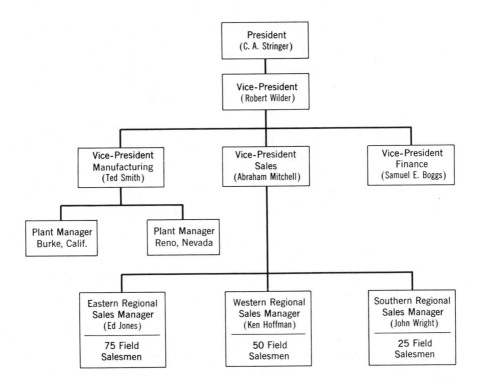

Regional managers recruited field salesmen from competitors and through newspaper advertisements. Salesmen sold directly to public-paid employees of municipalities and were paid a straight commission of 33 1/3 percent on net sales, from which they paid their own expenses. One-half of their commission was paid at the time the salesman wrote an order; the rest after the company received payment, usually about eight weeks later. Salesmen also had weekly drawing accounts, the amounts drawn being later deducted from commission checks. Sales quotas differed among salesmen because of variations in territorial sales potentials; the average quota was about $1,000 per week. Therefore, if he reached quota, the average salesman could expect to gross about $333 per week.

In July 1967 Ed Jones, eastern regional sales manager, phoned Abe Mitchell.

Ed: Hello Abe, this is Ed, I'd like to talk to you a minute or two on a few problems in my area that I think require some attention.

Abe: OK – shoot, Ed.

Ed: I've been getting reports from the field that we are consistently being undersold on our aerosol products and paint solvents. As you know, these items account for about 75 percent of our business and we're getting clobbered in our area. It seems our products are consistently higher priced than competitors' and my men say it's hard for them to get their foot in the door. I guess you know our sales reports haven't been too encouraging recently.

Abe: I know. . . . I'm not surprised to hear what you're saying, however, John and Ken are having the same problems. I'll tell you what. . . . I'm going to set up a meeting here for next Saturday morning and I want you to attend. I'll contact John and Ken today. I want to present a new promotional technique, and I want your opinions.

Ed: OK, Abe, I'll plan to be in your office this Saturday at nine. . . . is that OK?

Abe: That's fine; I'll see you then.

The following Saturday morning Abe Mitchell met with the three regional managers and the president, C. A. Stringer. Mitchell opened the meeting.

Abe: I called you together because I've been getting some alarming reports from the field. Our gross sales for the last two months have increased only 3 percent and we've hired three new salesmen during this period. Now, all of you have been telling me we're being undersold on our money-making items.

The way I see it we're doing one of two things wrong: One – we're selling our products either too high or our competitors are selling theirs too low. I'm inclined to think our products are priced higher. Or two – our salesmen are not aggressive enough to sell the products. I'm ruling this out because it seems all our salesmen are having difficulty. As you can see, I'm inferring that our products are too high priced for the market.

Stringer: Yes, that's true, but that's been my policy. As you know, our strategy is to maintain high gross margins. Our production costs can't be reduced much lower, so we have to maintain our present pricing. If we reduce our pricing, we may increase our sales; but, you can't convince me that we can still maintain our present dollar margin. What we have to do is increase our sales and maintain our present pricing.

Ed: That's fine, but how are we going to do it? I've had my salesmen say it's next to impossible to make a sale to a municipality that's already been covered by a competitor. It seems to me the only way we're going to sell our products is to cut our prices.

Ken: I agree with Ed.

John: So do I.

Abe: I'll have to agree with Mr. Stringer concerning our operating margin. I think I have an answer to our problem. You see . . . our customers are mainly commissioners of public works, town superintendents, or town clerks. Now, they have to keep within their yearly budgets, but they probably won't buy more than $3,000 a year from us, so keeping within their budgets is only secondary to them. Now, if our salesmen were to approach a prospect and offer him a gift for doing business, I'll bet you anything he would bite.

Ed: Wouldn't that be illegal?

Abe: No. The concept isn't much different than a retail store giving trading stamps.

Ken: How about the cost of this promotion? Wouldn't it lower your margin?

Abe: No. I have considered using a 5 percent limit in gift value for each order. If a salesman made a $300 sale, he would give away a gift worth $15. The $15 would come out of the salesman's commission. He would then gross $85 instead of $100.

Ed: I don't think my salesmen are going to go for it.

Abe: I think they will. They're now burning up gas trying to make a sale. If they have a gift in their car trunk, they will probably have a jump on our competitors. You must also consider the customer. I think if you bait the line, he'll bite every time.

Ed: We could at least give it a try. Are you sure we won't get into any legal trouble?

Abe: No, I'm not!

Questions

1. Do you agree with Mitchell's size-up of the behavior of buyers for municipalities? Why? Why not?

2. Evaluate Mitchell's proposal to present buyers with gifts.

2-7

GRIFFEN FEED, SEED, AND FERTILIZER COMPANY

Agribusiness—Problems in a Declining Market

As R. B. Evans, president and manager of R. W. Griffen Company, planned the 1969 selling season, he reflected upon the sales volume declines that had occurred since 1965 – the year Ralph W. Griffen, founder of the company, had died. Sales had declined about 3 percent each year since, and Evans hoped to forestall any further decline.

Griffen had founded the company in Douglas, Georgia, in 1934. At its inception, it was one of two seed and fertilizer dealers in this south Georgia community. Starting with two bags of seed peas, the company eventually became the world's largest independent fertilizer dealer. Griffen's early financial backing came from his other business – a cotton brokerage firm. He transferred needed capital into his seed and fertilizer business and it grew rapidly.

Griffen's liberal credit and loan policies aided in business expansion and in maintenance of a backlog of regular clientele. He extended generous amounts of credit to those farmers who were steady customers. He granted real estate loans to tenant farmers who were buying their own farms; they gave

Griffen nearly all of their seed and fertilizer business. In addition, Griffen frequently made personal loans to customers.

The Griffen organization handled a complete line of feeds, seed, and fertilizers. It sold five major makes of fertilizer produced by the country's largest manufacturers, from whom Griffen bought direct. According to Evans, customers exhibited very little brand preference for fertilizer; they regarded price as the most important consideration. Griffen's trade came mainly from farmers in Coffee and contiguous counties. Although it also sold fertilizer to the Georgia state government on a bid basis, this business accounted for a very small fraction of total sales.

The main warehouse in Douglas housed company headquarters and the sales office. Most company sales originated in Douglas, but Griffen had three other warehouses in small towns in Coffee County: one in Ambrose, 15 miles west; another in Broxton, 10 miles north; and another in Nicholls, 20 miles east. The four locations gave Griffen excellent coverage of Coffee County and adjacent rural areas.

Sales volume in 1968 approximated $3 million. This represented a decline of $120,000, about 3 percent from the year before. Fertilizer, with a 10 percent markup, accounted for 87.5 percent of sales; and feed and seed, with a 25 percent markup, made up the remaining 12.5 percent. In 1968 profits averaged about 4 percent of sales, but return on investment was 23 percent.

Griffen advertised locally in two newspapers and over two radio stations. However, total advertising expenditures in 1968 came to only five thousand dollars. Management emphasized quality products, fair prices, and efficient service; consequently, it had not stressed advertising and personal selling.

In 1968 six competitors (two local independent dealers, one farm cooperative, and three national fertilizer manufacturers running farm centers) operated in the trading area. Griffen's management regarded A. B. Swanson and Sons, one of the independent dealers, as its major competitor. Swanson sold a substantial volume of fertilizer but did not carry feed and seed. The other independent dealer sold small quantities of feed, seed, and fertilizer. While the farm cooperative had a large membership, its service was poor and many of its members traded elsewhere; Evans noted that Griffen made substantial sales each year to individual cooperative members. Of the three manufacturer-operated farm centers, Armour closed its center in late 1968, and those of Kerr-McGee and Mobil had relatively small sales of fertilizer.

Evans, manager and president, was also the company's main salesman. Three secretaries and three foremen helped in meeting customers, quoting prices, and taking orders. Occasionally, Evans and the foremen visited customers' farms and advised them on product use. However, most personal contacts occurred at the end of the crop year when farmers came into the office

EXHIBIT 1

Use of Commercial Fertilizer
State of Georgia and Coffee County

Place	*Year*	*Farms Using Fertilizer*	*Fertilized Acres*	*Tons of Fertilizer*
State of	1959	87,430	5,246,356	1,198,823
Georgia	1964	63,137	4,334,217	1,227,585
Coffee	1959	1,457	87,784	21,346
County	1964	1,219	68,060	20,750

Source: *1964 Census of Agriculture,* Vol. 1, Part 28, Georgia.

to settle their bills. At this time, farmers were encouraged to continue trading with the company.

During the period 1955–65, in spite of changing farming conditions, Griffen maintained a stable sales volume. The number of farms decreased considerably, but the average size of farms more than doubled.[1] With growth in the size of farms, increased quantities of seed, feed, and fertilizer were required, and competition among suppliers became more intense. Farmers also stepped up their fertilizer usage per acre (Exhibit 1), and although Griffen lost some customers, its sales remained fairly stable during the period.

One depressing influence on sales traced to the fact that some farmers had placed land in the Soil Bank and the Federal Feed and Grain programs.[2] This, coupled with a decrease in acreage used for cotton, corn, peanut, and tobacco crops (see Exhibit 2) contributed further to Griffen's declining sales. However, yields per acre of these crops increased, even though the amount of cultivated land decreased.

Evans attributed most of the sales decrease to the aforementioned agricultural trends; but he believed that other factors, such as inadequate personal selling, were also responsible. In a conversation with his three foremen, he expressed this view, saying, "We must begin to sell the farmer a complete

[1] From 1945 to 1964 the number of total acres of cultivated land in farms in Georgia decreased from 25,266,522 acres to 17,886,931 acres. The average farm's size increased from 101.0 acres in 1945 to 214.6 acres in 1964. Source: *1964 Census of Agriculture,* Vol. 1, Part 28, Georgia.

The number of farms in Georgia decreased from 106,000 in 1959 to 83,000 in 1964. Source: *Statistical Abstract of the United States, 1968.*

[2] Information concerning the amount of land taken out of cultivation and put in the Soil Bank Program and the Federal Feed and Grain Program was not available. However, U.S. Department of Agriculture officials agreed that more and more land was being taken out of cultivation and placed in the programs.

EXHIBIT 2

Selected Crops: Number of Farms and Acres under Cultivation — State of Georgia and Coffee Country

Place	Year	Cotton Farms	Acres	Corn Farms	Acres
State of	1935	199,436	2,157,099	232,038	4,398,659
Georgia	1959	42,555	639,326	75,293	2,428,442
	1964	22,941	616,508	47,740	1,638,700
Coffee	1959	697	6,012	1,243	56,777
County	1964	383	5,075	1,080	48,395

Place	Year	Peanuts Farms	Acres	Tobacco Farms	Acres
State of	1935	56,914	(NA)	18,116	50,773
Georgia	1959	22,773	465,332	19,559	68,895
	1964	15,965	408,109	15,027	63,596
Coffee	1959	473	3,542	1,078	4,252
County	1964	427	3,426	941	3,818

Source: *1964 Census of Agriculture,* Vol. 1, Part 28, Georgia.

crop program; we must assist him in the use of all our products. If we can do this, there will be less emphasis on price competition. If we can help him to become a better farmer, then we'll get and keep his business."

Questions

1. What "business" was this company really in ?
2. What steps should have been taken by Evans to forestall further declines in sales?

SECTION 3

PRODUCT MANAGEMENT

WORLEY-SEWELL COMPANY

Clothing Company—The Addition of a New Line

In 1964 Jack Worley, vice-president and salesman for the Warren-Sewell Clothing Company, organized the Worley-Sewell Company of Bremen, Georgia. He believed that the Sewell name, well known for suits and sports coats in the men's clothing trade, would carry over to Worley-Sewell's line of men's jackets and all-weather coats. In 1966 Worley-Sewell expanded its line to include ladies' and children's outerwear. In early 1969 management was considering adding a new line — boys' suits and sports coats.

Initially, an out-of-state contractor made Worley-Sewell's products. However, in 1966 Worley and George Turner, an employee of Hubbard Slacks, also a Bremen Company, organized T and W Manufacturing Company to make the Worley-Sewell line. The T and W plant, located in Waco, Georgia, finished piece goods furnished by Worley-Sewell. Title passed to Worley-Sewell upon completion of "trim" work, and the finished items were stored in warehouses in Bremen. Sales volume reached three hundred thousand dollars in 1964 and grew to $2 million in 1968, causing management to expand both the Bremen warehouses and the Waco plant.

Worley-Sewell regarded Campus and Cambridge Original as its principal competitors. Campus offered a wider product line and had annual sales of approximately $50 million. Cambridge Original of Duluth, Georgia, was about the same size as Worley-Sewell, had roughly the same territory coverage, and had a similar product line.

Worley-Sewell sold most of its output to retailers in small towns and in the smaller cities. Retailers in large cities were regarded as difficult prospects requiring excessive selling time. Competition was also more intense in the larger metropolitan areas. Management believed that middle-aged people constituted its largest customer group, as such people were not particularly brand conscious and generally shopped for medium-priced quality clothing. Worley-Sewell did not attempt to set fashion but produced current styles; however, Jack Worley frequently visited various large cities to study fashion trends.

In 1968 the product line included jackets, all-weather coats, three-quarter-length corduroy coats, parkas, men's formal wear, ladies' coats, and children's outerwear. Men's jackets came in sixteen colors and in sizes from Prep – 6 to 54, and they retailed from $9 to $15 depending on size and type of lining. All-weather coats were made in five colors and in men's and ladies' sizes from 6 to 54, with retail prices ranging from $14 to $35. Wholesale prices were usually lower for ladies' coats than for men's. Corduroy coats came in three colors and twenty-five sizes. Formal wear for men included pants and dinner jackets in five colors. Every item in the line was offered in two qualities of material. Jackets and all-weather coats were the largest sellers, accounting for more volume than any other items.

Worley-Sewell's nine-man sales force covered the southeastern United States. Salesmen traveled their territories in September and October selling the spring offerings and in February through May selling the fall offerings. They received a 6 percent commission on all sales made in their territories, whether they personally wrote the orders or customers ordered direct from the home office. Salesmen earned an average of $15,000 to $18,000 annually. Although many carried noncompeting lines, such as men's hats, ties, and umbrellas produced by other makers, all were regarded as Worley-Sewell employees.

Mather Muse managed the company's sales force and personally called upon "prime" accounts near Bremen. He received an annual salary of $20,000 and a 6 percent commission on his own sales. His job involved selection, training, compensation, and supervision of the salesmen. New salesmen were recruited rather informally; most salesmen were former shipping clerks.

Worley-Sewell used very little advertising. It provided "plates" and "slicks" to retailers for their use in local newspaper advertising. Most such advertising emphasized Mister 365, the brand name used on all company products except for the formal wear, which carried the name Black and White. On request, the company often sewed on a store's own label. Some salesmen gave away pens, pencils, tape measures, and other novelties imprinted with their name and the company's. Salesmen were not reimbursed for novelty costs and expenses incurred by them at trade shows.

Worley-Sewell sold its products to retailers at prices under the industry. Its markup for retailers averaged about 35 percent on the selling price as compared with other makers' markups of 45 percent. Unlike most of the industry, however, Worley-Sewell did not grant quantity discounts. It usually extended credit on a "net thirty days" basis, but "net sixty days" terms were allowed to those placing early orders. The company adhered to an industry practice in selling ladies' clothing which involved granting an 8 percent cash discount for prompt payment.

When sales of formal wear dropped and the company had idle capacity among the formal-wear workers, Worley considered adding a new line. He believed that addition of boys' suits and sports coats would solve the idle capacity problem; therefore, he recommended that T and W tool up for production. He was aware of the intense competition in the new field; in fact, two other suit manufacturers in Bremen had already introduced similar lines. He also realized that customers for children's clothing were often price conscious; however, the idle capacity problem at T and W demanded immediate attention. He assumed that the new line could be sold through the present sales force and would not involve additional promotional expenditures. Therefore, in early 1969 he recommended to Turner and Sewell, and to Muse, the sales manager, that production begin on boys' suits and sports coats for the 1969 fall season.

Questions

1. Should W-S have added the new line?

2. Evaluate the company's approach to structuring the product line.

3. Assuming that the company adds the new line, what should be the overall marketing strategy?

3-2

YORKTOWN MANUFACTURING COMPANY

Copper Fabricator—Adding a Secondary Product Line

Yorktown Manufacturing Company, a copper fabricator, had been an important supplier of copper products since 1801 when it built the first copper rolling mill in the United States. From its original copper sheeting and bronze products, Yorktown expanded into full lines of copper industrial products (such as tubing, sheeting, and wire) and a line of consumer products including stainless steel cooking utensils. Yorkware, the utensils line, was the leader in premium-priced cookware, with over 50 percent of the market. Not long after a competitor introduced a line of stainless steel cooking utensils (similar in appearance to Yorkware, but of inferior quality, and retailing at about 10 percent less), Yorktown experienced a sales decrease practically equivalent to its competitor's sales increase. Yorkware, because of its higher production costs, could not compete on a price basis with the competitive Brand X. Yorkware was stainless steel with copper bottoms; Brand X was "tri-ply" steel – a layer of stainless steel, a second layer of low-carbon steel, and a third layer of stainless steel.

Yorktown management did not want to cheapen Yorkware's reputation through price competition, so the desirability of adding an entirely new cooking utensil line was considered. Executives, however, thought the new line, similar in quality and price to Brand X, should carry a Yorktown brand to capitalize on the company's general reputation. The design of the new product line, Heritage Ware, fully differentiated it from Yorkware. Like Brand X it was tri-ply steel, but management regarded it as both more attractive and of better quality even though it would retail at a lower price. (See Exhibit 1.)

EXHIBIT 1

Retail Price Comparison Chart

Utensil	Yorkware	York Heritage Ware (proposed prices)	Brand X
1-quart saucepan	$5.50	$5.25	nil[a]
1½-quart saucepan	nil	nil	$6.25
2-quart saucepan	nil	nil	7.50
3-quart saucepan	8.95	8.50	nil
4-quart saucepan	nil	nil	9.75
6-inch skillet	6.95	6.50	nil
7-inch skillet	nil	nil	6.75
10-inch skillet	10.95	10.50	nil
2-quart double boiler	12.50	11.75	11.95
6-quart dutch oven	14.50	13.95	nil
6½-quart dutch oven	nil	nil	14.25
8-cup percolator	12.95	12.50	nil
8-cup dripolator	nil	nil	18.97
2-quart teakettle	7.25	5.25	nil
3-quart teakettle	nil	nil	7.50

[a]Nil – not in line.

Management intended to distribute York Heritage Ware, the new line, through the same marketing channels, using the same marketing techniques as for Yorkware. Yorktown's sixteen salesmen sold both through wholesale distributors and direct to hardware dealers, appliance dealers, jewelers, and small department stores. The company also sold direct to specialized accounts such as leading mail-order chains and trading-stamp firms (e.g., Sperry and Hutchinson, Top Value). Yorktown products were fair traded but, since management did not police all wholesale sales, some discount houses sold Yorkware at reduced prices. The suggested retail prices gave retailers a 35 percent markup and wholesalers a 15 percent markup.

Yorkware utensils were advertised in leading national magazines. In addition, a cooperative newspaper advertising program provided for reimbursing 50 percent of retailers' advertising costs. Under this program, a retailer was allowed to run up to six hundred lines of advertising monthly. Frequently, Yorktown also placed ads in hardware and housewares trade publications.

Questions

1. Should the new product line have been added?
2. If added, what should have been the marketing program for the new line?
3. What improvements might have been made in the marketing program for the Yorkware line?

PEPSI-COLA BOTTLING COMPANY OF ATHENS

Soft Drink Bottler—Private Label
under Consideration

Pepsi-Cola Bottling Company, Inc., of Athens, Georgia, a franchised Pepsi-Cola bottler and distributor, sold in thirteen northeast Georgia counties. Established in 1946 by Julian M. Rhodes, the president, the firm grew steadily and had 40 percent of its area's soft drink market. In early 1968 management was thinking of adding a private-brand soft drink for sale through grocery wholesalers. No other private-label product of this type was being sold in the market area at the time.

Don M. Rhodes, vice-president, favored the addition. He said, "The private-label brand will not require additional physical plant, and advertising and distribution expenses will be low. Also, concentrates used in producing the private label are less expensive than our regular ingredients." Other executives generally agreed, but some expressed concern over the possibility that the private brand might take sales away from regular brands. They also doubted that grocery wholesalers would promote the private brand adequately.

The Athens operation had grown consistently, expanding its physical plant on eleven different occasions. Industry trends featured increases in both expansions and mergers; there were thirteen bottlers in Athens in 1946, only three in 1968. Don Rhodes believed higher labor costs, the need for added promotional expenditures, and increased bottling efficiency by the larger firms had caused small and medium-size bottlers to drop out.

Sales of the regular product line (including Pepsi-Cola, Mountain Dew, and Diet Pepsi) totaled $3 million in 1967. Pepsi-Cola accounted for 79 percent of sales, Mountain Dew for 14 percent, and Diet Pepsi for 7 percent. Pepsico, the franchiser, maintained strict control over the regular product line, not allowing any franchisee to bottle a private-label cola; however, private-label "non-colas" were permitted. Pepsico also closely supervised product quality, insisting on usage of regular concentrates and product formulas.

Coca-Cola, as in most market areas, provided the main competition, being particularly strong because its Atlanta national headquarters was only sixty-five miles away. Coca-Cola had 50 percent of the thirteen-county market, and Royal Crown about 10 percent. Athens Pepsi-Cola avoided price competition, relying mainly on quality control, customer relations, and delivery service to hold its share of the market.

Athens Pepsi-Cola packaged its products in both glass and metal containers. In 1967 "one-way" canned drinks accounted for 18 percent of sales; management believed they would account for 60 percent by 1977, mainly because of rising costs of glass bottles. The Company's most recent expansion, added in 1955, was a modern canning plant. Management pointed to another trend in soft drink packaging — increased use of six-packs, which accounted for 45 percent of the firm's 1967 sales.

Athens Pepsi distributed in thirteen counties. Clarke, the home county and the most populous, accounted for 40 percent of 1967 sales. Management anticipated further growth here because of continuing increases in population. The other counties, primarily rural, had experienced population losses. In 1967 management estimated that the thirteen counties contained 250,000 potential customers.

The firm's sales organization consisted of a sales manager, an assistant sales manager, five sales supervisors, and twenty-three driver-salesmen. The sales manager directed and coordinated sales efforts. His assistant maintained contacts with large supermarkets, mainly to insure good customer relations; he also helped store managers erect Pepsi-Cola point-of-purchase displays. The supervisors set up routes for driver-salesmen and helped sell difficult accounts. Driver-salesmen called on customers and prospects, took orders, and made deliveries. Salesmen were paid base salaries plus commissions; supervisors and sales executives were paid straight salaries.

The company's 1967 advertising budget amounted to ninety thousand dollars. Sixty percent of it was used for television time on an Atlanta station, a program sponsored by the parent company. Athens Pepsi cooperated in this advertising with other Pepsi franchise holders who were within range of the Atlanta station's signal. Franchisees paid amounts proportionate to the number of potential customers in their market areas. Athens Pepsi-Cola used the rest of its advertising budget for local radio and newspaper advertising and point-of-purchase displays. The advertising budget was set on the basis of a fixed amount per unit of anticipated sales (about ten cents per case).

Questions

1. What factors should Athens Pepsi-Cola's management have considered in the introduction of its private brand?

2. If added, should the private brand have been distributed through grocery wholesalers?

3-4

DONNER HOSIERY COMPANY

Hosiery Manufacturer—Adding Fashion and Teen-age Lines

Donner Hosiery Company, a division of Donner, Inc., manufactured women's hosiery. The company was the successor to two firms – Sanderson Hosiery Company and Star Mills – which Donner, Inc., acquired in an effort to broaden its product base. Donner, Inc., operated the two acquisitions as separate companies until 1967 when they were combined into Donner Hosiery. The division's annual sales averaged over $2 million. However, in early 1969 sales dropped alarmingly, and management, concerned about the poor sales performance of the division's medium-priced national brands – Sanderson and Concord – sought new ways to strengthen sales volume.

Donner's nineteen-man sales force sold the line of branded products to department stores, variety chains, and women's apparel shops. Customers desiring private brands purchased them direct from Donner's home office. Company salesmen reported to seven regional managers responsible for brand sales in their regions. Regional managers reported directly to the vice-president of sales (Exhibit 1).

EXHIBIT 1

Donner Hosiery Company Organization Chart

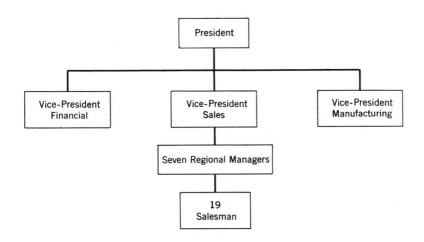

Donner's sales came from the lower- and medium-priced segments of the women's hosiery market. Snagproof, Donner's lowest-priced hosiery, outsold all competition in its price range. Although all Donner's prices were competitive, consumers seemed to prefer competitors' medium-priced brands over Sanderson and Concord. Industry sales had risen, but Donner's sales, especially in the medium-priced lines, had not increased proportionately. The company did not use national advertising, restricting its promotional efforts to counter displays in large department stores. Management believed that price was the most effective competitive weapon.

In late 1968 Donner's management conducted some marketing research. (See Exhibits 2 and 3.) Results led management to formulate certain definite opinions about the hosiery market: (1) fashion had increased in importance among hosiery buyers; (2) no company in the industry marketed true "high-fashion" hosiery; (3) teen-age girls were wearing more hosiery; (4) only one company sold hosiery especially designed for teen-agers; and (5) Snagproof was the largest selling low-priced brand, and Sanderson and Concord ranked sixth and eighth, respectively, in sales of medium-priced lines. Management, therefore, concluded that low-priced brands, teen-age hosiery, and high-fashion hose were the three major areas of growth in the hosiery industry.

Subsequently, Donner's marketing strategy was aimed at these growth areas. As Snagproof already led in the lower-priced market, management focused its strategic efforts on the teen-age and fashion market segments.

EXHIBIT 2

Excerpts from Secondary Data Contained
in Donner's 1968 Marketing Research
on America's Youth Market

	Total Population (in thousands)	Percentage of Population			
		0–5 Years	6-11 Years	12-17 Years	18-24 Years
New England States	11,466.4	11.1	12.1	11.0	10.7
Middle Atlantic	37,242.2	10.7	11.7	10.8	10.3
East North Central	39,758.7	11.3	12.8	11.9	11.1
West North Central	16,205.5	10.8	12.7	11.9	11.6
South Atlantic	30,144.5	11.8	12.6	11.7	11.9
East South Central	13,154.2	11.5	12.8	12.0	12.5
West South Central	19,336.9	11.8	13.1	12.1	11.7
Mountain	8,102.1	12.4	13.8	12.5	11.5
Pacific	26,095.2	11.7	12.5	11.4	10.8
U.S.A.	201,505.7	11.4	12.5	11.6	11.2

Source: Department of Commerce, Bureau of the Census; *Current Population Reports,*
Series P-25; No. 381.

Although both Sanderson and Concord were national brands, neither possessed
the needed fashion or teen-age appeal; so it was decided to upgrade Concord's
image to strengthen its salability as a high-fashion, premium-price line. At the
same time a new brand, Slimchick, was introduced to appeal to the teen-age
market segment. Sanderson was continued as the company's medium-price line.
This strategy was formulated in the hope of accomplishing three objectives: (1)
creation of a national brand image synonymous with high fashion; (2)
penetration of the expanding teen-age market segment, and (3) development of
effective and mutually supporting promotional programs for the new market
offerings.

EXHIBIT 3

Current and Projected Female Population
of the U.S., Age 10 through 24, 1960 to 1990

Year	*10-14 Yrs.*	*15-19 Yrs.*	*20-24 Yrs.*
1960 (Actual)	8,314	6,652	5,586
1965 (Est.)	9,323	8,305	6,794
1970 (Proj.)	10,169	9,407	8,551
1975 (Proj.)	10,181	10,257	9,558
1980 (Proj.)	10,586	10,245	10,401
1985 (Proj.)	13,454	10,699	10,394
1990 (Proj.)	15,318	13,532	10,817

Source: Department of Commerce, Bureau of the Census; *Current Population Reports,* Series P-25; No. 381.

FASHION LINE

The president, intrigued with the concept of a "boutique look" for the product, changed the Concord brand name to Concord Boutique and retained three internationally known fashion designers to design the product. Promotion of Concord Boutique was launched with a presentation in New York City. National advertising was concentrated in fashion-oriented magazines, including *Mademoiselle, Seventeen,* and *Vogue.* New packages and point-of-purchase displays were prepared for retailers' use. Cooperative advertising was also used, with Donner paying 50 percent of all retailers' ads featuring Concord Boutique. The total promotional effort focused on the fashion concept and the prestigious names of the product's designers. The product's prestige price allowed both Donner and its retailers higher markups than on other Donner brands.

Donner sought exclusive distribution for Concord Boutique, choosing only the largest department stores and the most prestigious women's shops. Company salesmen sold the new product and were paid the usual commission rate. Deliveries began in the fall of 1969, and market acceptance proved even better than anticipated. However, reorders were below expectations, largely because of retailers' complaints about poor delivery. Management was pleased that the product had bolstered lagging sales and profits; however, it was displeased with the sales force's effectiveness in promoting Concord Boutique and with the product's acceptance by department store buyers.

TEEN-AGE LINE

Donner introduced Slimchick in four colors, six styles, and a full range of sizes. Four styles were specifically designed for "school wear," while two were for "dress-up." Donner set a medium price on its teen-age line; however, retailers secured larger markups than on other medium-priced lines, including Sanderson.

Since management desired to coordinate the introduction and promotion of other new products, Slimchick, like Concord Boutique, was sold to retailers as an exclusive. However, Slimchick was promoted through advertising appearing on national television and in major teen-age magazines. Regular salesmen were responsible for selling Slimchick and were instructed to concentrate their efforts in metropolitan New York, Chicago, and Los Angeles. Sales were below expectations, although inquiries flooded the central office.

Questions

1. Evaluate the product planning approach used by Donner for Concord Boutique and Slimchick.
2. What additional factors should have been considered by management?
3. Discuss the relevance of the product life cycle concept for Donner's formulation of marketing strategy.

BEARDEN'S PIANO COMPANY

Piano Retailer—Loss of Franchise

Early in 1970 James Bearden, president of Bearden's Piano Company of Decatur, Georgia, an Atlanta suburb, was wondering how to compensate for the loss of one of his dealer franchises. Bearden's dealt in new and used pianos, but currently most of its sales were of used and rebuilt pianos. A short time before, the firm had severed relations with Yamaha International Corporation, its major supplier of new pianos, and had not yet found a suitable replacement.

Since its founding in 1952 Bearden's had specialized in selling new and used grand pianos, but it also carried a narrow line of vertical pianos. From time to time it stocked a few organs, even though the company considered itself a piano specialist. Bearden's also offered piano tuning and repair services, both of which became increasingly important sources of revenue after discontinuance of the Yamaha line. Bearden's did not provide piano-moving service, since it used hired trucks and part-time workers for its own deliveries. A music teacher worked part-time on a commission basis, instructing neighborhood children in piano. Exhibit 1 shows company sales for the period 1964 through 1969. Sales of new and used pianos constituted about 70 percent of total sales.

EXHIBIT 1

Bearden's Piano Company — Gross Sales

Year	Sales
1964	$40,000
1965	44,000
1966	69,000
1967	72,500
1968	76,000
1969	29,000

James Bearden looked upon the Atlanta metropolitan area as a good market for musical merchandise, particularly DeKalb County. This fast-growing county, in which Bearden's was located, ranked second in population only to Fulton County in the heart of Atlanta. Per household incomes in DeKalb County were among the highest in Georgia, nearly four thousand dollars above the state's average, and three thousand dollars higher than the United States average.

To keep pace with Atlanta's booming economy, Bearden's had recently enlarged its building, adding showrooms and offices; also housed were rebuilding facilities and a small music studio. Before losing the Yamaha line, business was good in the *string-street* location, although James Bearden knew that a significant amount of business was being lost to outlying shopping centers.[1]

Twenty-seven competitors, including Atlanta's two major department stores — Rich's and Davison's — sold pianos and related products in the metropolitan market. Except for Rich's and Davison's, central city piano retailers had experienced declining sales as more and more buyers bought at shopping centers and from suburban dealers. Alexander Piano Sales and Honey Music Company provided major competition for Bearden's in DeKalb County; both operated stores in nearby shopping centers. Generally, prospects visited all three stores before buying.

Bearden's management classified piano buyers into three groups:

1. Those searching for a piano to use exclusively as a piece of furniture

2. Those hunting for a fine musical instrument

3. Those looking for some combination of numbers 1 and 2.

---

[1] A *string street* is a street on which businesses locate with little or no effort to coordinate their merchandise offerings as in planned shopping centers.

"Furniture" prospects were interested mostly in style, appearance, and size. "Instrument" prospects sought performance and therefore regarded name brands as highly important.

Management believed that buyers thought of a piano as a "culture" item. Typical buyers wanted their children taught how to play; piano buyers were usually middle-aged, but piano players were generally young. Most buyers were members of white, middle- to high-income groups, many of them professional or management people. Most often, purchasing was a family decision, with husbands and wives commonly doing the prepurchase shopping together.

Bearden's handled two types of pianos: grand and vertical. Grand pianos ranged from the most popular models (five- or six-feet long) to concert grands (nine-feet long) designed for professional musicians. Upright pianos (those containing vertical plates and strings) included studios, spinets, and consoles. Bearden's sold studio models primarily to institutions; spinets and consoles, available in numerous styles and colors, were sold almost exclusively to private households. Grand pianos generally carried a higher dollar profit margin per unit than uprights.

Over the years Bearden's had handled various piano and organ lines. In 1954 management took on the Starck line, a medium-quality, medium-priced piano. In 1958 a little-known yet high-quality and high-priced line, Krakauer, was added. Bearden's had also carried, at one time or another, Gulbransen, Lowrey, and Thomas organs, although none were ever "pushed." Bearden's stock was high quality, but not particularly composed of name brands until it added Yamaha pianos and organs in 1965.

THE YAMAHA STORY

Nippon Gakki Company, Ltd., of Hammanatsu, Japan, maker of Yamaha (although better known by the United States general public for its motorcycles), was the world's largest piano manufacturer. Organs, guitars, band instruments, skis, boats, and archery equipment were also made under the Yamaha name. The first Yamaha sales office in the United States opened its doors in 1960, and Yamaha, along with a rival Japanese company – K. Kawai – soon came to dominate the United States piano market.

Yamaha piano production rose each year after 1960, and in 1968 the company turned out 120,000 pianos, two and one-half times as many pianos as Wurlitzer, America's largest manufacturer, which made 45,000 pianos. In 1966 Story and Clark Piano Company, a highly respected United States manufacturer, contracted with Yamaha to make Story and Clark grand pianos. About the same time Baldwin Piano and Organ Company, another United States manufacturer, made a similar agreement with Kawai.

Yamaha produced a high-quality piano. Employing low-cost but highly efficient mass-production methods and utilizing patents acquired from Beckstein, long recognized as a top European piano maker, Yamaha gained worldwide prominence. Numerous universities, churches, and individuals endorsed the Yamaha piano; it was purchased by such leading musical educational institutions as the Toronto Conservatory of Music, Oberlin College, and the University of North Carolina.

Bearden's sales increases during 1965–68 traced directly to the Yamaha line, although occasionally it "special ordered" a Starck or a Krakauer. Previously specializing in *rebuilt* grands, the Yamaha dealership now allowed Bearden's to offer a complete line of *new* grands, opening up new opportunities to sell to restaurants, night clubs, schools, and churches. Bearden's continued to rebuild pianos but greatly reduced its emphasis on this phase of the business. Yamaha's grand pianos were similar to other makes, but its vertical pianos were available in a variety of styles for which preferences existed in the American market: Early American, French Provincial, Italian Provincial, European, Contemporary, and Traditional.

Bearden's concentrated its promotion on the Yamaha products, advertising in local newspapers, neighborhood publications, high school annuals, and telephone directory "yellow pages." It also set up a Yamaha exhibit at Atlanta's 1965 Southeastern Fair, generating high interest and resulting in numerous inquiries and sales. Personal selling was aided by Yamaha sales brochures and pamphlets.

Yamaha suggested retail prices for all models (Exhibit 2). Bearden's

EXHIBIT 2

Retail Price Ranges for Yamaha and Similar Makes—1968

	Make	*Size*	*Price Range*
Grands	Yamaha	5'1" - 9'6"	$1,695 - $ 6,195
	Chickering	5'1" - 5'8"	2,275 - 2,890
	Knabe	5'1" - 9'	2,300 - 6,550
	Steinway	5'1" - 8'11"	3,325 - 7,500
	Baldwin	5'2" - 9'	3,018 - 7,700
	Bechstein	5'6" - 8'9"	5,300 - 12,000
	Bosendorfer	5' - 9'6"	5,600 - 13,800
	Kawai	5'1" - 9'2"	1,695 - 6,195
Verticals	Yamaha	41 - 48"	$ 695 - $ 995
	Chickering	40"	1,175 - 1,480
	Knight	41 - 45"	1,495 - 1,595
	Bechstein	45 - 50"	2,800 - 3,400
	Steinway	40 - 46½"	1,495 - 1,895
	Everett	41 - 45"	1,015 - 1,170
	Kawai	41 - 49"	650 - 995

margin averaged 45 percent. James Bearden believed that on a quality-for-the-money basis Yamaha was the best piano on the market. It was priced under all competitors except Kawai, which mirrored Yamaha's retail prices but allowed dealers a higher margin averaging about 51 percent.

In Atlanta, Yamaha dealers had exclusive community distribution but not exclusive metropolitan-area distribution. Initially, Yamaha had three Atlanta dealers: Bearden's handled the line exclusively in Decatur; Maddox Music Mart sold in southwest Atlanta; and Waggoner Music, Inc., covered northwest Atlanta (Marietta).

Two matters caused friction to develop between Bearden's and Yamaha. The first was that Bearden's management did not want to emphasize organs as suggested by Yamaha (only two were ever ordered). The second was that James Bearden refused to sponsor and conduct a music course recommended by Yamaha for all its American dealers; he believed that the initial cost of setting up the course for approximately $2,800 was too high (Exhibit 3) and that Yamaha's "typical" operating budget was unrealistic because it was difficult to enroll as many as three hundred students and even more difficult to hire qualified teachers, particularly at the rates suggested by Yamaha (Exhibit 4).

In June 1968 Yamaha's United States general sales manager contacted James Bearden and asked that he begin to offer the music course. Bearden refused. In October Yamaha's district sales manager visited Bearden and

EXHIBIT 3

Yamaha Music Course Specifications—Basic Course[a]

Equipment:	
Ten DS/49 Yamaha reed organs	$ 90.00 each
Kit of music materials	5.55
Rhythm instrument set	
1 small drum and beater	
1 tambourine, 7″ diameter	
1 set orchestra bells	
(Glockenspiel with mallets)	
3 sets sleigh bells	
1 5″ triangle and beater	
1 wood block and beater	
2 castanets	
1 rhythmica	37.00
One magnet board (resembles	
blackboard with music notes)	12.50
Attendance record forms	.02 each
Student registration cards	.02 each
Mailing brochures (optional)	.04 each

(continued)

EXHIBIT 3 (continued)

Teacher:
Qualifications
Age 23 - 26
College degree required
Piano and singing talents
Good worker with children
References required
Passing a Yamaha music test
Four training seminars required $300.00 cost to
                                                                         dealer

[a]Pre-school children — ages four to six.

EXHIBIT 4

Typical Operating Budget—Basic Music Course

Tuition received (300 @ $10 per month)		$3,000
Reserve for teaching (three teachers)	$1,200	
Royalty to Yamaha (10%)	300	
Reserve for church facility rental if used	600	
	$2,100	
Remainder for administration and profit		900
Profit on material sales, average per month		50
Total average profit per month		$ 950

strongly suggested that he start the music course or face losing the dealership. Again Bearden refused, and in early 1969 the association was terminated.

The dealership was moved to the Atlanta Piano Company, which had also recently acquired Maddox Music Mart, the Yamaha dealer in southwest Atlanta. Atlanta Piano planned to open two suburban stores in northwest Atlanta in early 1970 and agreed with Yamaha to offer the music course at all three locations. At about the same time the other Yamaha dealer in Atlanta, Waggoner Music Company, lost its dealership for selling to an out-of-state customer, a violation of its dealership agreement.

Subsequently, Bearden's found itself largely confined to the used piano business, since its stock of Starck and Krakauer pianos had also dwindled to nothing. Painfully aware of the seriousness of the situation, James Bearden explored the possibility of building up the offerings of Starck or Krakauer pianos, or of adding the Everett, Knight, or Kawai lines as possible replacements. Of these, the Kawai line seemed the best choice because it compared favorably with Yamaha in product offering, quality, and price. However, Kawai pianos could only be obtained through another dealer, a downtown Atlanta firm. This firm, headed by a personal friend of James Bearden, wanted a 5 percent commission on each unit ordered through it. But, since Kawai allowed a slightly higher dealer margin than Yamaha, Bearden was inclined to take on the line.

Questions

1. Was Yamaha justified in taking away Bearden's dealership? Why?
2. Should James Bearden have taken on a new line?

3-6

FACILITIES CORPORATION—TECHNICAL EQUIPMENT AND OFFICE MACHINE DIVISION

Equipment Manufacturer—Problem with New Product Line

Facilities Corporation of Buffalo, New York, made large-scale computers; electronic controls; industrial, agricultural, and construction equipment and systems; office machines and equipment; consumer products; and technical furniture. Two plants in upstate New York manufactured the technical furniture.[1] Founded in 1884, the company enjoyed a good reputation as a quality manufacturer of technical furniture, the Hi-Standard line. The school construction boom, beginning in 1954, increased market demand for desks, library furniture, and other technical furniture items, thereby causing many competitors to enter the field. Some of the new competitors produced inferior furniture with poor styling, design, and construction, but as most orders for technical furniture depended upon availability of public funds, a considerable

---

[1] *Technical* furniture contrasts with what might be termed *commercial* furniture. Technical furniture is custom built to meet certain definite requirements and specifications according to the particular function that it must fulfill. For example, a rare book display case for a library must be dustproof and equipped with a specially designed glass front which prevents sunlight from discoloring books on display.

market for lower-quality furniture existed. Facilities Corporation found itself unable to compete with respect to price as competitors consistently submitted the lowest bids. Management realized the need for corrective measures and considered taking action either (1) to lower prices on the present line or (2) to market a new line composed of lower-priced and lower-quality items. Ultimately, it was decided to introduce a new line, but subsequent results were disappointing, indicating the need for additional corrective measures.

Facilities Corporation marketed its products through five divisions. Exhibit 1 indicates a breakdown of 1968's sales by divisions.

The company sold its technical furniture through forty-six direct factory sales specialists calling primarily on architects and school administrators. These sales specialists covered the forty-eight contiguous United States and reported to regional sales managers for the West, Midwest-Southwest, Southeast, and East territories. Each regional manager supervised from eight to fifteen salesmen. Regional managers reported directly to the sales manager for division IV. Personnel turnover among salesmen had caused some recent concern, as an increasing number, discouraged by the difficulty of overcoming price resistance to Facilities Corporation's technical furniture, were leaving the company in early 1969. Many of those leaving were among the company's more experienced and competent salesmen, some having been in its employ for more than fifteen years.

For several reasons top management wanted, if possible, to avoid adding a new line. Considerable expense would be involved in developing and introducing a new line to the market. In addition, danger existed that a second — and lower-quality — line might damage the company's high-quality image. Therefore management moved to cut costs, hoping to maintain the same high quality while making it possible to sell at reduced prices, for example, certain costly production inspection procedures were dropped. This caused a higher proportion of defective items to get into the hands of customers and the volume of returns zoomed, causing, in turn, increased shipping costs and loss of customer goodwill. Other cost-cutting efforts produced similar disappointing results, eventually leading management to conclude that costs could not be reduced sufficiently to permit meaningful price reductions.

Finally, in desperation, management decided to develop a wholly new line of technical furniture which would sell at lower prices but which customers could still regard as high quality. The company launched an intensive product research and development program, utilizing both company research personnel and outside design consultants. Arrangements were made with a well-known paint company to develop a new finish for the furniture. As plans for the new product line took shape, the company purchased additional equipment and machinery, most of it rather expensive. For example, two new furnaces required for baking the new finish cost $150,000 each. Before project completion, three years had passed and several million dollars had been invested in research and development efforts.

EXHIBIT 1

Sales by Division, 1968

Division	*Sales*
I. *Information Handling and Retrieval Systems* Electronic digital computers Computer peripheral equipment	$ 544,000,000
II. *Aerospace* Airborne navigation systems Autopilots Compass systems Speed controls Airborne computers Missile guidance systems Air traffic control systems	304,000,000
III. *Industrial, Agriculture, and Construction Equipment* Hydraulic systems Combines Balers Livestock feeding systems Crop handling equipment	352,000,000
IV. *Technical Furniture and Office Machines* Adding machines Electric and manual typewriters Electronic copiers Office duplicators Office furniture Technical furniture	240,000,000
V. *Consumer Products* Electric knives Hair curlers and dryers Health and beauty care products	160,000,000
TOTAL SALES	$1,600,000,000 ($1.6 billion)

Note: Sales by customer classification were: 27 percent to military and space agencies, 53 percent to domestic-commercial market, and 20 percent to international market.

When the new line was ready for market testing, the company completely equipped a new "showcase" library in a public school without charge. Architects, building planners, school administrators, and other "influentials" were then invited to inspect the new line and give their evaluations. The line was generally well received, many "influentials" considering it years ahead in styling. For the full-scale market introduction of the new line, it was decided to include only those items to which 90 percent of the "influentials" had reacted favorably.

Next, management faced the problem of pricing the new line. It had originally hoped to price it competitively with other makes of cheaper technical furniture, but product development costs exceeded estimates, and the break-even point at competitive prices seemed unrealistically high. When all calculations were in, the indicated minimum prices for items in the new line were higher than those for items in the established high-quality line. Nevertheless, believing firmly that style, design, and construction of the new line was years ahead of competitors' offerings, management decided to proceed with the full-scale market introduction.

Market introduction began in early 1969. Management scheduled a preview of the new line at its new design center in New York, inviting architects, school administrators, and other "influentials," as in the testing phase. Product training was provided for the sales force, samples were shipped nationwide, and films were made emphasizing the new line's special features. To exhibit various items in the new line, showrooms were opened and, in some instances, entire libraries were furnished.

The new line began to take hold and showed promise of market success. Nevertheless, feedback to management indicated customer resistance to high prices and continuing sales force dissatisfaction. In addition, management belatedly recognized that the advanced styling was suitable for use only in certain newer, more modern, buildings.

Management moved first to improve short-run profitability and then to improve long-range marketing strategy. Pursuing the first goal, it decided to accept orders only for the most profitable items; this move proved disastrous — sales volume fell sharply, production lagged, and dissatisfaction reigned throughout the entire division. Management's long-range strategy called for major changes, beginning immediately. Facilities Corporation converted its New York furniture plants to manufacturing other products and decided to transfer the furniture manufacturing operation to a southern state. Management based this decision largely on two factors: (1) it believed the New York plants could never become more efficient in straight-line production of technical furniture, and (2) the major competitors based their production operations in the South where there were lower taxes, cheaper utility rates, and relatively low-cost labor. Management believed a new factory in the South would enable the company to compete profitably on a price basis while still maintaining quality standards.

Questions

1. What improvements, if any, could have been made in product planning procedures and practices in the technical furniture division of Facilities Corporation?

2. Should the new product line have been introduced?

3. What recommendations for future action would you make to Facilities Corporation's management?

PALMER CORPORATION

Industrial Equipment Producer—Entering
a New Market

Palmer Corporation had headquarters and main manufacturing facilities at Beaver Falls, Pennsylvania. It made a complete line of gear-type power transmission equipment, automatic valve controls, linear actuators, and fluid mixers. The company custom built most of its products to users' specifications and manufactured for stock only a few low-priced items, such as replacement parts. Total 1967 sales amounted to $54 million. In August 1965, during a ten-year expansion of the pulp and paper industry, the Palmer Corporation introduced a product line for sale to that industry; by 1968 management concluded that sales of this product line (fluid mixers) were not meeting earlier expectations.

All Palmer's product lines were marketed through a technically oriented sales organization. It consisted of 24 company salesmen working out of thirteen metropolitan sales offices, fifty-two manufacturers' agents using 127 salesmen to cover fifty-eight sales districts, and thirty-seven manufacturers' agents in thirty-one foreign countries. All the company's own salesmen had either engineering degrees or a minimum of ten years' experience in the mechanical power transmission area. Prior to assigning men to the field, the home office required that each man spend eighteen to twenty-four months as an inside sales engineer. This period of training stressed the acquisition of extensive product knowledge, and trainees were rotated through all corporate departments. The field salesman's duties involved application, preliminary design, and, in some instances, product servicing.

THE MARKET

In 1963 the pulp and paper industry began a ten-year expansion. Intermediate-range forecasts indicated that from 1965 to 1968 over $1 billion would be spent annually, increasing industry productive capacity by 12 percent. Industry capacity historically exceeded actual production by about 10 percent. (See Exhibit 1.) The buildup of industry capacity was along three main lines: (1) "pure" expansion required to keep pace with rising pulp and paper demand; (2) modernization involving new technology, making existing machinery and equipment obsolete; and (3) replacement of worn-out equipment. An estimated 51 percent of predicted expenditures would be for "pure" expansion and 49 percent for modernization and replacement. Pulp and paper industry expenditures on gear-type products, such as fluid mixers, were forecast at roughly $10 million annually.

Personal relationships pervaded the pulp and paper industry, and were maintained and encouraged through the various trade journals, magazines, conventions, trade meetings, and joint committees and the "open-plant" policy of most mills. Information concerning a particular mill's solution of a problem quickly spread to other mills and was generally soon being accepted as industry practice. Because of the open-plant policy, few developments, processes, or operating techniques remained trade secrets for long. This phenomenon carried over into selection and use of capital equipment — all industry members soon learned of specific instances involving a product's success or failure.

Zippy, Palmer's main competition, introduced its fluid mixers to the pulp and paper industry in 1956. Prior to Zippy's entry, the industry regarded mixing as more of an art than a science. Mixing knowledge and skills acquired over time by one man in using horsepower, speed, and propeller diameter were passed on to his successor. The end results of mixing operations often were not predictable and in many cases were unsatisfactory. Through application of chemical engineering and fluid dynamics principles, Zippy achieved consistent and predictable results in most mixing applications; consequently, its product line gained industry-wide acceptance and a commanding lead over competitors entering the market later.

United States Pulp and Paper Industry: Capacity and Production

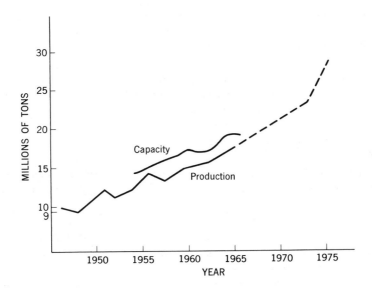

THE PRODUCT

A fluid mixer was basically an electric motor directly coupled to a mechanical speed reducer which, in turn, was attached to a shaft and an impeller. The mixer was mounted on a tank so that the shaft and the impeller extended into the fluid(s) or material(s) being mixed. From this basic arrangement it was possible to substitute other prime movers for the electric motor, incorporate special seals between the tank and the reducer section, extend shafts, and make the components of almost any metal from carbon steel to titanium. Modifications of the basic arrangement were the rule rather than the exception.

At the time of its market entry Palmer offered four basic mixer designs, more than any competitor. Palmer was also the only company to manufacture its own mechanical speed reducer; competitors purchased reducers from transmission manufacturers. Management believed that offering four designs and "in-house" manufacture of the speed reducer component were significant competitive advantages. Mixer prices ranged from seven hundred to fifty thousand dollars. Although Zippy mixers enjoyed wide market acceptance, prices and quality of Palmer mixers compared favorably with all major competitors, including Zippy.

MARKET ENTRY

In 1965, basing its decision on detailed market information and forecasts, Palmer introduced its mixers to the pulp and paper industry. The company had previously operated on the periphery of this market through selling speed reducers and valve controls both to the mills and to the many manufacturers of original equipment for the pulp and paper industry. Although Palmer was "known" in the industry, management recognized that the mixers required a sales approach different from that of other company products. In other words, to sell effectively, Palmer salesmen would need to understand not only pulp production and papermaking and mixing methods and techniques but customers' objectives in using particular mixing processes. This contrasted sharply with circumstances met in selling the other product lines where customers normally specified machine requirements, and Palmer's engineering department came up with needed designs.

Competing in the pulp and paper market, it was necessary to accumulate certain industry information, to have management assimilate it, and to teach it to field and inside salesmen. In April 1965 Mel Melrose, a man with twenty-five years' experience as a paper mill superintendent, was hired to assist in this effort. His first assignment was to assume responsibility for developing a design manual to serve as a reference source in mixer sales. This manual detailed proper methods of sizing mixers for different applications and provided related information on pulp and paper production. Next, he assisted in modifying existing mixer designs to meet specialized conditions in the pulp and paper industry, his role being that of adviser to the design engineers. He then visited numerous United States pulp and paper mills and wrote detailed reports on the industry's current problems for perusal by Palmer management. Finally, he was appointed as a manufacturers' agent for Palmer's mixer sales in the southeastern United States.

THE SALES FORCE FOR MIXERS

Mike Thomas, vice-president of sales, next analyzed the existing sales force with respect to (1) geographic areas that would require more selling emphasis and (2) salesmen and agents capable of selling the mixer line after additional training. Initially, five manufacturers' agents covering eight areas and sales personnel from two company offices were selected for special training. These agents and company offices fielded twenty-four salesmen in all, but only thirteen actually received the special training (see Exhibit 2).

EXHIBIT 2

Pulp and Paper Specialists

1965 *Company Sales Office*		*Received* *Training*	*1968* *Company Sales Office*	
New York AP P&P			New York AP P&P	
Salesmen	4[b]	2	Salesmen	5
Philadelphia AP P&P			Philadelphia AP P&P	
Salesmen	4	2	Salesmen	4
Manufacturers'			*Manufacturers'*	
Representatives			*Representatives*	
Southeastern U.S.A. P&P			Lakeland, Fla. AP P&P	
Mel Melrose[a]	1	1	Salesmen	4
Boston, Mass. M P&P			Lafayette, Ind. M P&P	
Salesmen	2	1	Salesmen	2
San Francisco M P&P			Louisville, Ky. M P&P	
Los Angeles			Salesmen	1
Salesmen	3	2	New Orleans, La. AP P&P	
Seattle, Wash. P&P			Salesmen	3
Salesmen	3	2	Boston, Mass. P&P	
Cleveland, Ohio M P&P			Salesmen	2
Akron, Ohio			Minneapolis, Minn. AP P&P	
Pittsburgh, Pa.			Salesmen	3
Salesmen	7	3	Kansas City, Mo. AP P&P	
Total	24	13	Salesmen	4
			Syracuse, N.Y. AP P&P	
			Salesmen	1
			Charlotte, N.C. AP P&P	
			Salesmen	1
			Akron, Ohio M P&P	
			Cleveland, Ohio	
			Pittsburgh, Pa.	
			Salesmen	7
			Cincinnati, Ohio M P&P	
			Salesmen	2
			Portland, Oreg. P&P	
			Salesmen	2
			Richmond, Va. M P&P	
			Salesmen	2
			Total	43

Code: AP—All Products, M—Mixers, P&P—Pulp and Paper mixers. Code indicates organization sales responsibility.

[a]Resigned after eighteen months.
[b]The number of salesmen in each organization qualified to sell pulp and paper mixers was not necessarily the same as the totals shown. In some cases only one man in the sales office was qualified in this special area.

The special training period varied in length from one to two weeks, depending upon the salesman's background. The training was conducted at the home office under the direction of L. Cobb, senior application engineer, who later was to manage inside sales. Trainees were expected to learn the technical advantages of the Palmer mixer line compared with competitors' lines, mixing techniques, equipment applications, and pricing methods.

On completion of training, the salesmen knew they were to handle routine sales only. Cobb was to handle all situations involving extensive equipment modifications or unusual applications. Inquiries directed to the home office were quoted on directly to customers, and copies were sent to the area salesmen. Salesmen would then follow up on quotes, answer questions, and, hopefully, get the orders. All Palmer quotations carried a guarantee that the mixer would perform as described or would be replaced at no charge. Two major competitors, including Zippy, used similar guarantees.

ADVERTISING

An advertising campaign started soon after sales training was underway. Models of the mixers were displayed at trade shows and conventions. Advertisements appeared in trade journals and magazines, and an attempt was made to promote a "showcase job" to point up Palmer's installation and operational efficiency and its industry know-how. This was partially achieved through an early contract Palmer obtained to supply all of the mixer requirements of Neptune Soap, a large detergent manufacturer, which had just begun producing facial and toilet tissue. However, Neptune regarded its manufacturing process as confidential, and since it was new to the pulp and paper industry, little testimonial benefit accrued to Palmer.

Despite its efforts Palmer did not reach its goal of 10 percent of the mixer sales to the pulp and paper industry. Only a few mixer inquiries emanating from within the pulp and paper industry came to Palmer, and Cobb had written salesmen several times urging them to generate more inquiries. One possible reason for the disappointing results was that Palmer delivered in from fourteen to twenty-two weeks and competitors in eight to twelve weeks. However, both Thomas and Cobb agreed that delivery was critical only for replacement sales, since most new construction programs had lead times well within Palmer's delivery schedule.

Questions

1. Should Palmer have initially entered the pulp and paper market? Why?

2. What advantages did Palmer have over competitors? What were the competitors' advantages?

3. What steps should Palmer have taken to attain its goal of securing a 10 percent market share in sales of mixers to the pulp and paper industry?

3-8

THE ALLEN-BRADLEY COMPANY

Manufacturer of Control Devices—
Addition of New Products

The Allen-Bradley Company of Milwaukee, Wisconsin, pioneered in making motor control devices for industrial use. Its products were distributed nationally through its own sales force and a network of electrical wholesale distributors. District sales managers reported directly to the president, who was responsible for marketing operations and managed the sales effort within the context of broad corporate policy. Voting control of the corporation was held by a foundation set up by the founders; consequently, this was the chief reason why company policy had been to expand through retained earnings rather than outside financing. In its quest for new products the company therefore emphasized research and development (R & D) and made no move to acquire competitors or firms producing complementary products. In 1968 this emphasis on R & D resulted in two new products not closely related to established product lines but believed to have strong marketing possibilities.

The backbone of the company's business had always been the manufacture and sale of high-quality motor control devices. One of the two major product lines included control relays, contactors, switches, rheostats, motor control centers, push buttons, pilot control devices, and control units for high-voltage equipment, such as those used in factories and utility installations. The second major product line was made up of condensers, resistors, and other related highly technical and scientific devices used by the electronic equipment manufacturing industry. Because of the close relationship of these two lines, both were marketed through the same sales organization.

Direct sales effort was of two types. One type was exerted by a small but select group of electrical wholesale distributors, each of whom sold Allen-Bradley products on an exclusive basis within a specified geographical area. Each distributor was required to carry a complete line of stock items at an inventory level determined by the Allen-Bradley Company. The other type of sales effort was made by the company's own sales force of highly trained, well-paid mechanical and electrical engineers. These men sought out new accounts, performed required engineering work, and determined the indicated product applications. Normally, the company's own salesmen saw to it that most stock items were ordered through distributors, but in certain cases customers were allowed to order directly from the factory. Company selling strategy, in other words, was that the company's own sales force should complement the selling efforts of distributors by ensuring correct engineering applications of the products and by making the missionary calls and contacts that distributors' sales personnel were unable to handle. Furthermore, in cases in which customers were disenchanted with distributors, existence of the company sales force provided an alternative source of supply for Allen-Bradley products. Prices quoted to customers were identical regardless of whether orders were placed through distributors or directly with the company. Also, as a matter of policy, the company did not compete on a price basis but strived instead to manufacture and sell the highest-quality products and to provide the best delivery time and service available anywhere.

In introducing new products to the market, company practice varied. The sales force attempted to pull new additions to the line of motor control products through the marketing channel by bringing them to the attention of architects and design engineers (who wrote the specifications for electrical installations), contractors (who made such installations), and industrial users (who paid for them). For example, a modular motor control center was introduced at a luncheon meeting with the executive committee of the Chicago Electrical Contractors Association. In other instances, company salesmen closely coordinated their efforts with distributors to introduce new products to industrial users. New additions to the line of condensers, resistors, and related products were introduced directly by the sales force to electronics manufacturers, to computer manufacturers, and to firms producing advanced technical devices.

In 1968 the R & D department completed work on two new products. The first was a machine for the sifting of powders or particles, which compared with sifters then on the market was much less noisy and required substantially less maintenance. Preliminary market research indicated that the individual in a prospective customer's organization who would give the final sanction to such a purchase would be a physicist, chemist, or other scientist in charge of a large laboratory, a type of contact with which the company had had no previous experience. Such laboratories were found in pharmaceutical, chemical, and other scientifically oriented companies.

The second new development was a decorative architectural building tile which was easy to clean and withstood the extremes of weather as well as any available competitive products. Market introduction of the tile also presented a sales problem inasmuch as it lacked the engineering nature of the established product lines and presented little possibility of being marketed through the established distributive network. Furthermore, it was felt that the existing sales force, because of its high degree of engineering orientation, would not be appropriate for use in introducing or in selling the new line of tile.

Questions

1. Should Allen-Bradley have attempted to market either or both of these new products? If so, how?
2. What should have been Allen-Bradley's product objectives? Product policies?

SECTION 4

MARKETING CHANNELS

CAMP-BELL CANDLE COMPANY

Candle Manufacturer — Using Rack Jobbers for Product Introduction

The Camp-Bell Candle Company, Syracuse, New York, made and sold a wide assortment of candles for both commercial and church use. The commercial line was distributed through department stores, gift shops, florist shops, and variety stores. An earlier effort to secure supermarket distribution had failed, but in 1966 John Bell, commercial sales manager, again began a campaign for supermarket distribution. By the close of 1967 Bell, aiming to expand both sales and geographical extent of supermarket distribution, was considering adding rack jobbers in five large eastern cities and on the West Coast.

Steven A. Camp organized Camp-Bell in 1925 after working some years for the Ware and Smith Candle Company. After twelve years of specialized production of church candles, Camp-Bell developed, in 1937, a line of staple dinner and decorative candles for home use. The new commercial line was introduced at a New York trade show, but although prospects showed interest, few bought. Somewhat discouraged, management considered underpricing the competition but finally decided to drop the commercial line.

However, the next year, in the summer of 1938, a buyer from an Indianapolis department store, L. S. Ayres, contacted Camp-Bell management and asked that the company produce an apple-shaped candle, an innovation for the industry. For exclusive selling rights until February 1939, the buyer promised to buy a minimum of 10,000 units. By the following spring the "Big Apple" dance craze had reached its height, and Camp-Bell had sold over 150,000 units to Ayres. Camp-Bell management, encouraged by this experience, proceeded to develop a wide line of novelty candles.

In the fall of 1939 Bell went back to New York City and at another trade show exhibited the novelty line and a new dinner candle line, both under the Cabel brand name. The novelty line sold well at the trade show, thus establishing a beachhead for Camp-Bell in the nonchurch market. Numerous customers who had originally bought only novelty candles at the trade show were also later persuaded to place orders for dinner candles.

From that time until 1967 nonchurch sales expanded rapidly, and the sales mixture tended to stabilize at 60 percent commercial candles and 40 percent church candles. Although the company had built a plant in California in 1957, the Syracuse plant continued to produce about 75 percent of the company's output. Exhibit 1 shows the geographical distribution of sales.

EXHIBIT 1

Geographical Distribution of Sales — 1967

Region	*Percentage of Company Total*
East	40
Midwest	35
South	8
Southwest	7
West Coast	10

Management estimated that Camp-Bell ranked second in total industry sales in 1967, but the company's showing with respect to different market segments varied. As the pioneer in novelty candles, the company had the number one position in sales through gift shops. Its poorest showing was in sales through supermarkets, where it stood fourth in the industry. (See Exhibit 2.)

From 1940 to 1967, as the company broadened its retail distribution, changes occurred in the relative importance of various types of retail outlets (see Exhibit 3). In 1940 sales were distributed evenly among department stores, gift shops, and florist shops. But by 1967 the major variety store chains (Woolworth, W. T. Grant, Kresge, J. J. Newberry, etc.) had become the company's most important retailers.

EXHIBIT 2

Industry Position by Sales Volume 1967

Total Sales:
  1. Ware and Smith Candle Co. (Syracuse, N.Y.)
  2. Camp-Bell
Church Sales:
  1. Ware and Smith
  2. Camp-Bell
Gift Shops:
  1. Camp-Bell
Hotel and Restaurant Sales:
  1. Chicago Candle Co.
  2. Camp-Bell
Department Store Sales:
  1. Victry-Lite Candle Co. (Oshkosh, Wis.)
  2. Colonial Candle Co. (Hyannis Port, Mass.)
  3. Camp-Bell
Major Chain Store Sales:
  1. Camp-Bell
  2. Columbia Wax Products, Inc. (Ozone, N.Y.)
  3. Candle-Lite (Cincinnati)
Supermarket Sales:
  1. Ware and Smith
  2. Halo Candle Co. (San Francisco)
  3. Capri Candle Co. (Pennsauken, N.J.)
  4. Camp-Bell

EXHIBIT 3

Percentage Distribution of Camp-Bell Sales
by Type of Retail Outlet

Type of Outlet	*1940 Percentage*	*1950 Percentage*	*1955 Percentage*	*1967 Percentage*
Department stores	33-1/3	30	22	10
Gift shops	33-1/3	30	22	20
Florist shops	33-1/3	30	21	15
Independent variety stores	—	5	10	10
Hotels and restaurants	—	5	5	10
Major variety store chains	—	—	20	30
Supermarkets	—	—	—	5
	100	100	100	100

In 1956 Camp-Bell's sales organization included a general sales manager, Samuel Bell; a church sales manager, Frank Tobey; and a commercial sales manager, N. J. Harvey. Two divisional sales managers, Joseph Bower and John Brant, reported to Harvey. Bell handled the major chain accounts, working with manufacturers' representatives. Harvey directed sales to department stores, gift shops, and florist shops. Bower managed hotel and restaurant sales, and Brant handled independent variety store accounts. These men worked directly with company salesmen, manufacturers' representatives, and rack jobbers. (See Exhibit 4.)

EXHIBIT 4

Camp-Bell Sales Organization

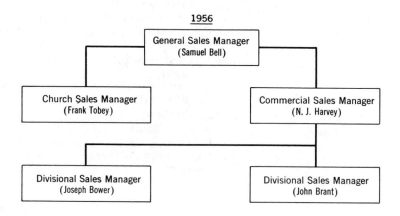

In 1957 Harvey died and Bower became commercial sales manager, with Brant taking over the hotel-restaurant accounts (see Exhibit 5).

In 1964 Samuel Bell's son, John Bell, joined the firm, replacing John Brant who became plant manager on the West Coast (see Exhibit 6).

In 1965 Bower resigned, John Bell became commercial sales manager, and his former assistant, Nancy Holt, was promoted to divisional sales manager. (See Exhibit 7.)

Selling methods varied with marketing channels. All company salesmen and some manufacturers' agents sold to department stores. Samuel Bell and certain manufacturers' agents sold exclusively to the major chains. Most company salesmen and most manufacturers' agents also sold to gift shops, hotels and restaurants, and variety stores. A small number of manufacturers' agents and rack jobbers sold to supermarkets, with agents accounting for 20 percent of supermarket sales, and rack jobbers for the rest.

EXHIBIT 5

Camp-Bell Sales Organization

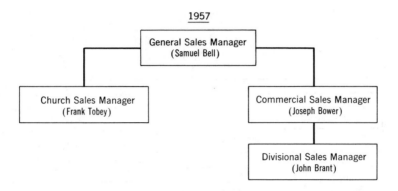

1957

Camp-Bell Sales Organization

EXHIBIT 6

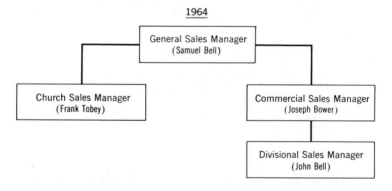

1964

1950 SUPERMARKET CAMPAIGN

In 1950 Camp-Bell's sales management sought to increase sales volume through widening retail distribution. After a market study it was concluded that (1) women were the main buyers of candles used in homes, (2) candles used in homes were bought mainly on impulse, and (3) most consumers had no particular preferences as to the type of retail outlet. Management was also convinced that price exerted very little influence on consumers' candle-buying decisions. In management's opinion, color and design, stimulated by impulse at the point of purchase, were the important factors.

EXHIBIT 7

Camp-Bell Sales Organization, 1965-1967

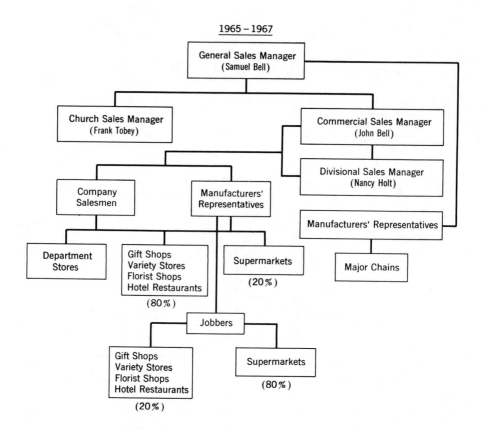

Management therefore decided that supermarkets would be ideal retail outlets for candles. Bower took charge of the commercial line, seeking to secure supermarket distribution through food brokers in major cities. At this time the line was made up of high-grade, high-priced candles, the same items as were distributed through gift shops and department stores. As a part of the introductory campaign, supermarkets received a free, simply constructed, point-of-purchase display rack.

Initial efforts to secure supermarket distribution proved unsuccessful. Company officials believed that the lack of market acceptance was due primarily to shortcomings of the food brokers. Brokers handled many different product lines, and many were unable to devote adequate attention to Camp-Bell's candles. A field investigation of supermarket outlets showed that, in many cases, inventories were low, displays were pushed into obscure corners, and candles were being mishandled and damaged. Supermarket sales did not reach expectations (less than 1 percent of total sales), and when Joseph Bower became commercial sales manager in 1957, the company abandoned the program.

1966 SUPERMARKET CAMPAIGN

When management resurrected the supermarket campaign in 1966 it set two sales goals, both to be reached within four years: (1) to achieve a number two industry ranking in candle sales through supermarkets, and (2) to make supermarket sales account for 15 percent of total sales. John Bell, now in charge of the effort to secure sales through supermarkets, (1) concentrated the initial distribution effort in New York City, New Jersey, and Connecticut, (2) sold through two manufacturers' agents and one rack jobber, (3) retained the traditional commercial line and prices, (4) provided buyers with modern display racks, and (5) designed new, bright, and colorful packages.

The rack jobber, who placed the line in the Food Fair and Grand Union supermarket chains, made 80 percent of Camp-Bell's total supermarket sales in 1967. Camp-Bell had given him a substantial discount from list prices, and he passed on a full 40 percent margin to the retailers. Camp-Bell split the cost of display racks (ninety dollars each) with the rack jobber. Food chains buying through the manufacturers' agents purchased display racks at full price but were allowed to deduct 5 percent from invoices until their investments in display racks were amortized.

By the end of 1967 Camp-Bell was the fourth largest candle seller through supermarkets, and supermarket sales constituted 5 percent of total sales volume. John Bell estimated that both major sales goals would be achieved a year ahead of schedule if the company secured rack jobbers in Boston, Philadelphia, Baltimore, Washington, and Detroit. He was also considering adding a rack jobber on the West Coast.

Questions

1. Why did Camp-Bell fail in its first effort to obtain supermarket distribution?
2. Why did Camp-Bell appear to be succeeding in its second effort to obtain supermarket distribution?
3. Should the company have expanded its use of rack jobbers to other cities throughout the country?

ACE MANUFACTURING COMPANY

Bat Manufacturer—Decision to Cultivate
an Additional Market Segment

Ace Manufacturing Company, founded in 1924, made baseball and softball bats in its Juniper, Alabama, plant and sold them throughout the United States and in Central and South America. Ace first manufactured ax handles, adding bats in 1940, which later became the only product line. The company used two marketing channels. (See figure on facing page.) Ace's major line, Linedrive, was sold through wholesalers and direct to large retailers; bats made according to retailers' specifications and those carrying private labels were sold direct. Ace had never tried to secure orders from professional baseball teams but, believing that the top-grade Linedrive models were of high enough quality for professional use, top management was currently weighing the advisability of cultivating this market segment.

Ace ranked fourth in total industries' sales in 1970, behind Hillerich and Bradsby (H and B), Hanna, and Adirondack, but ranked second in sales of softball bats. Regular brands accounted for 80 percent of its total sales of five hundred thousand dollars, with the balance being made up of private-label business. Linedrive brands were bought and used primarily by semipro, school, and youth teams.

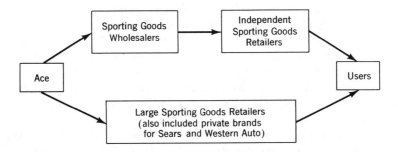

All industry members had difficulty in procuring raw wood for bat production. Smaller firms such as Ace had the most difficulty, as they had weaker bargaining positions. Ash grown in the northeastern United States was the best hardwood for bats. Used not only for making bats but for making skis, sleds, and furniture, ash wood was almost always in short supply, and fierce competition existed among buyers of the wood. This had led the larger bat makers to experiment with substitute materials, both other woods and some light metals. However, on laminated and aluminum models, product weight proved difficult to control in meeting required strength specifications. Players also balked at using the "new" bats, and industry executives concluded that the market wanted bats made of wood — preferably ash.

Ace offered twenty-eight models under the Linedrive name: four for semipro, college, and high school use; three approved for Pony and Babe Ruth leagues; six for Little League; and fifteen for playing softball. More expensive models were made of northern ash; less expensive models of hickory and other hardwoods. Bat models came in different finishes, colors (stains), lengths, weights, handle and barrel sizes,[1] and with or without handle wrappings (tape, foam rubber, or fiberglass).

Ace sold at competitive prices. The "top of the line" (used mainly by semipro, college, and high school teams) retailed at $5.20; comparable H and B and Hanna models retailed at $5.40. Little league models and softball bats carried lower prices. The "bottom of the line" retailed at $1.80. Retailers' markups averaged 40 percent.

Although some top-line Ace baseball bats carried the names of certain major league stars, none were either "signature" models or actually used by these players. All the stars had done was to "approve" certain styles as being similar to the bats they actually used. The rest of the baseball bat line and all softball bats carried names, such as Bomber, Swatter, and Slasher.

Ace employed thirty full-time people: twenty-four in manufacturing and six in sales. Salesmen called on sporting goods wholesalers and large retailers, selling Linedrive models. The main office dealt directly with private-label accounts. Salesmen received 15 percent commission on sales and paid their own

---

[1] The *barrel* is the bat's hitting portion.

expenses. In addition, each time a salesman covered a trade show or a convention, he received a flat fee of two hundred dollars.

In 1970 Ace spent its entire five-thousand dollars advertising budget on trade-journal advertising and product brochures. The ads, which appeared during the playing season, emphasized quality at reasonable prices. Product brochures stressed the modern manufacturing process, an aspect of the operation that had led to widespread industry emulation in the drying, curing, and finishing stages.

Ace's main competitor was Hanna, a company also serving the nonprofessional market segment exclusively. H and B and Adirondack dominated the professional market, and Ace's top managers were considering the advisability of invading this segment of the market. The sales manager, a former H and B employee, assured other executives of Ace's ability to compete both on a price and on a quality basis.

Questions

1. Should Ace have continued its existing distribution strategy or should it have invaded the professional market segment?

2. What changes in marketing strategy would have had to be made in order to invade the professional market segment profitably?

4-3

VENTRE PACKING COMPANY

Food Processor—Use of Food Brokers

In 1969 John Ventre, Jr., president of the Ventre Packing Company, makers of the Enrico spaghetti product line, became concerned over the line's distribution. The company had its main plant in Syracuse, New York, and a smaller plant in New Jersey. Distribution of the line was confined entirely to the area east of the Mississippi River. The product line consisted of (1) glass-packed spaghetti sauce (with or without mushrooms), (2) ravioli (with cheese or meatballs), and (3) instant pizza mix. Food brokers were used in distributing all products in the line, but John Ventre was not certain that this was the best possible system of distribution, particularly in view of his plan to increase production greatly.

Ventre started in business in Syracuse as a co-owner of Enrico's Italian Restaurant. This operation was a success from the beginning, and he soon recognized that his spaghetti sauce had considerable potential for sale through local grocery outlets. Thus before long, in 1960, he began bottling the sauce in the restaurant's kitchen and selling it to nearby small independent grocers. At first he personally prepared, bottled, and delivered the sauce. As market demand grew, he began to sell also to local wholesalers and food chains, thus expanding distribution.

In 1961 Ventre moved the food-processing operation from the restaurant to an old factory building and hired a sales manager to assist in selling the now greatly increased output. This move required additional capital, so he incorporated the business, selling stock to local investors. By 1963 not only the spaghetti sauce but the other products that had been added were being marketed in an area east to Albany and west to Buffalo. Four years later distribution was expanded further and Enrico's spaghetti products were on grocers' shelves from the Atlantic to the Mississippi. Ventre restricted his advertising to a "50-50" retailer cooperative program. By 1969 the company had more than quadrupled its business, causing the company to again relocate its main processing operation. The new Syracuse plant was a modern three-story structure, large enough to allow for substantial future expansion. Ventre expected to more than double the output with the new production facility and equipment.

During the preceding nine years, marketing channels had been changed three times. (See Exhibit 1.) Since 1967 all sales had been made

EXHIBIT 1

Changes in Marketing Channels

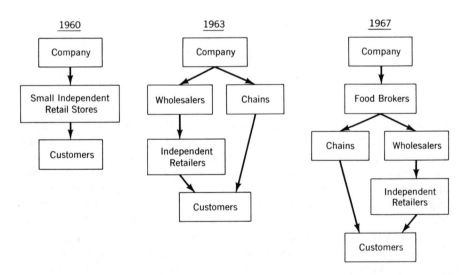

through sixteen food brokers (Exhibit 2). The food brokers received a straight 5 percent commission on sales. Each broker employed from six to ten salesmen who worked within a one-hundred-mile radius of the broker's headquarters. Brokers' salesmen sold the Enrico line directly to cash-and-carry wholesalers, voluntary and cooperative groups, corporate chains, and independent grocers.

EXHIBIT 2

Brokers Representing the Enrico Line

1. Syracuse, New York	9. Cleveland, Ohio
2. Greater Rochester, New York	10. Detroit, Michigan
3. Buffalo, New York	11. Chicago, Illinois
4. Albany, New York	12. Huntington, West Virginia
5. Greater New York City and Metropolitan New Jersey	13. Washington, D.C., to Baltimore, Maryland
6. Boston, Massachusetts	14. Richmond, Virginia
7. Columbus, Ohio	15. North Carolina and South Carolina
8. Cincinnati, Ohio	16. Greater Miami area and Jacksonville, Florida

In 1968 sales of spaghetti sauce reached 1 million quarts, but the company planned to increase its production in 1969 to 2 million quarts. It also planned to double production of the other products in the line. Ventre doubted that the present marketing channels were capable of absorbing the entire increased output. Therefore, he was searching for ways to improve the "throughput" of present channels and was thinking of exploring alternative marketing channels.

Questions

1. What might John Ventre have done to improve the "throughput" of the present channels?

2. What alternative marketing channels should have been explored?

4-4

THE ROSWELL COMPANY

Jewelry Marketer—Possible Change in Distribution Methods

The Roswell Company, organized in 1968, marketed novelty jewelry throughout the United States. It sold direct to retailers in every large metropolitan area; however, rapid product-line expansion and difficulty in getting and keeping qualified manufacturers' representatives caused management to consider using more indirect distribution methods. Roswell, the president, favored making a drastic change, but his partner, Dodd, did not.

Roswell and Dodd formed the company as a partnership, adopting Roswell's name because he was well known in the New York market area. Neither man had had previous experience in the jewelry trade, but both had worked as buyers for large New York department stores and were skilled businessmen. Roswell got the idea of marketing jewelry when his wife asked him to help open a pillbox. He talked to her about the pillbox, found it had cost eighteen dollars, and learned that most of his wife's friends owned similar items. Later, in the department store where he worked, he came across sales figures of expensive novelty jewelry and found them amazingly high. He and Dodd talked with several people experienced in the jewelry field, all of whom encouraged the pair to pursue the idea further.

The company's first product, an Italian coin-styled pillbox, consisted of two genuine Italian coins fitted on a golden frame with a clasp opener on the side. The opener could easily be activated by the thumb and the contents removed. Roswell and Dodd test marketed the pillbox through DePinna, a prestigious New York retailer. DePinna liked the product's design and sales were beyond expectations. DePinna advised the partners to devote full time to the new venture.

The business began on a small scale, using Roswell's home as the first base of operations. Roswell and Dodd purchased the Italian coins through a foreign exchange dealer, bought other raw materials from local suppliers, and had them delivered to Turner and Company, a small manufacturer. Turner assembled the pillboxes, packaged them, and made deliveries to Roswell's home. Turner did excellent work and made deliveries on schedule. In addition to DePinna, the partners sold directly to major New York department and specialty stores, each calling on those he knew from his previous retailing experience.

Consumers enthusiastically accepted the pillbox, retailers sent in large reorders, and first year sales were 30 percent above the forecast. Roswell and Dodd responded by introducing two other novelty jewelry items – a coin-adorned money clip and a watch, the latter with a design similar to that of the pillbox. The same components were used in making the money clips and the pillboxes; however, the Swiss-made watch components were purchased from local wholesalers. Turner and Company handled assembly of both new products. The company concentrated its early efforts on these three products.

Later Roswell developed additional designs, and by early 1970 the product line included twenty-eight products, such as coin cuff links, coin tie tacks, money-clip watches, ladies' cocktail money clips, and so forth. Company sales growth caused the business to move to a downtown office, which also provided greater storage space.

The Roswell Company used direct mail to promote its products to retail customers. Advertising copy featured new creations, special introductory offers, and prices. Retailers advertised at their own expense in national magazines such as *The New Yorker, Esquire,* and *Playboy* and in college magazines and newspapers. Many large-city stores also used local newspapers to promote the jewelry line.

Roswell and Dodd handled all the accounts in New York City. Eight manufacturers' representatives covered other metropolitan areas. Two were in the East, one in the South, three in the Midwest, and one in the Far West, but no specific territories had been assigned. "Reps" were not assigned sales quotas; they made calls at their own discretion. However, they did make monthly sales reports to Roswell. All reps received straight 12 percent commissions on sales.

Roswell believed that with the expanding product line the representatives could no longer perform satisfactorily. He said, "Initially, we were able to get good coverage and service out of our 'reps' because of the high commission rate and good market demand. I do not feel that they will be able to give us adequate support as our product line expands and as our customers increase in number. If demand falls, they certainly won't push our products. We have very little control over these men at the present and I foresee even less in the future." He thought that a switch to jewelry and novelty wholesalers would facilitate promotion, product introduction, and collection of market information.

Dodd favored continuing the manufacturers' representatives; however, he wanted to revamp the distribution system by clearly defining territories, setting sales quotas for reps, and establishing meaningful report and control procedures. He also wanted to retain the pricing structure, pointing out that middlemen performing additional tasks would demand higher margins. He feared, too, that if the company added wholesalers, it would be forced to raise prices. He was also concerned over the possible loss of "marketing control" to wholesalers. He said, "At present, we control the ownership and distribution of our products. We can sell them to whom we wish, at our prices, and in the quantities we desire; I like this arrangement. I am aware that we must improve our present representatives system and I think we can do this."

Questions

1. What should Roswell and Dodd have done in regard to distribution methods?
2. What other options might have been available for improving this situation? Elaborate.

GUARD-LINE CUTTER COMPANY, INC.

Manufacturer of Cutters—Marketing Program

Guard-Line Cutter Company, Inc., of Albany, New York, produced a unique hand-operated cutter designed for use with nonmetal sheet materials such as paper, vinyl, acetate, poster board, leather, and emulsion paper. This family-owned business, founded in 1963, had experienced little success in achieving sales volume, which barely reached one hundred thousand dollars in 1967. Donald E. Showalter, son of the owner and sales manager, was very much concerned with finding ways to increase sales volume substantially. His most recent plan had been to secure the interest of wholesalers capable of performing the marketing tasks necessary to have the cutters reach final buyers. Because of financial and manpower limitations, management regarded wholesaler distribution as the only feasible alternative, but this form of distribution had produced disappointingly small sales. Showalter was trying to determine what, if anything, could be done to improve the situation.

The company, essentially a one-product firm, produced three models of slide-type cutters. Originally, an eighteen-inch model was designed and put into production by Showalter's father, who believed that the product's inherent safety features and high quality would permit the cutter to be sold with minimum effort. Basically the Guard-Line cutter consisted of a flat base board with a bar and sliding blade attached. The user placed the material to be cut under the bar, applied downward pressure to the bar, and moved the blade along the distance to be cut. Maximum cutting length depended upon the board's length, for example, an eighteen-inch cut was the maximum possible on the eighteen-inch model. Various precise angles were imprinted on the masonite base board, and these made it easy to cut any angle with great exactitude. The maximum thickness that could be cut at a time was one-eighth of an inch. Besides the eighteen-inch cutter, twelve- and forty-two-inch models had been developed with different end users in mind.

When Showalter's father had first conceived the idea of the cutter, no formal market research had been conducted. A prototype was produced and displayed at a school suppliers' trade show. On the basis of favorable comments from the trade show attendants and encouragement from friends, management believed from the start that the cutter could not help but become a marketing success. The sales manager believed that the largest potential market for all three models was represented by the public school systems of the nation. However, he pointed out that considerable delay in selling this segment was typical because of school system annual budgetary limitations and administrative red tape. He also thought that other potential buyers could be found among architectural firms, photocopy finishers, blueprinters, general office suppliers, and art and photography schools.

List prices for the three cutter models were set at:

> 42-inch model $109.95
> 18-inch model . . . . . . $ 28.50
> 12-inch model . . . . . . $ 19.95

These prices compared favorably with those of competitive products. Management did not attempt to exercise any control over retail prices but based the discounts allowed to distributors on a percentage of list price. List price was set by deriving the unit cost of a single cutter and multiplying by a factor of six — this formula had been devised by a producer of a similar product, so Guard-Line's management regarded it as appropriate. Depending on the terms of the particular agreement made with individual distributors, they received discounts of from 40 percent plus 10 percent to 66 percent off list prices.[1] Insofar as could be determined, no distributor had yet ordered in large enough quantities to be regarded as doing anything but making a trial purchase.

---

[1] A discount of 40 percent plus 10 percent is the equivalent of 46 percent off list price. On an item priced at one hundred dollars, for example, the 40 percent discount (forty dollars) was deducted first. Then, from the remainder (sixty dollars), the 10 percent discount was deducted, leaving a net price of fifty-four dollars.

Guard-Line had no sales force other than the sales manager who personally attended various trade shows in the hope of interesting potential distributors in taking on the line of cutters. However, company budgetary limitations prevented him from attending as many trade shows as he would have liked. Direct mail flyers had been used in an attempt to contact distributors not reached at trade shows, and a large Chicago wholesaler, contacted initially through direct mail, had bought a fairly large number of cutters over the last two years, but nothing was known about the nature of his customers. The Chicago firm had been granted the right and the responsibility for contacting and selling retail outlets west of a line drawn from Washington, D.C., to Pittsburgh. East of this line no formal distributorship had been secured. Four mail-order wholesalers, known as *catalog houses,* carried the cutter in their catalogs, and all four served mainly the school and office supply markets.

The sales manager commented that he had never personally met nor discussed mutual problems concerning the cutter with the Chicago distributor. Monthly phone conversations, however, were held to resolve any difficulties that had arisen. In the East, the catalog houses and other prospective customers were contacted initially at trade shows, but there had been little communication since, other than that necessary to get the product included in catalogs or to fill small orders. Direct orders were accepted and filled both from retailers (who received 40 percent discounts from list prices) and from final buyers (who were charged list prices).

Originally the company had turned over the problem of promoting the cutter line to a large and well-known advertising agency. This resulted in numerous articles and photographs of the cutter being carried in trade magazines and journals. It also resulted in a few small orders from interested readers, but no repeat orders from this group had ever been received. It was at this point that management realized that the cutter would not sell itself "on sight." The sales manager concluded that to make sales it was necessary for someone to demonstrate the product's capabilities. Shortly thereafter, he personally began demonstrating the product at trade shows in New England and in New York City. He realized that this promotional method would limit the product's exposure to potential dealers, but he felt that this limitation might be counterbalanced by volume sales made to wholesalers attending trade shows.

As another method of promotion, direct mail flyers, pictorially describing the cutter's specifications and its uses, were circulated throughout New York State. These were addressed to prospective final buyers, such as school systems and photographers. Management hoped, in this way, to initiate a "pulling" effect on distribution — that is, when addressees asked their customary distributors for the product.

Similar cutting devices were on the market, but none were exactly like the Guard-Line in function or in appearance. Management thought that primary competition came from the familiar "guillotine" cutter, but no share-of-the-market data were available. The dangers involved in using the guillotine cutter, especially around children, were a main feature on which Guard-Line had hoped to capitalize. Four other competitive products possessed safety features comparable to those of the Guard-Line, but little was known concerning their method of distribution, promotion, or general marketing success. Showalter said that these competitive products were turned out by companies much larger than Guard-Line, so even if he could get such information it would probably be of limited utility due to Guard-Line's small size.

Question

What improvements should have been made in the marketing program of the Guard-Line Cutter Company?

4-6

SYRACUSE CHINA

China Manufacturing Company —
Multiple Marketing Channels

The pottery industry, brought over from Europe, arrived in the United States and became established in the last half of the nineteenth century. From a small obscure beginning, Syracuse China, organized in 1871, advanced to a position of leadership in the industry. Headquartered in Syracuse, New York, it was the country's largest producer of high-quality decorated chinaware. Syracuse manufactured and marketed prestigious products, competitively priced. The company's distribution strategy, operative for many years, had recently been identified as the cause of a major problem. Large organizations, such as hotel and restaurant chains, had become highly important buyers of china. As these chains grew larger and more sophisticated, many of their managements were refusing to buy their china requirements through dealers. One by one, they were demanding the privilege of buying direct from manufacturers.

The firm operated two plants in Syracuse employing about twenty-three hundred workers, the majority women. Although some automation existed, major reliance was placed upon the skilled handicraft of the large core of veteran workers. All production workers were paid in accordance with the provisions of an incentive compensation plan.

Creative artists and designers worked continually on new china patterns and shapes, from both marketing and production viewpoints, as roughly half of the output was made to individual customers' specifications. Syracuse distributed approximately eight hundred different designs throughout the United States, with California and certain large metropolitan areas, such as New York City and Chicago, being the best market areas; however, Florida had steadily increased in importance as a market for china.

The company's sales department was made up of two divisions: commercial and household. The commercial division accounted for the bulk of the sales, selling through franchised dealers to hotels, restaurants, clubs, hospitals, cafeterias, schools, and transportation companies. The household division worked mainly through retail outlets, although it also made some mail-order sales. There were twenty men in the sales force, ten in each division. Salesmen were assigned in pairs to ten sales districts, with the commercial salesmen acting as district sales managers.

The distribution network contained two hundred franchised dealers and two thousand retail outlets. Most of the franchise holders were exclusive dealers, but a few handled competitive as well as related product lines. The retail outlets were generally prestigious stores in their market areas. Syracuse's distribution policy emphasized selling through reputable and long-established dealers and retail outlets. The company, by working closely with its middlemen, adhering strictly to its distribution strategy, and providing middlemen with sales aids at low prices, had built up considerable goodwill. Consequently, most responded by turning in excellent sales performances.

The two divisions pursued separate promotional programs. The household division directed appeals to the mass market with all-purpose china and to the class market with fine china. These two lines were advertised nationally in consumer magazines such as *Better Homes and Gardens* and *Ladies' Home Journal*. The commercial division's main effort involved providing its dealers with display material and advertising mats, and advertising in business publications such as *Restaurant Management*. The advertising budget, however, amounted to only a small percentage of sales.

According to S. G. Starr, manager of marketing, the emergence of large hotel and restaurant chain buyers presented Syracuse with channel problems. Some chains bought through regular dealers, but most wanted to buy direct. A change in the company's distribution strategy could conceivably strain company-dealer relationships, but management believed that permitting chains to buy direct would expand sales volume considerably.

Questions

1. Should Syracuse China have continued its existing distribution strategy?

2. Under what circumstances should a marketer adopt a multiple channel policy?

3. Should Syracuse's products have been distributed exclusively? Selectively? Intensively?

4-7

WORTHINGTON CHECKWEIGHER CO., INC.

Manufacturer of Checkweighing Systems — Selling and Distributing Organization

Carlton A. James, a packaging engineer, founded the Worthington Checkweigher Company in Ithaca, New York, in 1950. The company's early success traced to the founder's development of a checkweigher for salt-filling machines used by Continental Salt Company. The company grew steadily, achieving sales increases each year, and with 1967 sales approximating $1.5 million, it had earned recognition as a worldwide leader in its field. However, the company found itself overly dependent on one large customer. In addition, management was concerned about the effectiveness of its salesmen and some of its manufacturers' representatives.

Worthington showed a profit each year and its strong financial position allowed it to search for growth opportunities. From its initial move into checkweighing systems, Worthington developed related skills in package-handling techniques. Thus, important new avenues of growth were opening up through the design and construction of specialized material-handling systems.

A checkweighing system measured discrete units and compared results with predetermined weights. Its basic components were a scale, a material-handling system, reject systems, and control devices. When properly integrated and synchronized, these components comprised a complete check-weighing system.

Worthington located its checkweighing systems in the assembly lines of its customers. Customers' products varied but included cake mixes, cereals, dry milk, meat products, salt, cookies, crackers, sugar, dried fruit, tobacco, chemicals, activated charcoal, freeze-dried foods, candy, ammunition powder, automatic ignition coils, plastic preform bricks, aerosol containers, and automotive parts kits. Among the company's customers were such internation-ally known firms as Anheuser-Busch, Armour, Colgate-Palmolive, Eastman Kodak, Du Pont, General Foods, Johnson and Johnson, National Biscuit, Olin Mathieson, Polaroid, and United States Tobacco.

The company sold its products throughout the world. Its salesmen sold directly to customers not only in the United States but in Canada, in Australia, and throughout Western Europe. However, because of foreign nations' product import regulations as well as service difficulties, management did not emphasize export sales; they amounted to only 10 percent of total sales. Worth-ington had set up eight United States territories; by 1968, all were manned except the South Atlantic territory. Company salesmen traveled two territories; five manufacturers' representatives worked five others.

Hugh Corcoran and Bill Clark were the company's only salesmen. Corcoran, a Worthington employee for five years, traveled out of the Ithaca headquarters and covered Ohio and Michigan. His job also included special assignments assisting representatives in other areas with engineering and servicing problems. His compensation consisted of a salary of $14,000 per year plus reimbursed travel expenses. Bill Clark, a Worthington salesman for two and one-half years, lived in and covered the New York metropolitan area. He also assisted with service problems in nearby territories of manufacturers' representa-tives. He received a salary of $12,500 and had his travel expenses fully reimbursed.

The five manufacturers' representatives, specialists in packaging techniques, had exclusive territories. One covered New England; one worked Chicago and a surrounding radius of one hundred miles; one, based in Dallas, sold in the Middle South and Southwest; and one traveled out of Los Angeles covering the West Coast. Representatives received a commission on sales of 10 percent plus an additional 5 percent if they handled equipment installation. The 10 percent sales commission was split when one representative wrote an order but the equipment was shipped into another's territory.

After 1958 the company grew especially rapidly, providing a backlog of orders for the engineering and production departments. Management spent little time in coordinating the different business functions. No executive was responsible for marketing, and three major problem areas developed.

The first traced to a checkweighing system Worthington had designed, several years earlier, for a large chemical company with substantial government contracts. In the years since, this account had produced hundreds of thousands of dollars in additional orders, but nearly all required special design and engineering. Carlton A. James personally handled this account, mainly because of his superior technical competency. Largely because of his concentration on this account, James did not personally solicit business from other regular customers or seek new accounts. However, he did become concerned over the large percentages of sales, engineering, and production effort directed toward a single customer. He anticipated a drastic and rapid reduction in sales should the chemical company lose its government contracts; and he saw no immediate replacement for lost sales, as Worthington specialized in products built to specifications, a process usually requiring several months.

The second problem area involved the two company salesmen. Although executives considered both men capable and proficient, they observed an alarming trend. Both Corcoran and Clark were devoting an increasing proportion of their time to solicitation, installation, and service assignments outside their assigned territories. Corcoran followed up leads and negotiated sales in all parts of the country, a task once handled by James, the president. Clark spent several days each month outside his territory handling service problems. Worthington's service department lacked extensive engineering talent and was swamped with service and reconditioning projects for local customers. Clark indicated to top management that there was a pressing need for additional salesmen in his territory. He also wanted to open up the Philadelphia and Richmond (Virginia) markets.

The third problem related to the performance of certain manufacturers' representatives. James, the two salesmen, and the Chicago and Los Angeles representatives produced 95 percent of the domestic sales. The other three representatives appeared reluctant to seek new business; in many instances, they failed to follow up company-provided leads and inquiries. Furthermore, some representatives did not keep abreast of latest product features, and the company had found no way to provide them with continuing updated product training.

Questions

1. Should Worthington have acted to reduce its great dependence on a single large customer? What actions, if any, should it have taken? Why?
2. How, if at all, could Worthington have improved its marketing and sales organization?
3. What should have been done to improve the performance of the manufacturers' representatives?

4-8

B. A. RYAN COMPANY

Franchised Distributor—
Choosing Dealers for a New Product

The Space-Saver Door Company, Cincinnati, Ohio, was the leading manufacturer of folding doors in the United States. In the summer of 1965, to diversify its product line and to make more efficient use of productive capacity, Space-Saver began manufacturing a sliding, translucent plastic, metal-frame bathtub door under the name Bath-Dor. All Space-Saver products were marketed solely through 148 exclusive franchised distributors, one of which, the B. A. Ryan Company of Syracuse, New York, obtained the exclusive rights to distribute the Bath-Dor in its territory. Individual distributors were free to select their own methods of retail distribution, and B. A. Ryan, president of B. A. Ryan Company, assigned J. E. Barr, who had specialized in selling Space-Saver doors, the task of determining the best retail distribution method for Bath-Dor.

The Ryan company had been organized in 1956 to sell quality building materials in the Syracuse area. Its sales organization contained three divisions organized around four salesmen: B. A. Ryan, who not only managed the firm but dealt with large accounts and special customers; T. R. Ryan (B. A. Ryan's son) and W. P. Hamilton, both of whom concentrated on aluminum window sashes, folding gym risers, steel roofing supports, commercial and institutional windows, and other building materials; and Elrod Barr, who handled the sales of Space-Saver doors. Ryan's 1965 sales of $11 million included $880,000 in sales of Space-Saver doors.

An exclusive franchise agreement, signed by the manufacturer and the distributor, controlled the distributor's policies regarding sales of Space-Saver doors. It limited each distributor to definite areas (usually by counties), set sales quotas, and established wholesale and retail prices and quantity discounts. The manufacturer reserved the right to cancel the annual agreement on thirty days' notice. The agreement for Bath-Dor was identical to those for other Space-Saver products.

Bath-Dor sold at retail for $88.50 with installation included in the price. This compared favorably with the two major competitive items — Easey Door at $86.50 and Swing-Gate at $90.00. Distributors paid $43.50 f.o.b. factory for the door, which came in five colors and whose package contained all necessary installation screws, frame mortar, and mastic. Bath-Dor was designed to fit all standard enclosed bath tubs from 4'6" to 5' long.[1]

Barr supervised Space-Saver folding door sales through thirty dealerships (most of them lumber retailers) within Ryan's seven-county territory (Exhibits 1 and 2). Folding doors increased usable space in rooms and hallways; they also served as room dividers. Dealers made residential sales, whereas Ryan sold direct to contractors and commercial builders. Residential units, comprising 90 percent of total sales, were for replacement of conventional swinging doors. Barr contacted each dealer at intervals of from six to eight weeks, helped them with special problems, demonstrated proper installation, filled them in on new ideas and sales techniques, and supplied promotional material and displays. Space-Saver door "setups" showed tub units displayed as they would appear installed. Dealers purchased regular units for use as setups.

Ryan had hinted that he believed it would be best to use the established dealer network for distributing the Bath-Dor, but Barr concluded that the present Space-Saver dealers were incapable of providing sufficient sales volume. From personal experience Barr knew that the retail lumber yards were poor merchandisers and were rarely aggressive in selling. Many of their salesrooms were poorly lighted, were crowded with merchandise, and lacked adequate display and demonstration space. Nor did he favor using the kitchen cabinet companies, the venetian blind companies, or the paint stores, since he regarded their operations as foreign to the selling of Bath-Dors. Furthermore, he looked upon the two large department stores as unsuitable because their clerks lacked training in selling such specialized products.

In March 1966 Barr submitted his recommendation for Bath-Dor

---

[1] An enclosed tub sits flush with the floor and has a level edge all around the top. Tubs must be recessed, as the metal frame is secured to the tub and two vertical walls.

EXHIBIT 1

Map of B.A. Ryan Company Exclusive Territory

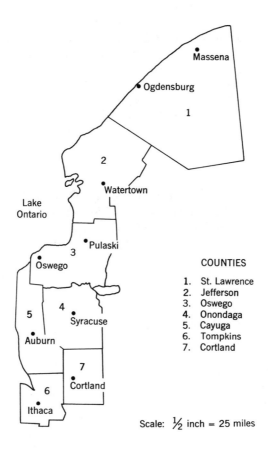

COUNTIES

1. St. Lawrence
2. Jefferson
3. Oswego
4. Onondaga
5. Cayuga
6. Tompkins
7. Cortland

Scale: ½ inch = 25 miles

EXHIBIT 2

Type of Space Saver Dealer	Number	Location
Retail lumber yards	23[a]	Throughout territory
Kitchen cabinet companies	2	Syracuse, Auburn
Venetian blind companies	2	Syracuse
Large department stores	2	Syracuse, Utica
Paint stores	1	Auburn

[a]Twelve retail lumber yards sold approximately 70 percent of the total volume of residential sales of Space-Saver doors. While these twelve dealers stocked Space-Saver doors, the remaining eighteen ordered from the Ryan Company only after they had made a sale.

distribution. He suggested four types of outlets: (1) plumbing stores because they were in direct contact with people needing plumbing services; (2) tile and floor dealers because Bath-Dor dovetailed well into their merchandise offerings; (3) plate glass companies because of their excellent installation service and closely related lines; and (4) storm window concerns because of their aggressive selling techniques. Barr, arguing in support of his recommendation, said: "The most effective distribution, the largest sales volume, and the best service and installation of Bath-Dor can be secured by adding these four new types of outlets. Our thirty present dealers will sell Bath-Dor on a special order basis. I will supervise installation, until we secure twenty of the new types of outlets and sign them up as exclusive Bath-Dor dealers."

Questions

1. Appraise the Space-Saver Door Company's policy with respect to allowing its distributors to choose their own retail distribution methods.

2. What retail distribution system for Bath-Dors should have been decided upon by Ryan?

T. A. DOLAN COMPANY

Food Broker—
Order Processing and Delivery

Tom A. Dolan, president of the T. A. Dolan Company — a food brokerage organization — sat at his desk one day in mid-March 1969 reading some canceled order forms his assistant had just handed to him. In the "Reason for Cancellation" space on the forms, one answer appeared time and again — "failure to make delivery." Dolan wondered what else he could do to overcome this reason for losing sales.

The Dolan firm began as a one-man operation in Atlanta, Georgia, in 1960. Initially, Dolan sold out of the basement of his home and represented two principals (manufacturers). By 1968 the company was distributing the products of fifteen principals (fourteen of them frozen food processors), and sales had reached the $8 million level. That year, also, two of the principals named Dolan their "Broker of the Year."

Dolan covered the Atlanta metropolitan area, the rest of North Georgia, and adjacent parts of Alabama, Tennessee, and South Carolina — the selling area having been designated by mutual agreement with the principals. The sales force was made up of fifteen salesmen, ten working out of Atlanta and five from such outlying centers as Chattanooga and Birmingham.

From the outset Dolan concentrated his brokerage operation in frozen foods. His previous experience included twenty-five years as a field sales representative for one of the nation's largest grocery manufacturers. Twenty of these years were spent in soliciting new frozen food accounts from among wholesalers and chain stores on behalf of brokers handling the grocery manufacturers' products. In addition, Dolan's vice-president had twenty years of frozen food selling and administrative experience, and the institutional sales manager had worked ten years for a marketer of frozen orange juice.

Three practices of the principals served to complicate Dolan's operations: (1) Principals often wanted Dolan and other brokers to secure orders for new products in advance of the launching of promotional programs; it was difficult to obtain such orders, since there usually was little to sell except the manufacturer's reputation. (2) Principals occasionally either failed to notify or gave late notices of price changes to Dolan; although manufacturers generally honored Dolan's price commitments, Dolan sometimes had to make up the difference between quoted and actual prices. (3) Manufacturers frequently either failed to ship orders to Dolan's customers or delivered them late.

Many of the difficulties involved in making deliveries traced to problems in production scheduling by the principals. For example, one principal scheduled production of its institutional line during lulls in production of standard retail (noninstitutional) items. Because the two product lines were processed to different specifications, their production could not be "mixed" together. In addition, standard retail products had their heaviest sale in winter, whereas institutional product sales peaked in summer. Customers, both retailers and institutions, had "stockouts" when the manufacturer was "running" the other product group. This caused Dolan's management to suggest to the manufacturer that he produce both groups of products to the same specifications, a suggestion under consideration by the manufacturer in early 1969.

However, not all delivery difficulties traced to problems in production scheduling. Dolan expressed dissatisfaction with order transmission and processing. Consequently, he had asked both his general sales manager and his institutional manager to submit plans for improving order cycle efficiency within the Dolan organization. He had also arranged to meet with all principals to explore ways to streamline inventory control and warehousing.

Questions

1. Appraise the steps taken thus far by Tom Dolan to improve delivery services to customers.
2. What else might have been done by Dolan to reduce order cancellations because of "failure to make delivery"?
3. What could Dolan have done about the other problems mentioned in the case?

SECTION 5

PROMOTION

FULLER BRUSH COMPANY

House-to-House Marketer—
Composition and Motivating of a
"Dealer" Sales Force

In October 1966 the Fuller Brush Company made two major policy changes: (1) using women as dealers and (2) accepting part-time dealers. Except during World War II, Fuller Brush had adhered to a policy of employing only full-time dealers. However, even after the changes had been in effect for two years, Stanley Lawrence, branch manager in Syracuse, New York, still found himself "selling the policies" to his field and unit managers. These subordinates were accustomed to working with and training men as full-time dealers; such dealers averaged sixteen hundred dollars in monthly sales. Women, as part-time dealers, required both more assistance and more motivation and had average monthly sales of only two hundred dollars.

Lawrence's branch had difficulty in implementing the new policies. Unit managers wanted the additional market coverage that women dealers (Fullerettes) could provide, but they experienced problems not only in recruiting women but in training and supervising them. Fuller needed more unit managers when the new policies went into effect, and it offered promotions to many veteran male full-time dealers, but not many accepted. Consequently, there was a perennial shortage of unit managers.

The company, incorporated in Connecticut in 1913, was famous for its "Fuller Brush men" and in the 1950s achieved sales leadership in the house-to-house field. Although its 1966 sales approached $75 million, during the early 1960s Avon, its largest competitor, had surpassed Fuller in sales volume. Avon attributed its success, in large part, to its use of part-time women dealers. Reacting to Avon's success, Fuller had expanded from a force of seven thousand full-time men to one including nearly thirty thousand Fullerettes in 1968. The goal was to have one hundred thousand Fullerettes by 1970.

Approximately four hundred products were sold under the Fuller name. Fuller made and marketed brooms, brushes, mops, and related cleaning supplies for household and commercial use. From other manufacturers it bought for resale such household items as cleaning and polishing fluids, pastes and waxes, dentifrices, toothbrushes, shaving cream, shampoo, cosmetics, vitamins, and food supplements. Although not so well known as the Fuller household products, the company also made and marketed a product line for industrial use.

Fuller dealer personnel worked out of one hundred branch offices, and orders were filled out of twenty-eight warehouse-distribution centers (Exhibit 1 shows Fuller's sales organization). Delivery from distribution centers to dealers was on an overnight basis by mail or truck. Dealers sent in their orders weekly, receiving billed merchandise from the distribution centers later the same week, which orders they then sorted and delivered to customers.

Dealers sold and delivered the products, and otherwise handled relations with customers. When delivering orders, dealers tried to secure additional sales. On exceptionally large orders, unit managers sometimes assisted the Fullerettes in making deliveries.

Dealers received 10 percent commission on sales, the highest in the direct-selling industry. While women dealers could easily earn two to three dollars an hour, their compensation varied, depending upon the number of hours worked. Fullerettes averaged from forty to fifty dollars in sales per week.

Unit managers not only recruited and assisted dealers but made sales themselves. They received the standard dealer's sales commission on their own personal sales plus a 5 percent commission on their unit's total sales. Since unit managers found it financially necessary to sell, they had a tendency to spend insufficient time in working with the full- and part-time dealers.

Field managers also did some selling, but most of their time was spent in recruiting, training, and motivating unit managers. With the shortage in unit managers, field managers were sometimes required to work directly with dealers. Field managers received fixed salaries plus 5 percent commissions on all territory sales.

Branch managers selected, trained, and supervised the field managers. They coordinated work of the entire branch, holding two monthly meetings: one with field managers and one with all branch personnel (Exhibit 2 outlines a

Sales Organization — Fuller Brush Company, 1966

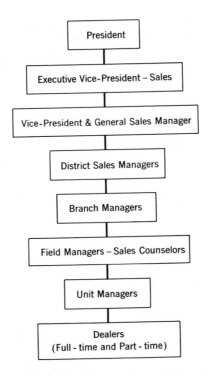

typical branch sales meeting); at such meetings, branch managers distributed and explained uses of all promotional materials. They received salaries plus small commissions on total branch sales.

The company had a promotion-from-within policy. Time required for promotion depended upon a person's ability to make sales and to supervise others. Ordinarily, it was possible for a dealer to move into a unit manager's job within two years and into a field manager's job in an additional two years. With the implementation of the policies concerning Fullerettes, management tried to move most of the seven thousand men dealers into unit-manager positions; however, those not desiring to "move up" were allowed to remain as dealers until their retirements.

Fuller recruited dealers from among enthusiastic customers who were recommended by field and unit managers and established dealers. Customers who knew Fuller's products were considered "prime" recruits, as generally they were presold on the products and were in a strategic position to

EXHIBIT 2

Branch Sales Meeting (once a month)

8:00 *p.m.*	Female unit manager told group about a "starter kit" for new Fullerettes that gave the new dealer something to work with, e.g., they were receiving $10-12 worth of merchandise for only $5. If the girls "worked out," they received a regular Fullerette sales kit.
8:15 *p.m.*	Field manager, Syracuse area, read a brochure on telephone solicitation. He listed four uses: (1) introduction as neighborhood Fullerette, (2) contacting interested parties, (3) selling over the phone, and (4) making appointments for home demonstration. He also explained the usefulness of record cards and continued sales contact.
8:45 *p.m.*	Field manager from the Utica area went over the specials for the next campaign. He explained features, uses, and aids in selling and demonstrated the items on special. He handed out samples so dealers could familiarize themselves with the specials.
9:10 *p.m.*	Telephone panel: Women who were successful in selling over the phone told of their experiences and answered questions.
9:35 *p.m.*	Mr. Lawrence gave pep talk to entire branch.
10:15 *p.m.*	Coffee: Small groups visited, discussed ideas and experiences.

sell their neighbors and friends. Fuller, like other house-to-house companies, had a high dealer turnover rate; many lasted only a few months. Management had found it increasingly difficult to provide both market coverage and good service through exclusive use of full-time dealers.

Fuller emphasized sales promotion rather than extensive advertising, averaging thirteen sales promotional campaigns per year. Each campaign featured different items, for example, mothproofer in the spring, garbage-can spray in the summer. Lawrence, convinced that word-of-mouth advertising was an important key to Fuller's success, said, "Public acceptance has, in the past, far outrun the service that we have been able to give. The Fuller dealer is known as the world's most famous visitor."

Fuller management believed that women dealers provided better market coverage, since they were assigned smaller areas, usually in their own neighborhoods, and could cover them thoroughly. Women could spend as little as three hours per day working, or work full-time if they desired. Fullerettes had a selling style different from that of Fuller Brush men; their calls were more of a social nature and lasted longer, and their sales per call were higher, perhaps because most of their customers were neighborhood housewives. By 1968 Fullerettes accounted for 38 percent of Fuller's total household business.

Fullerettes' performance was sometimes erratic. Schedules differed and income goals varied. Weather and sick children kept some at home in winter, and some worked sparingly during summer vacation months. Some worked for extra luxuries, some just to "get out of the house," and some to supplement their husbands' incomes, although many had difficulty convincing their husbands that they should work. However, the retention rate for Fullerettes was higher than that of full-time men.

Within Lawrence's branch, acceptance of Fullerettes had been slow. Some male dealers had quit, some unit managers wouldn't accept women, others found it hard to talk business with women. It took longer for Fullerettes to become oriented to the job, and they required constant encouragement and supervision. Unit managers, in particular, were reluctant to accept the part-time aspect of the Fullerette job, as it normally took eight women to equal one full-time dealer in gross sales. "Family first, business second" rubbed many managers the wrong way.

Unit managers were difficult to keep and more difficult to recruit. This situation was attributed to the policy of using Fullerettes. While Lawrence had tried outside recruiting of unit managers, this had proved unsatisfactory, as managers so recruited knew little about the company or its products. Successful women dealers were being encouraged to become unit managers, but most lacked the time and were not especially interested in full-time work as managers.

Questions

1. Appraise the wisdom of Fuller's decision to use part-time women dealers.
2. How should Lawrence have approached the problem of recruiting unit managers?
3. How might he have improved the supervision and control of Fullerettes?

5-2

FEDERAL OFFICE MACHINE COMPANY

Office Machine Manufacturer
and Distributor—Sales Organization

Early in 1966 all branch sales managers of the Federal Office Machine Company assembled at the home office in Hartford, Connecticut, to discuss future sales plans. Established in 1920, Federal experienced rapid growth and sales rose to $20 million in 1953 and $110 million in 1965. Several acquisitions, causing significant expansions of the product line, accounted for most of the recent growth. As growth continued, sales were expected to reach $180 million in 1968 and $200 million by 1970. Corporate officers, however, had become increasingly concerned about the sales organization's continuing ability to sell and service the expanding product line.

Federal specialized in machines geared to solve businesses' paper handling and mailing problems. It had, for instance, introduced the meter-mail system to business through its early development of a postage meter. Traditionally, salesmen pushed the desk-model postage meter as the company's best-known item, and management also viewed this item as a door opener to larger sales – an invitation to the customer to buy other items in the product line. Federal had pioneered in the postage-metering field, and it held an enviable position of market acceptance. All company products represented high quality at competitive prices; for example, the desk-model postage meter, priced at $15.00, was $3.50 cheaper than competing models. Prices ranged from $15 for the postage meter to $1,500 for copiers, one of the latest additions.

Prior to 1966 salesmen handled six product categories (a total of twenty-nine models):

Scales: eight models — determined weight and rate of postal items.

Mail Openers: three models — opened mail five times faster than by hand.

Postage Meters: nine models (desk model to electric floor models) — stamped, sealed, stacked, and counted up to fifteen thousand pieces per hour.

Folding and Inserting Machines: six models (desk models to fully automatic floor machines) — larger models opened and stuffed envelopes, counted, sealed, stacked, and printed postage at seventy-five hundred pieces per hour.

Counters and Imprinters: two models — counted and imprinted items such as checks, labels, tickets, and packages.

Tax-stamping Machines: One model — stamped taxable items such as cigarettes.

In 1966 three additional product categories (a total of twenty-one models) were introduced, thus bringing the company total to nine product categories (a total of fifty models). The new product categories were:

Addresser-Printers: four models — addressed mailing pieces.

Collating Machines: sixteen models — collated, stapled, stitched, folded, stacked, and counted.

Copying Machines: one model — copier warmed up instantly, produced eight copies per minute, and automatically cut copies to original's dimensions.

Management envisioned great potentials for the new products, especially the copier which compared favorably with four competitive machines recently introduced to the market. With the expanded product offering and to facilitate its further expansion, executives were considering restructuring the sales organization (Exhibit 1).

The company marketed its products worldwide. In the United States, there were four domestic sales zones — Eastern, Southern, Central, and Western. These contained a total of thirteen sales districts, which were further divided into 144 branch offices, out of which worked nearly six hundred salesmen.

EXHIBIT 1

Federal Office Machine Company Sales Organization

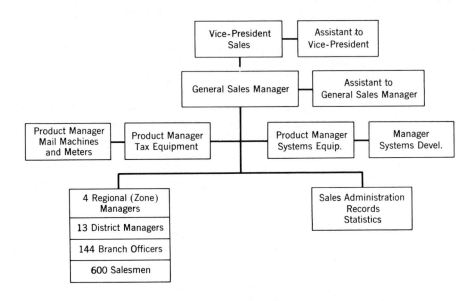

All salesmen sold all company products, contacting businesses of all sizes within their assigned territories. Each salesman averaged nine calls per day (three cold calls, three user calls, and three follow-up inquiry calls). Salesmen forwarded complicated service problems to service stations, which were charged specifically with handling such matters.

Federal advertised its various products through business and trade magazines and through direct-mail brochures to large prospects. Advertising copy stressed time and cost savings, customer pride, and the high quality and dependability of Federal's products. Recent advertising emphasized the company's broad line of systems equipment.

Branch managers selected, trained, promoted, and supervised salesmen in their territories. Although salesmen were held responsible for meeting their assigned sales quotas, they did not participate in setting them. Home office management established all sales quotas, basing them primarily on a formula heavily weighted by post office revenues in each territory. Branch managers submitted annual recommendations for territorial realignments which they regarded as necessary to maintain adequate coverage. They also reassigned salesmen and hired new men when the situation warranted.

Branch managers were also responsible for sales training. Each training cycle lasted approximately sixteen weeks. The first two weeks consisted of an orientation on company policies, discussion of sales techniques, and introduction to company products, with emphasis on metered-mail equipment (postage meters, scales, and mail openers). During the next thirteen weeks training focused on product knowledge and sales techniques for systems equipment (folding and inserting machines, counters, and imprinters). Twelve of these thirteen weeks consisted of on-the-job training under the supervision of experienced salesmen. A one-week review with branch managers completed the training cycle. Management believed that sales training for the addresser-printers and collators could be incorporated into the systems equipment phase. However, they thought that sales training for the copier would require an additional two weeks.

Experienced salesmen's compensation averaged fourteen thousand dollars annually. Trainees each received a salary of five hundred dollars per month plus a small sales commission. Salesmen usually went on straight commission after their first year with Federal. Commissions varied with each item's "dollar ticket value." As the ticket value increased, the commission percentage decreased (see Exhibit 2).

EXHIBIT 2

Compensation Commission

Product	Average Commission (%)
Postage meters	15
Scales	15
Mail openers	15
Folding machines	10
Inserting machines	10
Counter-Imprinters	10
Tax equipment	15
Addresser-Printers	10[a]
Collators	10[a]
Copiers	15[a]

[a]Proposed commissions. Salesmen selling copiers would also receive commissions on sales of paper supplies (20 percent for the first year, 10 percent for each succeeding year).

During the early 1966 Hartford sales meeting, the branch managers discussed various ways of achieving better results. They differed considerably as to how to achieve greater sales force effectiveness. Some suggested a reorganization along product lines and a specialization of salesmen by products. Others, convinced of the basic soundness of the present arrangement, argued that only minor changes should be considered. Top management concluded that some organizational changes should be made but was not certain what they should be.

Questions

1. What changes, if any, should have been made in the Federal sales organization?
2. As a company expands its product offerings, what problems may arise in sales force management?

STANAMER CORPORATION

Plumbing and Heating Company—
Sales Force Expansion

The Plumbing and Heating Division of Stanamer Corporation made and sold plumbing fixtures and fittings, hydronic heating and cooling equipment, food waste disposals, water softeners, and invalid bath lifts. The largest of seven corporate divisions, it operated fourteen plants from coast to coast. Toward the end of 1966 the general sales manager, J. B. Samson, was analyzing a problem concerning an increase in the size of the sales force.[1] The budget for 1967 provided funds for adding fifteen salesmen, and Samson compared two alternatives: (1) hiring salesmen with previous sales experience in the field and (2) following the company traditional practice of hiring and training inexperienced men.

Stanamer led the plumbing and heating industry in sales; its 1966 sales of $138 million was double that of the nearest competitor. Well known and respected, the company's market share was estimated at 50 percent. Although its position was enviable, company management recognized the dangers of

[1] See Exhibit 1 for Selling Section organization.

EXHIBIT 1

Selling Section — Marketing Department

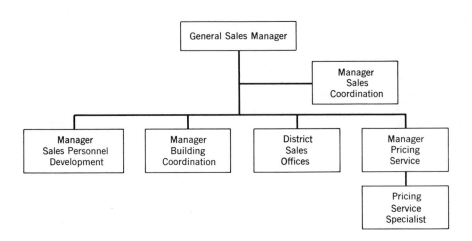

complacency, particularly as competition stiffened and market share showed signs of declining.

Activity in the home-building industry, the largest market for plumbing and heating supplies, fell off in 1966. There were predictions that new housing starts in the first half of 1967 would be below the 1966 level; however, an upturn was expected in late 1967. When new housing starts dropped, total demand for plumbing and heating products also declined; consequently, competition for available business increased. Most firms moved to hire additional salesmen to provide more intensive market coverage. Samson's decision to hire fifteen additional salesmen was made with the short-term objective in mind of reducing excess inventory. If housing starts recovered, top management might question the value of having fifteen extra men, since in such circumstances Stanamer normally received sufficient business to support its full productive capacity.

The company's products were of high quality, and as such commanded prices about 10 percent above those of competitors. All promotion emphasized the superior product quality. Company sales-training sessions, focusing on product information and selling techniques, also emphasized the price-quality relationship.

Stanamer's sales force sold exclusively through wholesale plumbing and heating distributors. The 250-man force called upon fourteen hundred wholesalers who, in turn, sold through fifty thousand contractors and plumbers.

Salesmen worked out of twenty-three sales offices located in some but not all of thirteen sales districts.[2]

Typical Sales District (Multiple Sales Offices).
Selling Section, Sales and Marketing Department

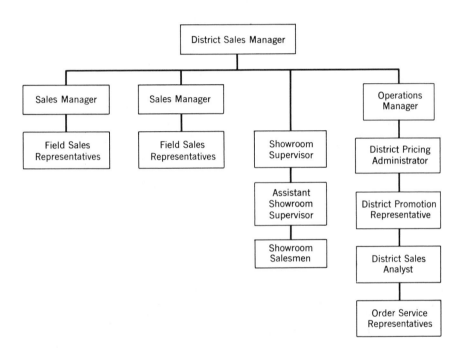

District sales managers performed administrative duties and reported directly to the general sales manager. Their responsibilities included recruiting and training of salesmen. However, the general sales manager determined the number and the qualifications of those hired.

The average salesman wrote orders totaling from $400,000 to $600,000 annually. Each received a straight salary of $10,000 to $12,000 a year. Salesmen maintained contact with distributors and assisted them in inventory control, in the training of their salesmen, and in the use of company promotional plans, programs, and materials. Salesmen also promoted the use of Stanamer products through their contacts with home builder and contractor

[2] See Exhibits 2, 3, and 4 for the organizations of the various types of typical sales districts.

E X H I B I T 3

Typical Sales District (One Sales Office).
Selling Section, Sales and Marketing Department

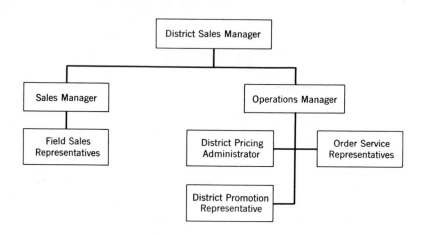

E X H I B I T 4

Typical Sales District (No Sales Office).
Selling Section, Sales and Marketing Department

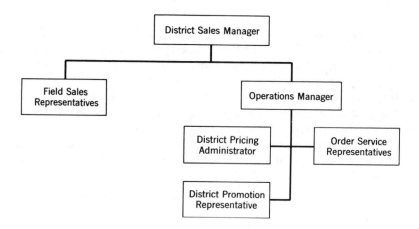

trade associations. In addition, they talked up the use of the division's products with key personnel in hospital and school administrations, public utilities, and governmental agencies. They also made inspections of consumer products and made service calls.

Traditionally, Stanamer hired inexperienced men and put them through a six-month training program. Sales recruits spent the first three months becoming acquainted with the company's products and policies. They then attended a formal three-month program emphasizing advanced product knowledge and sales techniques. Training costs amounted to approximately two thousand dollars per man. Once out of training, new men generally became fully operational and productive in from three to six months.[3]

EXHIBIT 5

Sales Personnel Development Unit.
Selling Section, Sales and Marketing Department

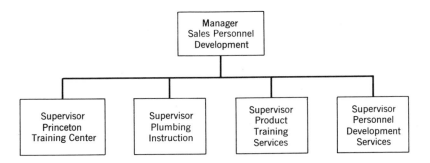

To lure salesmen with field experience away from competitors required starting salaries averaging ten thousand dollars annually. Also, considerable recruiting time and effort were involved, and there was the danger that competition might reciprocate. Men with previous field experience usually became fully operational Stanamer salesmen in about one month.

Samson wanted to hire the fifteen additional men, but he was not certain whether he should concentrate on men with or without previous selling experience in the industry.

Questions

1. How should Samson have gone about implementing the decision to add fifteen new salesmen?

[3] See Exhibit 5.

2. In alleviating the excess inventory situation, what other alternatives should have been explored?

3. Evaluate the appropriateness of Stanamer's various policies and practices relating to sales force management.

CONSTRUCTION SERVICE DIVISION (CSD)—
BETTER MACHINES, INC.

Distributor of Industrial Equipment—
Motivating Salesmen

Better Machines, Inc., founded in 1904, was an industrial distributor selling a broad line. It was organized into three divisions: (1) the Machine Tool Division, which sold metalworking equipment, (2) the Materials Handling Equipment Division, which distributed specialized handling equipment, and (3) the Construction Service Division (CSD), which sold and serviced construction equipment. Early in 1968 Ted Logan, CSD marketing manager, identified his division's most important problem as that of motivating salesmen to perform effectively. He remarked, "Sales executives can give employees incentives, but motivation must come from within the individual." The division's salesmen received considerably higher compensation than the average in the industry, but motivational problems persisted.

In 1967 CSD sold $23 million worth of equipment. It competed against thirty distributors serving the Indiana and southern Illinois market and attained a penetration ratio of 50 percent.[1] CSD's sales income came from

---

[1] A *penetration ratio* indicates the relationship between actual sales and market potential.

equipment ($15 million), parts ($5.7 million), and service ($2.3 million). Sales of Goliath equipment, the leading line, amounted to $11 million in 1967.

CSD represented four manufacturers of such equipment as graders, loaders, stone crushers, earthmovers, rollers, bulldozers, cranes, power shovels, and asphalt pavers. Prices of different pieces of equipment ranged from ten thousand dollars for small loaders to three hundred thousand dollars for larger, heavier products. Management made gradual changes in the items handled, discontinuing some pieces of equipment from time to time, but had dropped none since 1963. The high quality of the equipment it distributed was a source of pride throughout the division.

Central headquarters were at Terre Haute, Indiana, and the CSD's sales area extended over Indiana and southern Illinois. Branch offices, with parts and service facilities, were at Decatur and Mt. Vernon in Illinois, and at Indianapolis, Fort Wayne, and Terre Haute in Indiana. Branches, each with a full-time manager, operated autonomously as profit centers.

Of the nineteen CSD field salesmen, five worked out of Terre Haute, five out of Indianapolis, four out of Fort Wayne, three out of Mt. Vernon, and two out of Decatur. Each managed his assigned territory, made scheduled calls, prospected for new customers, developed mailing lists, and submitted weekly activity reports to his branch manager. Five specialty men, with engineering and application knowledge of certain equipment lines, covered the entire market area, assisting regular territorial salesmen. While on field assignments, specialty men were supervised by branch managers (see Exhibit 1 — Organization Chart).

Sales in different sales territories ranged from three hundred thousand dollars to $3 million annually. Territorial boundaries were drawn mainly on the basis of analyses of company and industry sales records indicating performances of both CSD and its thirty competitors. Further analysis of territorial sizes and potentials took into account the number of pieces of equipment already in each sales territory, their ages, and their models. After appraisal of these and other data, branch managers and the general manager determined market and sales potentials, made sales forecasts, and set the division's sales quotas. Experienced salesmen worked the larger-volume territories, newer men the rest

Management utilized a prospect classification system aimed toward improving control over field sales operations. All prospects for construction equipment were put into one of four categories:

1. Those who were *going to buy.*
2. Those who were *probably going to buy.*
3. Those *interested in buying.*
4. Those with almost *no interest in buying.*

EXHIBIT 1

Organization Chart

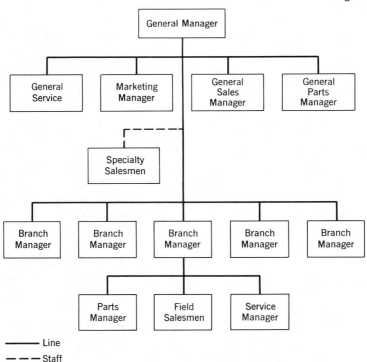

Prospects in category 1 received the highest contact priority. Prospects remained in category 2 for two weeks and in category 3 for three weeks; during these periods, contacts by salesmen were used to qualify these prospects for other classifications. This system forced salesmen to gauge the degree of buying intent in customers' minds. After a prospect bought equipment and became a customer, the division recorded the equipment's type, the date of sale, and the amount of sale. The company had recently computerized its prospect and customer classification system, utilizing the information to determine weekly routing schedules for the field salesmen.

Management assigned quotas to all field salesmen. Those failing to reach their quotas were required to submit written reports explaining the reasons for unsatisfactory performance. Branch managers reviewed these reports when considering salesmen's contract renewals.

Salesmen's compensation included a salary, averaging about 65 percent of the total income, and commissions on sales. Factors such as relative seniority, nature of territorial assignment, and recent performance compared with quota were used in determining base salaries. Commission rates varied according to the level of sales, and both rates and rate-break points differed among individual salesmen's contracts. In addition, certain product lines carried varying commission rates; for example, the contract of one salesman provided that on sales of Goliath equipment he be paid 1 percent up to $150,000, 1.25 percent from $150,000 to $225,000, and 1.5 percent above $225,000. Specialty salesmen also worked on a salary-plus-commission basis, sharing commissions on joint sales made with field salesmen. Shared amounts varied with the type of equipment, the selling effort exerted by each man, and the provisions of individual employment contracts.

CSD paid each salesman's travel and entertainment expenses in their entirety. In addition, all salesmen participated in a profit-sharing plan which paid up to 17 percent of base salary, depending upon company profits. Salesmen averaged between $14,000 and $17,000 in total compensation for 1967, compared with an average of from $9,000 to $11,000 for competitors' salesmen. Sales executives received base salaries plus profit-sharing bonuses. Top management reviewed all compensation plans annually; however, only minor changes had been made in recent years.

Salesmen reported to branch managers on their work plans, expense items, complaints and adjustments, and lost sales. They also submitted daily call reports. Copies of all salesmen's reports were sent to the central sales control unit, tabulated, and then forwarded to sales and marketing managers. Expense reimbursements occurred only after receipt of detailed expense reports. Selling expenses expanded rapidly in 1966 and 1967, though executives had been unable to determine the reasons.

When salesmen lost two or more consecutive sales to the same account, branch managers immediately tried to determine if the reason was salesman-customer incompatibility. On occasion, management reassigned certain customers to different salesmen. Branch managers, the sales manager, and the marketing manager all spent considerable time traveling with the salesmen.

CSD did not use sales contests or other devices involving special recognition for improved or outstanding sales performance. The management regarded such frills unnecessary in view of the high level of monetary compensation. CSD held seven formal sales meetings during 1967. Participants discussed such topics as new products, updating of sales techniques, and changes in company policy. "Improving morale" was a recurring and stated goal of such meetings.

CSD's annual salesman turnover rate was 12 percent; this compared with the industry's rate of 9 percent. The company did not conduct exit interviews, but management was of the opinion that most salesmen leaving did so because of greater monetary opportunities elsewhere. Three of the last five salesmen leaving the company, however, had gone to work for competitors.

Questions

1. What, if anything, should have been done to motivate CSD's salesmen to perform more effectively?
2. Had you been called in as a management consultant to CSD, what would have been your recommendations?

5-5

BRISTOL LABORATORIES

Pharmaceutical Company—Sales Contests

Bristol Laboratories, a division of Bristol-Myers, was one of the world's largest manufacturers of antibiotics and pharmaceuticals. It had 725 salesmen deployed throughout the United States. With a sales organization of this magnitude, Bristol faced managerial problems in motivation and in balancing the selling emphasis given its product lines. In 1967 sales force management used sales contests to motivate and direct salesmen. These ran continuously each month throughout the year.

Bristol's major brands included Tetrex, Saluron, Syncillin, Kantrex, Naldecon, Polycillin, Staphcillin, Prostaphlin, and Salutensin. Hospitals and drug wholesalers purchased direct from the company. Ultimate consumers bought Bristol's products from retail druggists on doctors' prescriptions. Sales for the parent company, Bristol-Myers, reached $468 million in 1966 (see Exhibit 1).

Bristol's sales force was organized into ten regions containing sixty-five sales districts. Salesmen were distributed within districts according to the sizes of individual territories and relative sales potentials. Their duties included calling on doctors, hospitals, and drug wholesalers, and making service

EXHIBIT 1

Sales — Bristol-Myers Company

1966 — $468,452,682
1965 — $391,433,053
1964 — $265,014,018
1963 — $232,354,202
1962 — $198,765,810
1961 — $164,420,656
1960 — $146,716,017

Source: *Moody's Industrials,* 1967.
Note: Bristol Laboratories accounted for roughly 17 percent of the corporation's annual sales.

calls on retail drugstores. Each man visited an average of 120 doctors, ten hospitals, and two wholesalers per month.

The sales force compensation plan consisted of a relatively small salary plus a relatively generous 5 percent commission on territorial sales volume. K. J. Ryan, sales manager, believed his salesmen were among the highest paid in the drug field. In 1966 they averaged thirteen thousand dollars, the top man earning thirty-nine thousand dollars.

Through its sales contests, Bristol sought to direct salesmen toward emphasizing all products in the line instead of only the high-commission, easy-to-sell items. While contests ran continuously, different products received emphasis each month. Ryan regarded money less important as an incentive than merchandise and travel awards, especially to a highly paid sales force. Salesmen competed against predetermined territorial sales goals; management believed that using other bases for contests would have caused morale problems, as salesmen worked different territories and had varying selling abilities. In all sales contests, the closer a salesman came to his established targets, the greater was his reward.

Maritz, Inc., a firm specializing in the organization and operation of sales incentive campaigns, planned and administered Bristol's contests. Four different drugs were promoted each month. In December 1967 these were Polycillin, Tetrex, Kantrex, and Naldecon. The marketing department estimated dollar sales and the percentage of each drug that should comprise a salesman's total effort. December's target mix was 65 percent Polycillin, 23 percent Tetrex, 9 percent Kantrex, and 3 percent Naldecon.

The contest scoring system involved awarding prize points in two categories: (1) total sales of the four drugs and (2) performance relative to the target sales percentage mix. For each dollar of total sales, one-half of one prize point was awarded (for example, $12,000 total sales = 6,000 prize points). Points awarded in the second category, "mix points," were based on performance relative to the target sales mix. For example, salesman X had actual sales in December as follows:

Product	Target Mix	Target Sales	Actual Sales	Performance Rating
Polycillin	65%	$ 6,500	$ 9,800	150%
Tetrex	23	2,300	1,650	72
Kantrex	9	900	360	40
Naldecon	3	300	360	120
Total	100%	$10,000	$12,170	

If X's sales had equaled the target sales, all the performance ratings in the last column would have been 100 percent. This column represented the percentages of drugs sold relative to the mix goal. Prize points ("mix points") were calculated by multiplying the lowest performance number by the "sales factor" established by management (see Exhibit 2). X's mix point total was 11,000 points (40 x 275 = 11,000). The lowest performance number was used in an

EXHIBIT 2

Memorandum
Bristol Laboratories
Division of Bristol-Myers Company

The contest items, product mix, and payoff for the sales month of December 1967 are as follows:

	$	Mix
Polycillin	3,400,000	65
Tetrex	1,235,000	23
Kantrex	485,000	9
Naldecon	220,000	3
Total detail sales	5,340,000	100
Total sales estimate		$6,750,000
Total budget estimate (.9% of sales)		$60,750
Less ½ point per $ sales		16,875
Mix payoff dollar budget		$43,875

Mix payoff in points
    ($.005 x dollar budget)   8,775,000

Total detail items   5,340,000
60% of detail items*   3,204,000

$$\frac{3,204,000}{100} = \text{Sales factor} \qquad\qquad 32,040$$

$$\frac{\text{Mix points}}{\text{Sales factor}} = \frac{8,775,000}{32,040} = \frac{275 \text{ Points/Sales}}{\text{Factor}}$$

Note: Determined by management

effort to motivate salesmen to make sales proportionate to management's target percentages. Total prize points earned by X were:

Total sales of promoted drugs ($12,179 ÷ 2) . . . . . 6,085 points
Performance relative to target (40 x 275) . . 11,000 mix points
Total . . . . 17,085 prize points

Had X sold the exact targeted product mix, his mix point total would have been 27,500, and his total prize points 33,585.

    "Prize-point" checks were mailed monthly, and were exchangeable for merchandise described in the Maritz catalog. Each prize point was worth $.005 (17,085 points = $85.43). Management withheld the proper income tax each month. Points could be exchanged for almost any item imaginable, from airplanes to pearls. Travel awards consisted of trips to such places as London, Casablanca, and Tel Aviv.

Questions

1. Should Bristol have used sales contests? As many as it did?
2. What improvements, if any, might Bristol have made in its program for motivating and directing salesmen?

5-6

KALO LABORATORIES

Pharmaceutical Company—
Sales Manager Training

In early 1968 Stephen Young, manager of personnel development, Kalo Laboratories, began planning the fall Sales Executive Seminar (SES) for district sales managers. This was to kick off a new program of continuous training for district managers. In Young's opinion, training sales managers was Kalo's main problem. Dennis Baily, recently promoted from district sales manager, was to assist in setting up the SES and in conducting it. Young awaited Baily's arrival at the home office so that the fall program's planning could begin.

Kalo Laboratories of Trenton, New Jersey, produced ethical drugs and certain pharmaceuticals. It was a subsidiary of Standard Products Company, a large conglomerate, whose 1967 sales exceeded $400 million, with Kalo accounting for $80 million. Kalo had four sales divisions: (1) hospital, (2) pediatric, (3) physician, and (4) government.

There were three groups of Kalo salesmen: (1) "detail men" who called exclusively on either physicians or pediatricians, explained product features and uses, and urged the prescribing of Kalo products, (2) salesmen who called on hospitals, performed "detail" tasks, and wrote orders, and (3) men who visited veterans' hospitals, military medical facilities, and large government installations, and who were skilled in negotiating and bidding on large contracts.

Each of sixty district managers supervised from 8 to 12 of Kalo's 650 salesmen. Each district manager reported to one of twelve regional managers. The company adhered to a promotion-from-within policy, and all district managers had prior experience in ethical drug and pharmaceutical sales. The sales organization manual outlined district managers' duties in seven areas:

1. *Office Procedures:*
   General reports, correspondence, inventory of supplies, and supervision of office personnel.

2. *Field Supervision:*
   Improvement, training, evaluation, demonstration, assistance, and personal supervision of the field sales force.

3. *Personnel Improvements:*
   Determination of need and organization of a personal improvement plan for each salesman. Relate to appraisal and evaluation.

4. *District Progress:*
   Accountable for territorial profit and service.

5. *Reporting Function:*
   Preparation of general and specific reports and communication with the regional manager and the home office.

6. *Personnel Selection:*
   Recruiting, screening, interviewing, and assisting the regional manager in the final selection of applicants.

7. *Special Duties:*
   Conducting sales meetings, attending annual SES, terminations, policing expense accounts, and other special assignments.

Early in 1967 Kalo adopted a new sales-training philosophy stressing customer orientation, the buyer-seller communication process, and advanced selling methods. Implementing this new philosophy involved using the latest developments in individualized training and participation techniques. Therefore, a new personnel center, complete with modern conference rooms and equipped with the latest and most advanced audio-visual equipment, was built in Trenton. All salesmen received training there before assignment to sales districts. Young gave his evaluation of the results thus far achieved by saying: "I believe the initial sales training program is good but our continuous training is suffering a breakdown as our district managers still stick to outdated techniques and continue to emphasize a product-oriented approach. We must do a better job of training the trainer." He believed they should coordinate and conduct on-the-job sales training continuously rather than sporadically. Young also voiced concern for the district managers' performance in field supervision and personnel improvement.

The district manager training program consisted of intensive study of the sales organization manual, exposure to topics covered by past seminars, case studies, problem solving, and general discussion. The annual SES constituted the only continuous training program for district managers. In December 1967 Young asked Jerry Chambers, a district manager from the southeastern region, to appraise the current state of district manager training and to submit a proposal for its improvement (see Exhibit 1). No decision on this proposal had been reached by early 1968, since Young was awaiting Baily's arrival. The forthcoming SES included a computerized marketing game emphasizing bidding, pricing, budgeting, and certain aspects of marketing. Young wondered if this game should be replaced with a different type of program. He faced the twofold problem of training both new and old district managers and of organizing the SES.

EXHIBIT 1

FROM	J. L. Chambers	DATE	December 18, 1967
TO	S. H. Young	SUBJECT	Proposal: New and
			Senior District
			Manager Training

PROPOSAL: New and Senior District Manager Training

I. Objective – The implementation of this program will minimize the maturation time of the early appointed District Manager, as well as maximize the managerial capabilities of Senior District Managers.

II. Procedure –
   A. Field Contact – Rather than a formal introductory meeting, the new District Manager will meet his personnel through scheduling himself into their respective territories. Since this contact will be made prior to a review of personnel records or Regional Manager counseling on this subject, the new District Manager will not have preconceived opinions of his salesmen's capabilities. The resultant atmosphere will be conducive to open, candid discussion allowing both parties to meet on common ground.

   B. Orientation with Regional Manager – After completing the above step, a thorough personnel discussion will also be reviewed at this time. Selected confrontations will then be shown the new District Manager. Because he will view his knowledge inadequate to handle the situations depicted, he will be motivated to search out the necessary information. Based on his recognition of those areas that require primary effort, the District Manager will outline a course of study with the Regional Manager which will be encompassed by the seven categories enumerated below. Case histories from former seminars and tape recorded discussions of those topics listed below the categories mentioned will provide a reservoir of applicable information.

1. Office Organization — Procedures
   a. Value of Basic Organization
   b. Preparation for Field Contact
   c. Report Evaluation
2. Field Supervision
   a. Training New Men
   b. The Hospital Man — Hospital Penetration
   c. Personnel Evaluation Techniques
   d. Capturing Government Business
   e. Drug & Wholesale Working
   f. The Pediatric Salesman
3. Personnel Improvement
   a. Understanding the Man — Application of Drive Patterns & Motivational Interviews
   b. Motivation of Senior Men
   c. Counseling Techniques
4. District Progress
   a. Gathering Distribution Data — Territory Construction Procedures — Pool Allocations
5. Reporting
   a. Written Communication Techniques
   b. Field Contact Report Construction
6. Personnel Selection
   a. Applicant Screening — Sources of Candidates — Interviewing the Applicant
7. Special Duties
   a. Organization of District Meetings

The Regional Manager orientation session will require approximately two weeks. Upon completion, the Regional Manager will contact other District Managers of the region and arrange for a one-day introductory visit, with each manager, for the new District Manager.

C. *Personnel Central*
   1. *The New District Manager* — The new District Manager will participate in a two-week training period in Trenton. During his stay, he will occupy the District Office, which has been established at Personnel Central. Since this office has been organized to be representative of a typical district office, he will have an opportunity to become acquainted with systems and procedures applicable to his new position. Upon entering training, the District Manager will be requested to bring personnel files relative to his salesmen.

   These records will be valuable in conducting routine district business while in training, as well as providing search material for

(continued)

confrontation assignments. Training will proceed in accordance with the steps enumerated below.

    a.   *Video Confrontations* – Two video confrontations will be completed on primary district problems. Through telephone contact with the Regional Manager, the District Manager counselor will explore specifics required for role play setting. On completion, the counselor will suggest search of similar case histories, confrontation, and a review of personnel records involved before rescheduling further tryout.

    b.   *Sensitivity Training* – The District Manager will participate in sensitivity training through being assigned two salesmen upon their entering the course. He will occupy the third chair, counsel the men assigned and, in turn, discuss his progress with the District Manager counselor.

    c.   *Recruiting, Screening, Hiring* – The District Manager will be required to complete confrontations as well as select four (4) candidates for hiring. Basis for selection of personnel will be discussed with District Manager counselor.

    d.   Time remaining, the District Manager will complete selected confrontations as suggested by the Regional Manager during the phone call previously mentioned, or through selection by the District Manager counselor.

    e.   The District Manager will complete the confrontations mentioned in (a) above and accept as his Back Home Commitment the completion of these confrontations with the personnel involved.

  2.   The Senior District Manager – The senior District Manager will complete steps (a), (b), (d) and (e) as listed under New District Manager training. The exception will be that he need only bring those records pertaining to the personnel that form the basis for confrontations listed under (a) above.

Since emphasis will be devoted to primary areas of weakness, the District Manager counselor should thoroughly discuss these with the Regional Manager prior to commencement of training. Concentration in these areas can then be implemented as outlined in (d) above. Senior District Manager training should require one (1) week.

III. *Materials Required* – As stated in II.B., Confrontation Capsules, selected case histories from former seminars, and the seventeen (17) taped topics listed under subheadings 1-7 will require duplication and distribution to the Regional Managers. As well, each Regional Manager will require one Fairchild projector.

While the majority of our Regional Managers currently have facilities to implement Regional Personnel, those that do not will be required to secure adequate additional office space.

IV. *Implementation* – Implementation of this program depends upon several factors. First, a District Manager counselor must be appointed to fulfill this new responsibility in Personnel Central. Second, as stated, Regional office facilities must be approved and secured by those that currently do not have such space available. Finally, reproduction of those materials noted will have to be accomplished.

It is anticipated that all three requirements mentioned can be accomplished in order to institute this program by January 15, 1968. At that time, it is recommended that a continual rotation schedule be developed that will allow simultaneous training of four (4) District Managers. Since Personnel Regional will be instituted coincident with this date, the Regional Manager will then have adequate decentralized training aids to augment the proposed central program.

V. *Conclusion* – The need for formalized managerial training has long been recognized. Implementation of this program not only fulfills current requirements, but offers an excellent base for future meaningful expansion in areas helpful in maximizing managerial skills. It is felt that an early decision to implement this program, by the date suggested, will further insure our continued progress in the years ahead.

J. L. Chambers

Questions

1. Should Chambers's proposal have been accepted and implemented?

2. What further recommendations for training the district sales managers would you have made?

5-7

PACIFIC FEDERAL SAVINGS AND LOAN ASSOCIATION

Financial Institution—Advertising Program

As C. H. Barksdale, executive vice-president of Pacific Federal Savings and Loan Association, contemplated presenting the association's objectives for the coming year to the board of directors, he wondered what modifications, if any, should be made in marketing strategy, particularly in promotion. He was aware of the board's keen interest both in advertising and promotion and in his own proposals for adding new services. He attributed much of Pacific's past success to advertising, and although he felt sure that the board would approve the new promotional budget and his overall recommendations, he realized that he needed additional information to support them.

Pacific Savings and Loan Association started in 1926 as a state-chartered association, the Pacific Building and Loan Company. It was the first financial institution in Armstrong County set up to attract savings for use in making long-term home loans. Assets stood at about $77,500 in 1934 (Exhibit 1) when the organization received its federal charter and thus became the Pacific Federal Savings and Loan Association.

Pacific's Growth in Assets (1926-69)

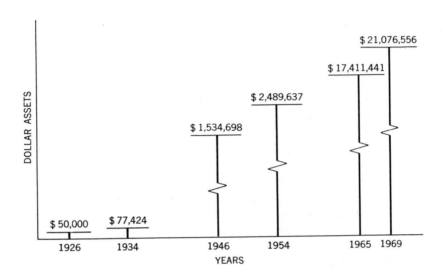

In 1961 Pacific Federal opened two new branch offices in adjacent counties. By 1969 the branch in Butler County had assets of $4 million; and the one in Clark County $3.5 million. In addition to the usual savings and loan facilities, each branch featured a community room for use, free of charge, by civic clubs and other groups.

In 1968 Pacific retained the Financial Advertising Agency of Cincinnati, Ohio, which specialized in producing ads for savings and loan associations. At that time the association increased its advertising expenditures, and management regarded the agency's help as essential in meeting the ever-increasing competition from local commercial banks. Barksdale believed that the added money spent on advertising was worthwhile, especially when new deposits became harder to attract during the tight money situation of 1969.

Management set the 1970 advertising budget at $32,000, an amount some board members considered high.[1] Barksdale sought to justify the size of the budget, citing both stiffening competition for deposits and industry information derived from various surveys (Appendixes A-C). Furthermore, he had complete faith in the Financial Advertising Agency's ability to produce effective advertising.

[1] Advertising expenditures were $23,636 in 1967 and $28,501 in 1968.

Surveys had indicated that savings depositors looked for some combination of safety, high return, and convenience; consequently, Pacific had featured these three themes in its advertising (see Appendix D). In addition, Barksdale wanted to emphasize in future promotion the five new services which he hoped to add at all Pacific's branches:

1. Safety deposit boxes
2. Free notary public services
3. Financial classes for families
4. Legal advice on certain matters
5. Estate planning

He predicted that adding the proposed services would generate increased traffic and create new savings accounts.

Marketing planning and programs had always been very informal at Pacific. None of its marketing plans, for example, had ever been put in writing. Such unstructured marketing planning pervaded most of the savings and loan industry. Barksdale, however, was convinced that Pacific could benefit considerably from increased formalization in its marketing planning. As he prepared for the approaching board meeting, he was acutely aware of Pacific's failure to move in that direction.

Questions

1. How should Barksdale have gone about justifying the increase in the advertising budget to the board? What use, if any, should he have made of the information contained in the various appendixes?
2. What steps should have been taken by Pacific to improve the effectiveness of its marketing activities?

Appendix A

Extracts from a Survey of
Advertising Budgets of Savings Associations *

FOREWORD

This survey was conducted so that individual associations seeking guidance might study comparative practices of 441 reporting Associations.

FIGURE 1

Nationwide Annual Advertising Expense as a Percentage of Gross Operating Income

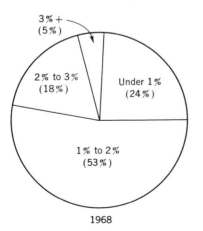

1968

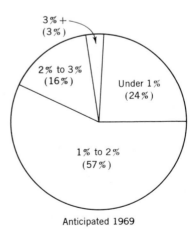

Anticipated 1969

*Conducted by the Advertising and Public Relations Committee, United States Savings and Loan League, 1968.

The majority (53 percent) of associations surveyed spent 1 percent to 2 percent of gross operating income for advertising during 1968. Nationwide, associations anticipated dollar increases in their advertising budgets for 1969.

As associations' assets grew, a higher percentage of their gross operating income was spent for advertising, especially in the $35-$75 million asset-size group (see Table 1).

TABLE 1

Association Assets	Number Reporting	% of Advertising Expense to Gross Operating Income		
		1967	*1968*	*1969*
Under $2 million	13	1.02%	1.03%	1.00%
$2 - $5 million	54	1.26	1.23	1.26
$5 - $10 million	84	1.41	1.42	1.35
$10 - $20 million	100	1.42	1.43	1.40
$20 - $35 million	59	1.60	1.57	1.54
$35 - $75 million	80	1.72	1.75	1.71
$75 - $150 million	31	1.66	1.66	1.60
Over $150 million	20	1.81	1.74	1.66
All Groups	441	1.68%	1.67%	1.61%

Appendix B

Extract from a Report
in Savings and Loan News *

The major finding of the survey is that a detailed written marketing program is the exception rather than the rule in the thrift business. Among the largest institutions only one of three had a written marketing program. In the smaller institutions, the number drops to one out of six.

This lack of solid planning results in lots of impulse buying, constant change of advertising directions and fast response to gimmicks, gadgets and shallow sales promotions. . . . The survey indicates that setting an advertising budget should be a matter of hiring a top flight advertising agency, explaining the institution's goals and letting the agency set the price for accomplishing these goals.

Marketing Program in Writing

Size Institution	Yes	No
Under $25 million	16%	84%
$25 - $75 million	21	79
$75 - $200 million	23	77
Over $200 million	33	67

*October, 1969

Marketing Dollars per $1,000 Assets

Size Institution	Median	Highest	Lowest
Under $25 million	$1.25	$3.10	$0.60
$25 - $75 million	1.00	2.50	.30
$75 - $200 million	1.00	2.40	.30
Over $200 million	1.00	2.90	.30

Mr. McDonald, President, Professional Development Corporation, St. Paul, expressed his feelings about the lack of planning:

1. There is no feeling of urgency in the Savings and Loan business.

2. There is very little desire to do better.

3. There is no well designed and tightly implemented philosophy of wanting to do business.

Appendix C

Gallup Survey (1969)—Major Conclusions

These conclusions were drawn by the Savings and Loan Foundation after a study of some findings by The GALLUP Organization. The comments are excerpted from an October, 1969, Gallup Report to the Savings and Loan Foundation.

Conclusion #1: Share of savings accounts is increasing.
Conclusion #2: Share is highest in the most important market segments.

MARKET SUMMARY

Incidence of any savings account	71%
Incidence of a S&L account	20%
Incidence of a bank savings account	55%
Ratio of bank accounts to S&L accounts	2.7
	(3.1 in '59)
S&L share of consumers with savings accounts	29%

Conclusion #3: Awareness is high.

Savings Institutions	Percent of adult population	
	Unaided Awareness	*Aided Awareness*
S&L associations	47%	85%
Building and loan associations	9	67
Mutual savings banks	14	62
Commercial banks	6	77
Full service banks	2	57
Banks (general)	70	a

[a]For aided awareness of banks (general), see commercial banks.

Conclusion #4: Image is good.

	Best Way to Save Money	+	*Second Best Way to Save Money*	=	*Best and Second Best Way to Save Money*
Bank savings accounts	31%		18%		49%
U.S. savings bonds	14		17		31
Real estate	11		8		19
S&L savings accounts	9		14		23
Life insurance	7		9		16
Savings account in an employee's credit union	7		7		14
Stocks, bonds	6		9		15
Home mortgage	5		6		11
Mutual fund shares	3		5		8

Conclusion #5: Advertising awareness is high.

Awareness of Advertising for S&Ls in Past Six Months

	Percent of adult population		*Percent of adult population*
Total yes, have noticed	60%	Comments Commercial/ad mentioned	23%
Where noticed		Specific S&L	
On TV	41	association	4
On the radio	14	Personalities/	
In the newspaper	15	situations	3
In mail circulars	1	Give gifts as	
In magazines	1	inducements	2
On billboards	4	Disliked format	1
Don't know	3	Liked format	1

Conclusion #6: A higher savings rate is still the feature that best distinguishes S&Ls from other institutions. This differentiation was more noticeable at the start of the 1960s, however.

Image of Financial Institutions

Description	*Percent endorsing S&Ls in '60*	*Percent endorsing S&Ls in '69*	*Percent endorsing comm. banks*	*Percent endorsing savings banks*
High interest	75%	55%	33%	41%
Safe	68	73	73	77
Friendly	68	73	67	73
Growing	61	71	66	68
Concenient	a	63	66	71
Progressive	74	46	41	41
Full range of services	a	35	59	56
Insured by government	43	54	61	69
Money available on demand	56	56	57	64

[a]not measured

Appendix D

Samples of Pacific Federal's Advertising

EXHIBIT 1

Special Letter Used in Advertising Strategy for Mailing to Prospective
Customers . . . Including Neighboring Counties of Butler and Clark

Dear Neighbor:

Here is excellent advice for everybody living in Armstrong, Butler
and Clark Counties. *Before you invest, take a good look at Pacific's 5-1/4%,
6-Month Certificate.*

This ideal investment keeps your money close to home . . . pays
5-1/4% on just $1,000 . . . and gives you a long list of important advantages!

- YOU EARN NATION'S HIGHEST RATE on Insured Certificates
  permitted by law.

- YOUR DIVIDENDS ARE COMPOUNDED QUARTERLY within
  your Certificate, or Paid Quarterly by Check.

- INVEST ANY AMOUNT in $1,000 multiples.
- LOW $1,000 MINIMUM meets Everyone's Needs.
- FUNDS NEVER FROZEN. Your Money is Always Available.
- INSURED SAFETY by the Federal Savings and Loan Insurance Corporation.
- YOUR CERTIFICATE RENEWS AUTOMATICALLY at Maturity.

There is no question about it. Pacific's 5-1/4% Certificate is one of today's finest opportunities for high-dividend investing. I personally invite you to take advantage of it in person or by mail.

Sincerely,

C. H. Barksdale
Executive Vice-President

EXHIBIT 2

Examples of Pacific Federal's Advertising
on Local Radio Stations in Armstrong County

Radio-T.V. Script

Client: Pacific Federal Savings and Loan Association
Description: Highest Rate, Greatest Flexibility

Script No.
FB-10sec-1

Earn Highest Rate with Greatest Flexibility at Pacific Federal. 5-1/4% per annum compounds quarterly on First Federal 6-Month Certificates, thousand-dollar units.

E X H I B I T 2 (continued)

Radio-T.V. Script

Client: Pacific Federal Savings & Loan Association
Description: Big Dividend Action

Script No.
FB-10sec-2R

Get BIG-DIVIDEND ACTION at Pacific Federal. Earn 5-1/4% per annum compounded quarterly with Pacific's Six-Month Certificate!

Radio-T.V. Script

Client: Pacific Federal Savings and Loan Association
Description: Now!

Script No.
FB-19sec-3

Now! Dividends Compound Quarterly on Pacific's 5-1/4% Six-Month Certificates. Earn highest rate with maximum flexibility at Pacific Federal.

DELTA AIR LINES

Airline—Marketing
and Advertising Strategy

In the summer of 1969 T. M. Miller, senior vice-president for marketing, Delta Air Lines, was analyzing certain factors related to the development of new market areas and was reviewing existing marketing strategies. Recent Civil Aeronautics Board (CAB) route rulings had caused him to foresee not only possible system expansion for Delta but also the growth of more vigorous competition from other trunk carriers.

Since 1961 Delta had enjoyed monopolies over southern transcontinental routes from Atlanta to California and on certain other shorter routes. Based upon its fundamental belief that competition best served the public interest, in mid-1969 the CAB authorized Eastern Air Lines and National Airlines to compete with Delta on the profitable Atlanta-Los Angeles and Atlanta-San Francisco routes. At about the same time the CAB granted Braniff Airways, a new competitor for Delta in the Atlanta market, a new route – nonstop Atlanta to Hawaii. Miller regarded these CAB decisions as generally unfavorable to Delta. From 1960 to 1969 Delta's return on investment had exceeded industry norms; in most years, Delta's "R-O-I" ranked first, second, or third among the eleven major United States trunk carriers.[1] Therefore, management viewed the newly authorized competition as a potential threat to Delta's continued profitability.

However, in 1969 the CAB also authorized Delta to compete with National Airlines on the Miami-Houston and Miami-San Francisco routes. Delta also gained a new Dallas-Phoenix route and permission to expand its Chicago-New Orleans system to include routings via Nashville and Birmingham. These decisions, in Miller's opinion, provided attractive marketing opportunities.

A key element in Delta's marketing strategy was its policy of maintaining and developing service to the many small cities that had formed the original backbone of its route structure. The degree to which a particular carrier provided really adequate service to its small city markets, however, had an important impact upon its "system operating results" in terms of "average aircraft hop" and "average passenger haul" results. To the extent that a carrier removed itself from the "short hop-short haul" market by decreasing the number of small cities served, or by holding down frequency of small city service, it improved its system operating efficiency through "longer hop-longer haul" service. Consequently, most trunk line carriers had voluntarily removed numerous points from their systems, and the CAB had involuntarily removed others. Delta management felt strongly, however, that it had an obligation not only to serve both large and small cities within its original territory but to provide the highest possible level of service. In addition, management believed that small city traffic was capable of contributing significantly to the line's overall economic well-being.

Aggressive marketing effort in competitive markets had secured for Delta more than its theoretical share of local traffic (see Exhibit 1). Management pointed to these market shares as evidence of the success of its service policy, which involved scheduling a frequency and variety of services adapted to local, as well as to long-haul, market needs. An example of Delta's long-haul success was the Atlanta-Kansas City route, where Delta and TWA competed under identical, compulsory one-stop restrictions. Delta carried 73 percent and TWA 27 percent of the 1968 trunk carrier traffic on this route.

---

[1] The year 1968, in which the airline industry marked the tenth anniversary of scheduled American jet service and the end of ten years of unprecedented growth, was a disappointing one for the industry as a whole. Revenue ton miles, the basic measure of service, both scheduled and charter, reached a record high of 18.12 billion ton miles, more than four times the level of service of 1958 and a 15.5 percent increase over 1967. However, earnings declined from 1967's $415.4 million to $216.1 million in 1968.

Stimulated by the greater speed and comfort of the jets, the number of passengers flying on the United States scheduled airlines tripled in the ten years of the jet age, from 50 million to 150 million annually. Revenue passenger miles flown more than tripled from 31.5 billion to 113.9 billion over the ten years and increased 15.4 percent over 1967.

EXHIBIT 1

Market Share Comparison

Market Pair	Percentage of 1968 Trunk Carrier Traffic
Atlanta-Chattanooga	
Delta	71
Eastern	29
Atlanta-Macon	
Delta	66
Eastern	34
Atlanta-Memphis	
Delta	63
Eastern	37
Chicago-Cincinnati	
Delta	70
American	18
Eastern	12

Delta's management firmly believed that the success of United States carriers in promoting and developing air traffic traced mainly to the industry's willingness to allocate a high percentage of revenue dollars to advertising and sales promotion. However, in the opinion of both Miller and Henry Ross, Assistant vice president for advertising and sales promotion, some carriers had overspent on advertising. Their view was that unwise media choices had resulted in considerable waste of industry advertising funds. In 1968, among industry members, Delta ranked sixth in magazines, first in newspapers, tenth in television, fourth in radio, and fifth in total advertising expenditures (Exhibit 2).

Management regarded the air passenger travel market as selective; therefore, it used advertising and salesmanship selectively. Ross contended that certain mass media, such as prime time network TV and high-circulation consumer magazines, while low cost relative to audience size, were actually expensive. He pointed out that consumer magazine audiences contained disproportionate numbers of nonprospects.

Delta's practice was to concentrate its advertising in newspapers, local spot TV, local radio, and outdoor media, allocating about 85 percent of its total budget to these. Management maintained that Delta had a unique story to relate to each city's traveling public and that the most practical way to tell it was through messages individualized for each locality. For example, in Chicago, Delta emphasized its nonstop flights to Miami, featured package tour prices, and promoted "Discover America," "Family Plan," and "Youth Fares." In Dallas,

EXHIBIT 2

1968 Advertising Expenditures of Domestic Trunk Line Carriers

Advertising Expenditures ($000)

Trunk Carrier	Magazines	Newspapers	Television	Radio	Total
American	$ 1,370	$ 3,846	$ 6,556	$ 1,923	$13,695
Braniff	858	2,656	3,374	43	6,931
Continental	771	1,330	1,168	332	3,601
Delta	777	4,376	207	1,725	7,085
Eastern	2,459	3,889	3,910	1,124	11,373
National	143	1,853	2,602	744	5,342
Northeast	–	354	1,041	547	1,942
Northwest	461	1,246	8	1,900	3,615
TWA	1,663	3,807	5,617	2,062	13,149
United	3,004	4,328	8,020	1,527	16,879
Western	621	1,324	334	771	3,050
Total	$12,127	$29,009	$32,837	$12,698	$86,662

Carrier Rank Order By Advertising Media

American	4	4	2	2	2
Braniff	5	6	5	11	6
Continental	7	8	7	10	9
Delta	6	1	10	4	5
Eastern	2	3	4	6	4
National	10	7	6	8	7
Northeast	11	11	8	9	11
Northwest	9	10	11	3	8
TWA	3	5	3	1	3
United	1	2	1	5	1
Western	8	9	9	7	10

Source: Travel Research International, Inc., *1968 Advertising Expenditures of Major Public Carriers in Measured Media within the United States,* May, 1969.

Delta promoted flights to Los Angeles, San Diego, San Francisco, Las Vegas, and connecting services (with Pan American) to Hawaii.

Delta, however, had not neglected the image-building potential of national advertising. But it had placed a lower priority on national advertising, allocating roughly 10 to 15 percent of the total budget to national media. Delta advertising campaigns appeared in *Time, Newsweek, U.S. News and World Report, New Yorker, National Geographic, Look, American Aviation Magazine, Air Transport World, and Travel Agent.*

Delta's advertising strategy, as outlined above, differed significantly from those of its main competitors. Eastern spent over $3.7 million on four TV specials in its fiscal year ending June 30, 1969, equivalent to twenty-two and one-half cents per passenger enplaned. (See Exhibits 3 and 4.) Eastern's total advertising expense during the same period was $14.9 million. Thus TV specials accounted for approximately 25 percent of Eastern's advertising expenditures.

EXHIBIT 3

Examples of Eastern Air Lines Advertising Associated
with National TV Specials

Date	*Sponsorship of*	*Approximate Cost*
October 1968	*The King and I*—Movie (Full sponsorship)	$1,361,000
January 1969	Rose Bowl Game (5-½ minutes)	500,000
January 1969	Eight sports network PGA telecasts (One-third sponsorship)	1,300,000
April 1969	Tony Awards (One-third sponsorship)	625,000
Total		$3,786,000

Source: *American Aviation*, July, 1969.

For fiscal 1969 Delta realized an 8 percent increase in net income to $39.2 million and a 20 percent increase in operating revenue to $516.1 million. Delta's share of the national trunk line market, in revenue passenger miles, continued the uptrend of the preceding two years, reaching 9.3 percent compared with 8.6 percent for the year before. Robert Oppenlander, senior vice-president of finance, dismissed as "insignificant" the potential impact of the newly created route competition on Delta's fiscal 1970 revenue and earnings. He reasoned that competitors would need considerable time to become strong rivals in their newly won markets because National "had not established an identity" in Atlanta and because Eastern was nearly as new to the California market. He also pointed out that Delta was already well established in Miami; therefore, it could move quickly to exercise its new authority to compete on National's former monopoly routes from Miami to Houston and San Francisco. He also

EXHIBIT 4

"Low to High" Ranking of Total Advertising Expense, 1968[a]

Carrier	Per Psgr. Enplaned	Rank	Per Revenue Psgr. Mile	Rank
American	$1.09	6	$0.0014	4
Braniff	1.36	7	0.0027	10
Continental	1.78	10	0.0024	8
Delta	0.74	2	0.0012	2
Eastern	0.79	3	0.0015	5
National	1.45	8	0.0018	7
Northeast	1.36	7	0.0026	9
Northwest	0.39	1	0.0006	1
TWA	1.47	9	0.0016	6
United	0.95	5	0.0013	3
Western	0.83	4	0.0014	4
Average	$1.02		$0.0015	

[a]In terms of cost per passenger enplaned and cost per revenue passenger mile.
Source: *American Aviation,* July, 1969.

predicted that Braniff would have a difficult time in siphoning off much of Delta's West Coast traffic through its new Atlanta-Hawaii nonstop flights. Miller and Ross, while generally agreeing with Oppenlander, were more sensitive to, and aware of, recent concentrated marketing efforts by both Eastern and National in Atlanta and elsewhere.

Questions

1. How, if at all, should Delta have altered its advertising strategy?
2. Appraise the appropriateness of the overall marketing strategies of Delta and Eastern.

CALVERT DISTILLERS COMPANY

Liquor Company—Promoting a New Brand

In 1962 Calvert Distillers, attempting to increase its share of the distilled spirits market, began making Leilani Hawaiian Rum. After required product aging, the company introduced the product to the market in Hawaii in 1965. Calvert then expanded the new rum's distribution to the mainland market. Leilani sales proved satisfactory in most United States market areas, but response in the sales district comprising the metropolitan New York market, which included the five city boroughs and Nassau, Suffolk, and Westchester counties, fell short of expectations. All liquor companies experienced resale price cutting in New York in 1965 at the time the state abolished fair-trade liquor pricing, but E. J. Morrow, district sales manager, believed that shortcomings in the performance of other marketing activities had also contributed to Leilani's disappointing sales. He explained, "It normally takes time to achieve success with new brands. Our sales can be improved with proper promotional efforts."

Calvert — a sales division of Joseph E. Seagrams and Sons, Inc., which was in turn a wholly owned subsidiary of Distillers Corporation, Seagrams Limited of Montreal, Canada — was set up in 1933 after repeal of the Eighteenth (prohibition) Amendment. In 1967 the division had sales totaling roughly 3 million cases ($120 million) for its seven different products:

> Calvert Extra
> Canadian Lord Calvert
> Canadian Masterpiece
> Calvert Gin
> Calvert Cocktails (mix)
> Mariachi Tequila
> Leilani Hawaiian Rum

Calvert Extra, a domestic blended whiskey, was the largest seller of the seven products.

In "open" states, such as in New York, Calvert relied heavily on liquor wholesalers for distribution; these sold to bars, hotels, restaurants, and retail stores.[1] Wholesalers exercised substantial influence in the marketing channel, particularly in securing new product acceptance. For that reason Calvert allowed only one or two wholesalers to handle its line in each major market; management believed wholesalers' salesmen gave more push to exclusive brands than to nonexclusive lines.

Morrow's New York staff consisted of an assistant, ten salesmen, and seven "window trimmers." Salesmen called on Calvert distributors and did missionary work with the retail accounts, developing sales ideas, explaining promotional programs, and stimulating interest in the products. Window trimmers set up window displays and assisted with point-of-purchase and shelf displays. Calvert's five distributors in New York fielded a total of approximately 475 salesmen. Two of these, employing 110 and 105 salesmen respectively, were selected as exclusive distributors for Leilani. In metropolitan New York fifteen thousand outlets handled Calvert products, twenty-five hundred of these were retail stores accounting for 70 percent of district sales.

When Calvert management first considered the introduction of a rum, it decided not to use a West Indian rum. There were already twelve West Indian rums on the United States market, not one seemingly able to distinguish itself from the leader, Bacardi, which had 50 percent of the market. However, management wanted to offer the market a quality product, and since sweet Hawaiian sugarcane produced an excellent rum, Leilani was chosen. Leilani was the only United States Hawaiian rum, and this helped considerably in securing initial market acceptance. Morrow was convinced that continuing market success

---

[1] Each state has the power to legislate on the sale of liquors and wines within its own boundaries. Some require that all liquor be sold exclusively through state-owned outlets (these are the "closed," or "monopoly," states). Others permit liquor sales through privately owned licensed outlets (these are the "open" states). In certain states "dry laws" permit local option by counties.

EXHIBIT 2

We get a little help from paradise when we make our rum.

Making great rum is a cinch when you have a volcano in your backyard.

Due to a few major eruptions, Hawaiian soil is rich in volcanic ash. This ash helps make the soil ideal for growing juicy sugar cane. It's the cane that helps Leilani rum acquire its delicious flavor.

4,000 hours of sunshine per year.

Aaah sunshine. And moisture in the air. We call it help.

We of Calvert Distillers are grateful to paradise. But due to our long years as distillers, we must take part of the credit for Leilani rum. True, we get help. But then we know best how to use that help. Try Leilani rum and you'll taste what we mean.

To capture the spirit of paradise when you serve Leilani, we offer these mugs in the form of the god Tiki. You can have 4 for only $3 (where legal). Send check to Tiki Leilani Mugs, P.O. Box 798, Dept. N, Mayfield, Kentucky.

Made in Hawaii by Calvert.

HAWAIIAN RUM • 80 PROOF • CALVERT DIST. CO. • HONOLULU, HAWAII also depended upon follow-up sales campaigns by the distributors. However, he had learned that many distributors' salesmen did not so much as mention the brand, even during its introductory promotion period (see Exhibits 1 and 2).

Distributors' salesmen typically handled thirty or forty "discounted" items each month. They generally relied on selling such items for most of their commissions, as their customers usually bought greater quantities of discounted items than of nondiscounted items. After allocating most of their time to selling the discounted items, salesmen could spend very little time selling special items, such as cordials, rums, and tequilas. Although distributors' salesmen gave more push to special items that were exclusives, it was still true that, as a rule, most salesmen were ineffective as sales builders for a brand.

Question

What steps should have been taken to improve Leilani's market acceptance in the New York sales district?

5-10

HUMBLE OIL AND REFINING COMPANY

Petroleum Marketer—Use of Consumer "Game" Promotions

In 1959 Humble Oil and Refining Company became a wholly owned subsidiary of Standard Oil Company of New Jersey. It engaged in the exploration for and production of crude oil and natural gas, and in transporting, refining, and marketing petroleum, petrochemicals, and related products. Its gasolines and oils were marketed under the ESSO brand in twenty-three eastern states and the District of Columbia, and under the ENCO brand in twenty-two other states. In 1965 two competing marketers introduced consumer "game" promotions, and Humble, desiring to counter this new type of competition, faced the problem of planning and launching a similar promotional effort.

W. W. Bryan, vice-president for marketing, stated the company's basic marketing objective "to sell quality products at reasonable prices through a distribution system which will best serve the needs of the consumer." Humble's goal was to obtain a 10 percent share of new markets. The "sales-mixture" goal for gasoline in all markets, new and old, was 40 percent premium-grade, 15 percent middle-grade, and 45 percent regular-grade. Humble marketed its gasolines through a distribution system made up of thirteen hundred terminals and bulk plants and over thirty-one thousand gasoline service stations.

Because of the wide diversity of market conditions throughout the country, there was no single most economical marketing channel, so Humble used multiple marketing channels. It sold directly at retail through nearly three thousand company-owned and company-operated service stations. It owned and leased an additional approximately eight thousand stations to independent operators. The remaining roughly twenty thousand Humble outlets were either owned by dealers or leased by dealers from third parties.

Petroleum marketers relied mainly on two types of sales promotion: (1) short-run traffic building and (2) long-run patronage building. The short-run type tended to intensify competition, while the long-run type usually helped to insulate a company against competition. Trading stamps and credit cards, for example, were long-run types of sales promotion. Both were based on the notion that stamp savers and credit-card users were likely to be better and more loyal customers than others. Long-run promotions tended to become permanent features of marketing strategy. In contrast, the chief purpose of short-run promotions was to stimulate new business through attracting buyers of competitors' brands and thus obtaining new users of the brand. Among the many forms of short-term traffic-building promotions were self-liquidating premiums (e.g., knife sets, glassware, and antipest strips), giveaways (e.g., light bulbs and aerial toppers), and consumer games. One of the most attractive aspects of short-term promotions was that they did not necessarily have to become permanent features of a company's overall marketing strategy.

Prior to 1965 the most widely used short-term promotions in the petroleum marketing industry were premiums, "sweepstakes," coupons, and consumer contests. In late 1965 and early 1966 two of Humble's competitors first introduced games to gasoline marketing. It soon became evident that games had a much broader appeal than other more traditional short-term promotions. At Humble it was not long before the company's northeastern region asked the central office's advertising group to meet this new form of competition.

Tidewater had demonstrated that a game could be highly effective in building short-term traffic. In January 1965 Tidewater began with a Win-A-Check game promotion in California and saw its gallonage climb as much as 50 percent over the preceding year's figures. Once Tidewater introduced this innovative form of promotion, competition soon followed. Shell moved with its Americana game into selected markets. Mobil came along with Play-Safe, a game based upon its national safety campaign. American Oil began an All Pro game in October, calling it "the richest and largest single game ever conducted in this country" (with more than $1 million in prizes). Nearly all other major petroleum marketers launched their own consumer games.

By lending his support to a game, a gasoline dealer had an opportunity to acquaint hundreds of new customers with his operation. Experience showed that if a dealer ran a good station and gave customers good service, he could retain many new customers, even after a particular short-term promotion ended. Short-run promotions, however, resulted in a shuffling of customers among dealers. Those dealers who served their customers best came out ahead.

Humble's advertising group sought the advice of Marden-Kane, Inc., a New York firm, about developing its first game. Marden-Kane advised using the following approach to introduce Humble's first game, Tigerino. In Tigerino, no set figure as to the total value of prizes would be advertised, but point-of-purchase displays would highlight the fact that there would be hundreds of winners at each service station — the "instant cash" winners. Larger prizes were to be packaged randomly with other tickets. Consumers were to be advised, in all advertising, that they had a chance to win up to $1,000. But in order to win $1,000, a participant would have "to achieve a striped 'T-I-G-E-R' on one or more cards." The odds against achieving this particular feat were a million to one. The next highest prize was $549, and again the odds were a million to one against winning. The lowest prize was $3.23. Odd amounts were selected for most prizes to add realism to winning — a figure of exactly $100.00 was not regarded as having the same degree of "realism" as $111.20.

Marden-Kane arranged with Dittler Brothers, Inc., of Atlanta, Georgia, to produce and print the Tigerino game tickets. Pinkerton guards were hired to provide maximum security during ticket production and distribution. To provide effective coordination and supervision of the game, Humble management appointed a Tigerino coordinator for each marketing district. His duties involved validating the tickets of winners receiving more than ten dollars and paying all winners. Management hoped that the validation requirement would discourage ticket counterfeiting and tampering. An invisible fingerprint was placed on the face of the tiger on the front of each ticket. Tigerino coordinators validated tickets by exposing them to an ultraviolet light which exposed the fingerprint, enabling them to determine if the ticket was genuine.

Bryan decided to test Tigerino during September 1966. The game was so designed as to provide a substantial number of winners at each participating station. To keep the company's promises to its dealers, and to assure the gasoline-buying public that winning tickets were available at every dealer's station, every box of one thousand tickets contained a predetermined number of "instant winners." It was decided to include 104 "instant-winners" tickets in each box. Therefore, in the printing of Tigerino tickets, a forty-group collation order was employed — that is, forty groupings of tickets in each box of one thousand tickets. A dealer, opening the box at either end, passed out the tickets one at a time to game players, thus spreading the cash winners among a large number and thereby increasing the chances that each would obtain a different ticket every time he came into the station. Hopefully, players would not be disappointed too frequently by receiving duplicate tickets. The distribution of "win" and "no win" tickets was programmed at the printing plant in Atlanta to assure a fair distribution of winners throughout all areas in which Tigerino was played. Each box of tickets, therefore, contained 102 small cash winners per thousand tickets. In addition to the instant winners in every box, 135 high-value winners were packaged at random in every 1 million tickets.

Questions

1. Was Humble well advised to launch the Tigerino game?
2. What problems might have been encountered in promoting Tigerino among the various types of Humble outlets?

SECTION 6

PRICING

C. C. CHESTELLE COMPANY

Fruit and Vegetable Wholesaler—
Pricing Produce

C.C. Chestelle Company, a fruit and vegetable wholesaler located in a Rochester, New York, suburb, sold to small-town retailers in an area extending from Rochester to Syracuse. Chestelle early experienced pricing difficulties in competing with chains, supermarkets, and large-city wholesalers. Consequently, its selling strategy was to concentrate on serving the needs of retailers in the small towns and in the smaller cities rather than those of retailers in the two large metropolitan areas.

Two major factors influenced adoption of this strategy:

1. Established produce wholesalers, operating in the two metropolitan areas, had a strong local competitive advantage because they had cultivated both large and small retailers for many years.
2. City grocers customarily made daily early-morning visits to wholesale produce markets, buying directly from commission houses, various specialized wholesalers (such as banana specialists, lettuce and celery houses, and potato and onion dealers), and local growers and truck farmers.

In the small towns, Chestelle met its main competition from two firms. One operated out of Rochester, selling in the western part of Chestelle's selling area. The other, a Syracuse wholesaler, made calls in the eastern part of Chestelle's area.

C. C. Chestelle, the proprietor, set up four sales routes, assigning a salesman and a helper to each. Salesmen bought produce to meet their customers' anticipated requirements from commission merchants and farmers at the Rochester regional market in the predawn hours each morning. They began making deliveries at 7:00 A.M., completing them by 2:30 P.M. Sales and deliveries were made routinely five days per week; "special" deliveries were sometimes made on Saturdays. Besides supervising general operations, Chestelle personally acted as the salesman on one of the routes. He planned to hire a salesman to take over this route, but he had been unable to recruit an acceptable man.

Chestelle emphasized high-quality produce, selling low-quality items only when specifically ordered by customers. Chestelle based prices on the assumption that produce quality was more important than price to his clientele. He attributed much of the company's success to strict adherence to this pricing strategy plus its ability to provide individualized account service. Through Chestelle's personal selling efforts, his thirty-five years of experience in the wholesale produce field, and his managerial ability, sales increased from $200,000 in 1959 to $580,000 in 1968. He predicted a 10 percent sales increase for 1969.

Chestelle sold to 175 retailers, with the greatest volume coming from nonaffiliated medium and large independently operated grocery stores and supermarkets. Many retailer accounts, however, were members of either the I.G.A. or the Red and White voluntary chains. Chestelle's other accounts included fruit stands, open only during the summer, and a few restaurants. During the winter, to maintain volume, Chestelle pushed sales to small neighborhood grocers.

The company's largest-selling and most-profitable produce items were bananas, lettuce, and potatoes. These three items accounted for 65 percent of the total sales volume. The average dollar markup on cost ranged from $0.25 to $1.50 on lettuce in eighteen- and twenty-four-head crates, $0.50 to $1.00 on bananas in thirty-five-pound boxes, and $0.50 to $1.00 on potatoes in one-hundred-pound lots.

Although bananas, lettuce, and potatoes were Chestelle's "bread and butter," other items, including apples, citrus fruits, onions, and watermelons, brought in substantial profits during certain seasons. For example, at harvest time Chestelle bought apples from local orchardists and stored them until sold. During the 1968 season Chestelle sold twenty-five thousand boxes of cellophane-packed apples. One year, during a heat wave, the company sold five thousand watermelons in a single week.

The firm also handled other produce items, such as green onions, beets, radishes, cucumbers, mushrooms, endive, and escarole. As these were highly perishable items, spoilage sometimes wiped out characteristically low profit margins. However, since customers frequently wanted these specialty items, Chestelle insisted on handling them.

Markups varied widely, and Chestelle gave four major reasons why:

1. *Size of customer.* (Larger customers purchased larger lots and demanded lower prices.)
2. *Market conditions.* (When wholesale buying prices rose much above normal levels, Chestelle found it difficult to secure standard markups.)
3. *Produce type.* (High unit value items, such as cantaloupes and grapes, carried higher markups than lower-valued items, such as locally grown cabbage and onions, because of both greater investment and higher risk of spoilage.)
4. *Intensity of retail account competition.* (When large chains and supermarkets threatened serious price competition, lower mark-ups were taken on certain items, particularly those sold to larger accounts.)

As a pricing goal, Chestelle aimed for an average markup of 20 percent on cost, but he actually realized only about 13 percent. He believed that his direct competitors, operating out of Rochester and Syracuse, had similar pricing goals and had experienced comparable difficulties in pricing so as to permit their customers to meet retail price competition from large chains and supermarkets.

For the most part Chestelle concentrated his purchases with a select group of commission merchants and farmers at the regional market. This, he believed, resulted in his paying lower prices because he also bought in larger lot sizes. It also enabled him to strengthen business ties with a small group of sellers, leading to special discounts and improving his chances of getting supplies during market shortages. Frequently he bought staple produce items in advance, storing them in his own modern warehouse.

Buying practices of Chestelle's retail-level competitors varied. Chain store outlets bought through central buying points, and large independent supermarkets bought direct from regional-market commission merchants. Typically, chain store buyers purchased full carloads of shipped-in produce, stored it in regional warehouses, and dispersed it to individual outlets. Fairly often, however, chain store produce managers received short shipments or shipments of items not ordered. Chain store produce managers also had little to say about produce buying and pricing, such decisions being made at chain central buying offices.

Chestelle's customers chronically complained about the low prices featured by chain and large supermarket competitors. Such complaints increased when competitors promoted weekend, holiday, and other specials. In helping his larger accounts to meet such competition, Chestelle sometimes lowered prices on specific items. However, it did not always take a competitor's special promotion to cause a customer to complain, since chain stores and supermarkets seemed always able to sell at lower prices. Chestelle's accounts argued that they could not maintain adequate margins if they cut produce prices to competitive levels.

Questions

1. To become more competitive, should Chestelle's policies on quality and price have been changed?
2. How appropriate was Chestelle's selling strategy?

CORNING GLASS WORKS

TV Bulb Manufacturer—
Pricing an Industrial Product

In the late 1960s the sales manager of Corning Glass Works' TV bulb department sent a letter to key customers, covering three main points:

1. Results of a study by Corning of demand for small TV sets
2. Encroachment of Japanese imports on the United States small-set market
3. News of Corning's new small bulb and the new small-bulb pricing policy

The new bulb was designed to replace all existing 12-inch models and was priced at 5 percent less. At the same time Corning increased prices on all other small bulbs by 5 percent. Packing material, which had previously been included in the price of bulbs, was now priced separately. With the new pricing policy and the new model, management hoped to stimulate the TV picture-tube-making industry's interest in the cost-reducing possibilities of standardization. Savings could, therefore, be passed on to their customers – the television set manufacturers. Corning management believed introduction of the lower-priced standard bulb and the simultaneous price changes, although not complete solutions, would help the industry meet import competition.

In 1851 Amory Houghton started a glass business in Massachusetts. He moved to Corning, New York, in 1868, establishing the Corning Flint Glass Company, which later was incorporated as Corning Glass Works. As the company grew and became an international corporation, much of its success traced to its skills in scientific research and development and in product innovation. There were fifty-one Corning plants in fifteen states, turning out nearly fifty-eight thousand glass items for use in scientific research and by industry and consumers. Working out of twenty-six sales and service offices, company salesmen brought in sales of over $400 million in 1965.

Corning operated six major divisions: consumer products, technical products, television products, lighting products, electronic products, and international operations (Exhibit 1). The TV bulb department was part of the

EXHIBIT 1

Corning Organization

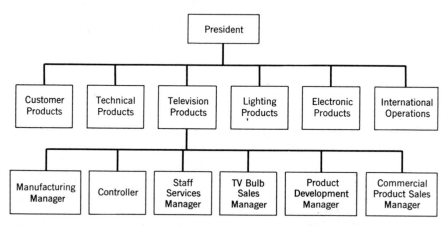

television division; the departmental sales manager reported directly to the divisional vice-president (Exhibit 2). The sales manager was responsible for budgeting, sales policies, pricing, coordinating sales with engineering and manufacturing, and salesman selection, control, and evaluation.

In the TV bulb market, Corning competed primarily with two other glass manufacturers: Owens-Illinois and Lancaster. Owens-Illinois, predominantly a glass container maker, was a strong competitor in both color and monochrome markets. Lancaster, the smallest firm of the three, sold mostly in the small-bulb market. All three sold to picture-tube manufacturers who in turn

EXHIBIT 2

Sales Organization

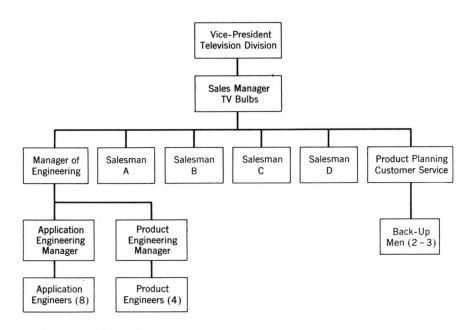

sold to television set manufacturers (Exhibit 3). In RCA and other integrated firms, this merely involved a transfer from the tube division to the set division.

The television bulb market consisted of twelve picture-tube manufacturers, ranging in size from RCA, which operated three picture-tube manufacturing plants, to Empire Company, a small tube rebuilder. On a quarterly, a semiannual, or an annual basis, picture-tube manufacturers submitted "blanket orders" to glass manufacturers for bulbs, that is, one order covering the quantity required over the entire period. This simplified invoicing and allowed purchasing agents of picture-tube manufacturers to "release" against the blanket orders on a weekly or a monthly basis. The tube manufacturers normally desired to receive shipments daily by the truckload.

General Electric had introduced the first small black-and-white portable TV set in 1963. The success of this model, which had an 11-inch screen, and the subsequent inroads made by Japanese imports with similar size screens, confirmed the existence of a huge potential market for small sets. By 1965 all major set manufacturers were producing small-screen portables.

Corning made a variety of glass bulbs used in manufacturing television picture tubes, but it had been unable to produce smaller types as

EXHIBIT 3

The TV Industry, 1966

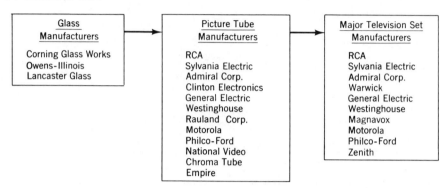

Glass Manufacturers	Picture Tube Manufacturers	Major Television Set Manufacturers
Corning Glass Works	RCA	RCA
Owens-Illinois	Sylvania Electric	Sylvania Electric
Lancaster Glass	Admiral Corp.	Admiral Corp.
	Clinton Electronics	Warwick
	General Electric	General Electric
	Westinghouse	Westinghouse
	Rauland Corp.	Magnavox
	Motorola	Motorola
	Philco-Ford	Philco-Ford
	National Video	Zenith
	Chroma Tube	
	Empire	

economically as its competitors. In investigating the possibility of adding a more efficient production facility for small bulbs, the company retained a marketing research agency to study demand for small TV sets. The agency focused on estimating demand for the years 1966 to 1975. First, the agency undertook a mail survey and conducted personal interviews with set owners, nonowners, and prospective buyers in an attempt to determine consumer interest in buying a fifty-dollar portable black-and-white small-screen set. Next, it contacted set manufacturers, suppliers of set components, set distributors, and TV retailers to determine the industry's willingness to supply small sets of low price and good design.

In late 1965 the agency submitted its report which said, in part:

A strong demand for television sets 16 inches in size and under (hereinafter called "small sets") for use as a second set in and around the home, or as a third or even a fourth set, exists today. This demand will grow over the forecast period, as *low cost,* convenient sets become available, and as householders increase their awareness of the advantages of multiple set ownership.

There is little industry resistance to supplying these low cost sets. On the contrary, many set makers, component makers, sales people, and broadcasters and programmers are aware of the potential for additional sets and are taking positive steps to meet the demand.

These two positive factors — strong consumer demand and active industry interest in filling it — should result in a steady increase in small set purchases (mostly for secondary set use in all types of family households) from an estimated 3 million small sets in

1966 to 7.5–8 million sets in 1970 and projected to 9–10 million sets per year by 1975.

The report clearly pointed up the importance of price to consumers and the fact that Japanese models sold at low retail prices. Japanese imports rose from 127,000 units in 1962 to nearly 1.2 million sets in 1966. Sales of these imports accounted for roughly 56 percent of the United States small-set market.

Increasing multiplication of picture-tube sizes and types by domestic manufacturers also characterized the small-set market. Prior to Corning's introduction of the standard bulb, its customers had requested the development and production of fifteen different models of new bulbs, all under sixteen inches. Customers, it appeared, were always seeking ways to achieve greater product differentiation, so they frequently requested bulb variations.

Corning's previous pricing policies on small bulbs were also thought to have contributed to size and type proliferation. When customers requested a variation in an existing bulb, Corning quoted it at the same price as that for other bulbs of the same size. For instance, the company produced twelve-inch bulbs with anode buttons on the short (back) side, but when customers had requested bulbs with anode buttons on the long (front) side, Corning had charged the same price even though the adaptation required costly alterations in manufacturing operations.[1] Other customers had asked that changes be made on bulb neck diameters and lengths; these also had resulted in increased costs.[2] However, to remain competitive, Corning had not charged higher prices for such design variations. By 1965 Corning was producing two or three varieties of each bulb measuring less than sixteen inches.

Customers' reactions to announcement of the new small-bulb policy varied. Some felt that the new bulb contributed to further proliferation of sizes, but others considered it a step in the right direction. The policy achieved limited success as the newer and more profitable color market increased in importance, temporarily overshadowing the small-set segment.

The sales manager believed that as small-set market trends continued, the TV industry would find itself in a situation similar to that of the domestic radio industry. Japanese radio imports rose from virtually nothing in 1947 to almost 60 percent of the market by 1965. Although Japanese TV competition was concentrated in the small-set market, it seemed likely that imports would soon invade the entire domestic market, including the market for color sets.

---

[1] Anode buttons allow electrical contact to be made in a finished tube.
[2] *Necks* are pieces of glass tubing that are sealed to bulb backs.

Questions

1. Was Corning's attempt at bulb standardization advisable?
2. Should management have changed prices on both the new bulb and the existing line of small bulbs?
3. What else might have been done by Corning to meet Japanese competition?

U. S. PLYWOOD CORPORATION

Plywood Manufacturer—Pricing Plywood

The U.S. Plywood Corporation was the largest plywood maker in the United States, with annual sales of approximately $200 million. It manufactured a high-quality line of plywood panels for both interior and exterior use. Its salesmen, however, received numerous complaints from dealers in regard to U.S. Plywood's high prices relative to those of competitors. Justifying prices to dealers was regarded by management as an important step in acting on these complaints.

Company management, in justifying the company's relatively high prices, pointed out (1) that its costs for high-quality raw material, labor, and manufacturing were higher than those of competitors and (2) that it offered more services to dealers, including handling complaints, advising customers on special problems, guaranteeing panels against manufacturing defects, and, most importantly, providing dealers with warehouse facilities. Because of the warehouse services, dealers did not have to handle a complete line but could secure almost any quantity of any item in it on relatively short notice. Advertising and sales promotional material were also provided for dealer distribution to final buyers. Each of these services added to total costs, but management considered them essential to proper marketing procedure. The company's distribution system included one hundred branch warehouses located throughout the United States and Canada. Salesmen working out of these were responsible for sales and servicing of industrial buyers and retail lumber yards within their assigned territories.

Competing plywood makers sold at prices considerably lower than those of U.S. Plywood. In selling comparable items, U.S. Plywood often both charged higher prices and offered smaller discounts. Even when competing with low-priced building materials, such as gypsum wallboard, the company insisted upon adhering to the highest quality standards; therefore, its prices were higher throughout its entire product offering.

Plywood panels were manufactured from a variety of domestic hardwoods and softwoods, as well as from imported woods. The product was made in various panel dimensions and in different grades for each type of wood. In the hardwood furniture and interior paneling lines, additional products were made by utilizing chipcore and solid core backing materials instead of standard veneer plies. Using white oak, as an example, for face veneer, panels differed in overall size, thickness (number of plies), grade of face and back veneers, and panel construction. Panel construction also included differences in style, bonding, and backing.

All U.S. Plywood plants adhered to production standards designed to insure uniform quality products. Bolt logs and flitches used for making face veneers were carefully selected from high-quality stock to minimize the amount of defective raw material.[1] In addition, quality control personnel took special care to see that cores and crossbands were free of major defects which might cause future breakdown or deterioration. Hardwood face veneers, used for interior wall paneling, were cut and marked so that adjacent veneers were incorporated in the same finished panel. Also, panels made from the same or similar flitches were marked and carried in stock together so that builders could decorate whole rooms with panels of similar appearance. All panels were "hot-press" bonded with high-quality adhesives, even though this was more expensive than "cold-press" bonding; management believed that hot bonding was essential to long-lasting plywood.

After panels were assembled, they were graded according to company standards. U.S. Plywood's standards for softwoods were higher than those set by the Douglas Fir Plywood Association. All hardwood grades maintained by the company were equal to or better than the comparable association standards.

---

[1] A *flitch* is a log that has been sawed lengthwise one or more times to expose desired grain patterns.

Panels were guaranteed against delamination or manufacturing defects, insuring users against these frequently encountered hazards. The company replaced any defective item and assumed responsibility for all or part of the replacement expenses. Management cited a case in which a contractor laid a subfloor for a new home just prior to the onset of winter, then left without covering the panels, and returned the next spring to find the panels severely warped. He asked U.S. Plywood to replace them, and, in spite of his obvious negligence, the company replaced the whole order without additional charge.

Salesmen called on each account at least twice a month. During these calls salesmen handled complaints, explained product quality, and trained lumber dealers in product uses. Salesmen were provided with films, literature, and other promotional material designed to help retailers sell the products. Company salesmen held periodic open houses at the warehouses to familiarize dealers, contractors, and architects with the full product line. Warehouses were located near most retailers, so they did not have to carry extensive inventories and could get needed items by ordering a day or two in advance.

While a limited amount of advertising was placed in selected consumer magazines, most U.S. Plywood promotion appeared in trade journals directed to contractor and architect audiences. All products were branded, but many brand names gave little or no indication of the product type or its uses. Moreover, the various brand names were not closely associated with the company, especially by household consumers who bought in small quantities for do-it-yourself projects.

Questions

1. Was the U.S. Plywood Corporation justified in asking higher prices for its products?
2. Should the company have maintained quality specifications above those recommended by the Douglas Fir Plywood Association?
3. What alternative pricing strategies might have been pursued by U.S. Plywood?

6-4

FLOYD'S INCORPORATED

Photographic Supplier—Pricing Policy

Floyd's Incorporated, San Diego, California, acquired a franchised Eastman Kodak distributorship in 1960. In eight years it became the largest seller of photographic supplies in southern California. Originally, the company sold to wholesalers and retail dealers, but top management later decided to confine the business exclusively to retail and commercial sales. In early 1969 Floyd's retail competition intensified in San Diego, and this caused R. D. Jones, the president, to wonder about the impact on company pricing policy. Although Floyd's maintained its position in the commercial market, discounters were selling high-turnover items at lower prices, and management detected a slight sales decline. Floyd's policy had been to price in such a way that "the customer would get a fair deal." Management wanted to retain this aspect of its pricing image.

Of the eight Floyd's salesmen, five "inside men" sold to amateur and professional photographers, while three "outside men" called on commercial accounts. Outside men sold audio-visual equipment and dictating machines as well as photographic supplies to governmental agencies, schools, and businesses throughout Southern California. Floyd's had 1968 sales of $1.5 million, of which retail sales accounted for 40 percent.

Floyd's salesmen emphasized customer service and satisfaction. Management believed that the company's past success largely traced to this emphasis and to "fair-deal" pricing. Repeat business predominated, but many new customers resulted from word-of-mouth advertising.

Advertising expenditures for 1968 were four thousand dollars. The company used newspapers, direct mail, and the San Diego telephone directory yellow pages. Floyd's participated sparingly in cooperative advertising arrangements offered by its suppliers. A catalog was used to contact the commercial market; its costs in 1968 were eighty-five hundred dollars.

Jones regarded the pricing policy as fair, but he believed some pricing action might be needed to counter competition; at the same time, however, he wanted to keep his retail price structure consistent. He advocated a pricing system similar to that of the discounters — each item of merchandise would carry a price tag reflecting both a regular price and a Floyd's price. "This system," he said, "would accomplish two goals: (1) meet discount competition, and (2) encourage pricing consistency among both new salesmen and veteran employees."

A. W. Flaschner, sales manager, argued that while Jones's system would work for some items, he felt that Floyd's should retain its present pricing method for "big ticket" items. Currently, big ticket items were marked with manufacturers' suggested prices, but salesmen negotiated the actual selling prices, as well as any trade-in allowances. Thus, salesmen enjoyed considerable discretion when "pricing" major pieces of equipment. Some other items, even though carrying suggested list prices, were actually discounted by an average of about 15 percent as a standard practice. A third group of items, composed of high-turnover items, such as photographic film, paper, and chemicals, were traditionally discounted at from 10 to 17 percent of suggested retail list prices.

Questions

1. Should Jones's proposed pricing system have been implemented "across the board"?
2. What other alternatives for meeting discount competition should have been explored by Floyd's?

6-5

CENTRAL SOYA

Agribusiness—Pricing Poultry

Central Soya, founded in 1934 in Decatur, Indiana, was the largest domestic processor of soybeans, as well as a leading manufacturer and distributor of concentrated livestock and poultry feeds. Other corporate efforts included grain merchandising and poultry production and processing. Mainly because of depressed broiler prices, Soya's net operating income declined from $14.5 million in 1966 to $9.3 million in 1967.

Management reorganized the company into four operating divisions: (1) Soya processing, (2) chemurgy, (3) feed sales and field operations, and (4) grain operations. In 1967, 44 percent of sales traced to soybean processing, 37 percent to feed and poultry, and 19 percent to grain merchandising.

In the early 1960s Central Soya launched a poultry-processing operation, as did other diversified feed manufacturers. Management predicted rapid growth for not only the poultry industry but the feed market. Management was attracted by the opportunity for increasing feed sales without increasing additional selling costs. The first Central Soya processing plant began operations in Athens, Georgia, in 1962. By 1967 two additional broiler-processing plants were operating at Canton, Georgia, and Chattanooga, Tennessee (Exhibit 1).

EXHIBIT 1

Central Soya's Poultry-Processing Capacity—1967

	Maximum Production Capacity per Hour (number of birds)	*Hours of Operation per Day*
Athens, Ga.	9,600	16
Canton, Ga.	5,000	16
Chattanooga, Tenn.	7,200	8

Soya faced three types of competition: (1) meat packers doing poultry processing, including Armour, Swift, and Wilson, (2) other feed manufacturers, such as Pillsbury and Ralston Purina, engaged in poultry processing, and (3) specialized poultry processors, such as Rockingham and Southeastern Poultry.

As Soya and other feed manufacturers became more deeply involved in broiler production, they recognized the need for coordinating and controlling the various broiler-processing activities. Therefore they either combined or coordinated diverse activities formerly performed by separate organizations — breeders, hatching egg producers, hatcheries, broiler growers, feed dealers, and processors. Soya's management accomplished this through vertical integration and contractual arrangements.

Contractual arrangements reflected a continuing shift of management and risk from growers to contractors. Generally, growers furnished the land, buildings, equipment, water, electricity, and labor. Contractors provided other inputs, such as management services, medicine, feed, and labor to catch and transport the broilers to processing.

As the number of contracts increased, processors assumed an inflexible commitment. With a forty-week production cycle from establishment of a breeder flock to marketable broilers, and a two- to-four-day optimum marketing period, processors had to forecast market requirements nine months ahead or suffer the consequences of oversupply or undersupply. If insufficient demand existed during the marketing period, the processor had three alternatives: (1) overproducing, thereby reducing the market prices, (2) destroying the broilers, or (3) maintaining and continuing to feed the broilers until a demand existed, at which time they might be too old to be marketable. Processors ordinarily chose to overproduce and endure depressed prices. Processing costs depended primarily on the plant's hourly capacity. Soya, for instance, experienced significant economies of scale as the processing rate increased to six thousand birds per hour; however, rates of six thousand to ten thousand birds per hour resulted in no significant cost reductions.

Three salesmen, located in the central poultry marketing office in Atlanta, sold Soya's poultry products, primarily broilers. A fourth salesman sold out of the Fort Wayne corporate office; however, he specialized in credit checks for new customers and in handling customer complaints. In overproduction situations, "plant salesmen" assisted the four regular salesmen in finding outlets. The four regular salesmen reported to the general manager of field operations. The plant salesman's job was mainly to handle customer complaints, coordinate and process orders from the central office, and make processed broiler shipments.

Central office salesmen spent most of their time processing and following up customers' orders. They devoted little time to developing new prospects or contacting existing customers. About 90 percent of the orders came by telephone. Salesmen consolidated orders weekly and transmitted them to processing plants.

Soya's marketing channel included large grocery chains, institutions, poultry distributors, and, on an "emergency overproduction" basis, smaller grocery stores and retail outlets near processing plants. The largest customer, Kroger, bought approximately 85 percent of Soya's production. Occasionally, Soya sold to A & P. Commercial buyers included such outlets as Colonel Sanders's Kentucky Fried Chicken. Soya also sold to distributors in Virginia, North Carolina, and Georgia, who in turn resold broilers to restaurants, independent grocery stores, hospitals, schools, and other outlets.

Soya fit its broiler-pricing strategies, to a large extent, to customers' purchasing policies. For example, Soya priced to Kroger on a mutually agreed price base, such as USDA's[1] daily *Dairy and Poultry Market News Report.* Soya also used the *Urner Barry Report,* another common price index, which summarized market conditions as to current production levels, market requirements, and wholesale and retail prices. It billed Kroger at the published price on the shipment date. The pricing procedure for sales to A & P differed, as processors submitted bids to A & P's corporate office and made shipments when notified that their bids had been accepted. Soya's prices usually included shipping, ranging from one to one and three-quarters cents per pound, from plant to destination.

Soya's average prices ranged from twenty-five to twenty-eight cents per pound. Kroger's retail prices varied from thirty-nine to forty-one cents per pound, a markup averaging about eleven cents per pound on whole broilers. Kroger secured an additional five- to thirty-cent premium by packaging select broiler pieces. Food distributors' resale prices ranged from twenty-eight to thirty-one cents per pound, giving them a three- to five-cent markup per pound.

---

[1] U.S. Department of Agriculture.

Retail outlets, supplied by poultry distributors, priced broilers at thirty-nine to forty-one cents per pound, thereby obtaining an eight- to eleven-cent markup per pound.

Primarily because of reduced earnings tracing to depressed broiler prices, Soya's management decided to centralize broiler marketing, with the goal of reducing pricing volatility. It also began using computers for controlling broiler production and distribution. Analyses were also made to determine the feasibility of freezing excess production in times of inadequate demand.

However, studies showed that additional costs incurred in freezing and storing made frozen broilers less competitive, with regard to price, than fresh broilers. In addition other problems existed: (1) consumers preferred fresh broilers, and (2) because it was difficult to know when to market frozen broilers, the usual result was to add to the oversupply, depressing prices further. Consequently, management sought to minimize shipping time from plant to retail outlet because of demand for fresh broilers.

Surveys conducted to identify factors influencing buying decisions identified six factors retailers regarded as important in choosing a supplier. These factors, in order of importance to buyers, were (1) product quality, (2) price, (3) supplier reputation, (4) supplier location, (5) supplier-provided merchandising and other services, and (6) established supplier relationships.

Up until 1960 the commercial broiler industry expanded output annually and sold all of it at profitable prices. After that time, however, rapid technological developments in broiler production and processing created an imbalance between broiler supply and demand. Noting this, Soya's management reevaluated its marketing program to determine the actions required to reduce price volatility inherent in broiler operations.

Questions

1. What improvements, if any, could Soya's management have made in its pricing strategies?
2. Contrast the pricing of agricultural and other products.

6-6

B. B. SANDERS

Food Distributor—
Adding and Pricing a New Line

The B. B. Sanders Company, founded in 1850 at Hartford, Connecticut, built an outstanding reputation over the years as a distributor of high-quality food products. Its prestige products carried the B. B. Sanders's Gold Seal. In the fall of 1970 Richard Sanders, president, asked Robert Borden to make recommendations concerning the possible addition and pricing of a line of liquors and wines.

Sanders did not handle the actual packing of any of the approximately forty-five hundred items in its offering. Borden described the company's chief function: "Our job is to create demand for our products via advertising and personal selling and to use sound distribution methods to meet this demand." Most Gold Seal products were processed, packed, and labeled to Sanders's specifications by large manufacturers such as Libby and Del Monte; other Gold Seal products, such as imported specialties, were secured under similar arrangements from smaller producers.

The Sanders organization employed approximately seven hundred people in its two divisions — "wholesale grocery" and "retail stores." Thirty-two wholesale salesmen called on about three thousand selected retail stores throughout the United States and Canada. The retail division's ten wholly owned outlets featured company products — eight were in Hartford and two in Boston.

John Gallant managed the wholesale grocery division. Reporting to him were four sales managers, each responsible for eight salesmen. Salesmen sold direct to selected retailers, each of whom had been carefully screened by Gallant and one of the sales managers. The Sanders organization sought retailers with a reputation for quality, prestige, and clean stores. Gallant described the wholesale distribution system as "quasi-franchise," although the company did not use written agreements. Salesmen kept management informed on the current state of each retailer's operation.

Company marketing efficiency and low cost of merchandise procurement allowed Sanders to offer retailers an average markup of 27 percent on resale prices, compared with an average of 15 percent obtained by them on national brands. Almost always, the company managed to buy the items in its line at low prices, since the suppliers had no promotional expenses. Sanders used these "purchasing savings" for promoting its Gold Seal label; consequently, the firm built up a prestige image, and its products commanded premium resale prices. As a key policy, the company refused to continue selling to retailers who had been detected attempting to use items in Sanders's line as "price leaders."

In late 1970 Richard Sanders became interested in the liquor and wine market and its apparently large sales potential. He wondered if his company should enter this field. As Borden was in charge of new product development, Sanders asked him to make specific recommendations concerning the possible addition of liquors and wines. Borden seriously questioned the company's ability to use its normal distribution methods for liquor products, and he asked the advice of John Gallant of the wholesale grocery division.

The two men discussed, at some length, liquor laws, pricing, and distribution methods. Distillers, rectifiers, and importers marketed liquor and wine through wholesalers and retailers in "open" states, and through state commissions and state stores in "closed," or "monopoly," states (see Exhibit 1).[1] Liquor marketing differed markedly from food marketing, and Borden hesitated to recommend entry into the new market.

Borden feared that in "open" states the company's prestige label might be the subject of discounting, which could adversely affect the food line. He realized that the liquor line could carry a different label; however, liquor retailing was highly competitive, and significant selling advantages were attached to established brand names. Also, through use of the Gold Seal label, it would be possible to get by with lower promotional expenses. Borden was also concerned about the possible need for changes in the sales force and marketing channels.

Gallant favored adding the liquor and wine line. He did not believe it was necessary to use selective distribution, pointing out that, in most states, it

---

[1] See Case 5–9: Calvert Distillers Company, fn. 1, p. 182.

EXHIBIT 1

Marketing Channel—Liquor and Wine

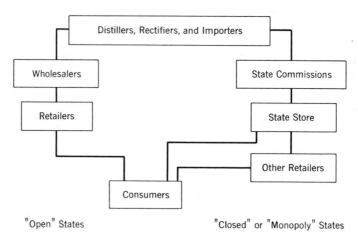

"Open" States   "Closed" or "Monopoly" States

would not be legal. He wanted to retain the Gold Seal label to help in securing market introduction and acceptance, but he cautioned that any effort by Sanders to obtain premium prices might lead to price cutting by liquor retailers. He proposed selling the new line under the Gold Seal label, but at competitive prices. He also suggested that quality be emphasized in advertising the liquor line, increasing the chances that customers would associate it with Gold Seal food products. He felt that prices should not be mentioned in liquor advertising as this might detract from the prestige appeal, might prove difficult to handle in different states, and would be clearly impractical when using national media.[2]

Questions

1. Should this company have added the liquor and wine line? If so, how should it have been priced?
2. Would Sanders's pricing and other marketing strategies used for the food line have been appropriate for the line of liquor and wine?

---

[2] The McGuire Act of 1952 supported fair-trade legislation in liquor prices. However, its provisions become operative only if supporting state legislation is enacted. Some states have not enacted such enabling legislation, and in these, the brand owner has no control over retail prices. In other states, the producer or importer may establish specific retail prices, but there is no provision for their enforcement by the state. Still other states permit the fixing of resale prices, and state enforcement is automatic. In a few states, mandatory markups exist, and middlemen must conform to fixed percentages specified by state law.

STADIUM COMFORT, INC.

Producer of Specialty Blankets—
Acceptance of Private Brand Order

Stadium Comfort, Inc., of Portland, Oregon, specialized in making blankets for spectator use at outdoor sports events. Distributing its output through selected dealers, both in large cities and in university towns, the company won recognition as a leading maker of sport blankets, and operations proceeded smoothly and profitably over the first several years. Recently, however, a general business recession had set in, causing sales to decline to the point where the production rate was cut to 55 percent of plant capacity. About this time a large retail organization asked Stadium Comfort to produce the identical sports blankets for it, but under a private label. Executives were divided on the question of whether to accept the order.

The founders, both of whom had considerable experience in textile manufacturing, set up the business to cater to the "comfort" needs of spectators at outdoor sports events, such as football and baseball games, track and field meets, winter sports carnivals, crew races, and rodeos. With continuing expansion of both intercollegiate athletics and professional sports, they visualized spectators as an already large and growing market segment for items designed to make spectatorship more comfortable, particularly in cold weather and at night events. While various products had been tried, such as stadium seats and cushions, eventually management decided to concentrate on making blankets of synthetic fibers (many of them in "team" colors), which spectators could use either for warmth or for sitting upon.

The large retail organization, which had never bought from Stadium Comfort before, offered to contract for fifty thousand private-label blankets for delivery over the next twelve months at a price of $5.50 each. It refused to accept the sales manager's counterproposal to supply the fifty thousand blankets under Stadium Comfort's label at the established selling price of $7.00 each. The retail organization operated a chain of sports shops and leased departments, mainly located in cities along the Atlantic Coast from New England to Florida.

Various executives pointed out reasons favoring or opposing acceptance of the contract. A few opposed acceptance on the grounds that the company had a long-standing policy against producing for private-label customers, since they might take business away from customers selling the Stadium Comfort label. The president and the production manager wanted to accept the order because, they said, it would make it possible to keep the plant operating and the skilled work force intact. The sales manager, in arguing against acceptance, emphasized that the offer was below the "hitherto uniform selling price" and would likely cause bad relations with established accounts. At an executive committee meeting called to discuss the chain's proposal, the controller presented the figures shown in Exhibit 1.

EXHIBIT 1

Output Level (in units)	100,000	150,000	200,000 (Plant Capacity)
Selling price/Unit	$7.00	$7.00	$7.00
Cost/Unit	$7.70	$6.50	$5.95
Margin/Unit	($0.70)	$0.50	$1.05
$ Sales volume	$700,000	$1,050,000	$1,400,000
Costs:			
General, administrative and other fixed costs	$210,000	$210,000	$ 210,000
Factory overhead and other semifixed costs	150,000	285,000	420,000
Direct labor, materials, sales commissions, and other variable costs	410,000	480,000	560,000
Total costs	$770,000	$975,000	$1,190,000
Profit (Loss)	($70,000)	$75,000	$210,000

Question

Should Stadium Comfort have accepted the private-brand order? Why or why not?

SECTION 7

MARKETING RESEARCH

WASHITA GLASS WORKS, INC.

Glass Manufacturer—
Measuring Sales Potentials

Washita Glass Works, Inc., a specialty glassmaker, produced items used in all phases of household food and beverage preparation and consumption. For some time Edward Paris, general sales manager, had been concerned because sales potentials for many of Washita's fifty-five sales territories did not parallel the corresponding "Buying Power Indexes," as reported by *Sales Management* magazine. He was convinced of the logic of relating sales potentials and sales territorial design, but he had not found a really good way to accomplish this under Washita's existing wholesale distribution system.

Paris knew that certain statistical discrepancies traced to the duplicate sales coverage given to some markets by local and nonlocal distributors. Although, for example, a local distributor in San Diego, California, covered that area, so did the Los Angeles distributor. A prime retail account in San Diego buying through the Los Angeles distributor would have its purchases credited to Los Angeles, but its potential would be part of the San Diego total. Thus, relative to the indicated sales potentials, actual San Diego distributor sales would be lower and actual Los Angeles distributor sales higher. Numerous "cross-buying" instances of this sort made it extremely difficult to estimate the real sales potentials open to individual wholesale distributors.

PRODUCT LINES

Washita's initial and still best-known product line was Chipruf, a clear glass thermal shock-proof bakeware. Since its introduction this line had been expanded to over one thousand items in ten product classes. Chipruf was a high-volume, low-profit line, having reached the maturity stage in its product life cycle.

Washita Ware, made up of cookware, beverage makers, bakeware, electromatics, and similar items, contributed the most to company net profit. Consumers had enthusiastically accepted the attractive and practical glass ceramic items. Consequently, Washita Ware sales had boomed from 1956 up until 1964, when a leveling off occurred (Exhibit 1).

In 1959, as an outgrowth of product research on the Washita Ware line, the company introduced Slimline, a tableware line. Items in this line had great physical strength but the feel of fine china. However, because of relatively high prices, the line had not experienced the sales success that management had anticipated. Among the factors contributing to this disappointing sales performance were high manufacturing and marketing costs, and problems in applying decorative designs to individual items. While the profit margins the company secured on most Washita Ware items ranged from 30 to 35 percent, its average margin on Slimline was under 15 percent.

Washita was considering introducing a plastic tableware line "positioned" to compete in the plastic dinnerware market. Management anticipated high volume sales for this line, as it would combine the physical strength and low cost of plastic with the scratch resistance, attractiveness, and feel of glass. While problems in manufacturing the plastic line were expected, management was confident that its skilled engineering and production personnel would find appropriate solutions.

MARKETING CHANNELS

The company sold Washita Ware and Chipruf through 350 wholesale distributors throughout the United States. Distributors' salesmen called on such retail outlets as specialty houseware stores, jewelry stores, department stores, hardware stores, variety stores, drugstores, gift shops, university co-op stores, and a few discount houses. Contrasting with this distribution system was that for Slimline, which

EXHIBIT 1

Washita Ware and Chipruf Sales, 1959 to 1967

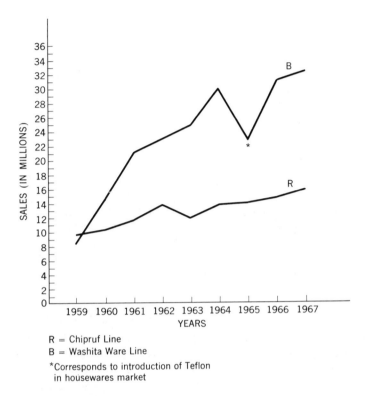

R = Chipruf Line
B = Washita Ware Line
*Corresponds to introduction of Teflon
in housewares market

was sold direct to retailers through Washita's own sales force. Management anticipated also selling the new plastic line direct (Exhibit 2).

Washita's sales force consisted of seventy salesmen: fifty-four territory salesmen calling on distributors; the rest, retail salesmen selling Slimline to retailers and assisting with store display and stocking problems. Territory salesmen linked Washita with its distributors, keeping them informed on changes in the company's marketing offering. Territory men were also responsible for training distributors' salesmen, explaining all changes in product, price, and promotion. In addition, they spent roughly 30 percent of their time making sales calls on key retail accounts of the distributors.

The company regarded its retail salesmen as trainees for territory men's positions. They operated in areas where there were large Slimline retail accounts, their jobs consisting of helping retailers in merchandising, inventory

EXHIBIT 2

Marketing Channels—Washita Glass Works, Inc.

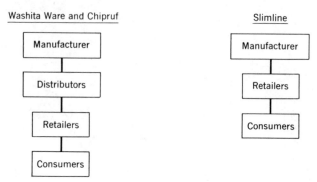

planning, and erecting in-store displays. Their training period covered eight to eighteen months, depending upon each man's rate of progress.

Territory salesmen reported to district managers. Each of the eight sales districts comprised from five to eleven sales territories. Retail men generally worked under, but were not subject to the "administrative" control of, the senior territory salesman in their districts. The eight district managers reported directly to the general sales manager.

Sales territories differed greatly in size, as well as in the number of distributor and retailer accounts. Sales potential also varied among territories, and as part of an effort to provide an equitable sales compensation plan, management had defined four classes of territories: A, B, C, and D. Class A territories contained the highest sales potential, Class D the lowest. The four classes of sales territories corresponded to four different sales job categories, each with a different salary range. Older and more experienced (though not necessarily the most productive) salesmen were assigned the better territories. Under this compensation plan, the highest sales salary was ten thousand dollars higher than the lowest sales salary.

Also paid to salesmen were quarterly and yearly bonuses on sales over quota. Usually it was easier for a man to exceed quota in a Class D territory than in a Class A territory, so a good salesman's compensation in a less fertile territory tended to approximate that of a poorer salesman in a more fertile territory. All in all, management was pleased with the sales compensation system.

As Paris reviewed 1967 sales, he again noticed differences between the company's sales figures and data in the November 1966 issue of *Sales Management* (Exhibit 3). As he analyzed the figures, he recalled a letter received

EXHIBIT 3

Comparison of Buying Power Index and Percentage of
Washita Sales in Selected Metropolitan Areas

Metropolitan Area	Buying Power Index	Percentage of Total Washita Sales
Baltimore	1.0045	1.1122
Detroit	2.3536	1.4091
New Orleans	.4910	.9053
Chicago	4.1723	6.1125
Los Angeles	4.3668	7.9956
Boston	1.8547	2.7715
Atlanta	.6800	2.1057
Dallas	.7505	1.2341

several weeks earlier from the company's only distributor in Akron, Ohio. The letter explained the wholesaler's somewhat-less-than-spectacular 1967 performance. In essence, the three largest retail accounts in Akron were supplied from Cleveland, and the Akron distributor had had to settle for smaller, lower-volume accounts.

In another instance, a distributor's salesman told the Washita district manager in Chicago why he had not called on certain important retail accounts. "Those are served by Cleveland, why should I waste my time and let Cleveland have the sales credit?" Many similar situations existed elsewhere, and Paris believed that the problem partially traced to the company's inability to define sales potential more precisely. He wondered how he might measure sales potentials with any degree of accuracy, how he could improve his evaluation of distributors' sales performance, and how he could increase the influence of Washita's sales force on retail sales volume.

Questions

1. What approach should have been used for establishing sales potentials for distributors and retailers?
2. What actions might have been taken to improve the evaluation of distributors' sales performances?
3. What could have been done to increase the influence of Washita's salesmen on the movement of Washita's products through retail outlets?

7-2

TEXIZE CHEMICAL, INC.

Chemical Company—
Product Concept and Product Development

Texize Chemical, Inc., a division of Norwich Pharmacal Company, manufactured liquid detergents and other household cleaning and laundry products, specialty chemicals for the textile industry, and industrial maintenance and metal treatment compounds. Texize was a relative newcomer to the household-laundry market, and its management was excited over the success of the division's new extrastrength household cleaner, "Janitor-in-a-Drum." Henderson Advertising Agency of Greenville, South Carolina, assisted Texize in developing the product concept, in collecting and interpreting marketing research information, and, subsequently, in introducing the product. In an effort to capitalize further upon the success of the 32-ounce size, management had tried adding a half-gallon (64-ounce) size (Exhibit 1), but both the Texize management and the ad agency executives were dismayed by its disappointing sales. Both groups sought reasons for the poor showing; they began by reviewing the original product concept.

In working on the original product concept, Texize and its agency directed their effort toward developing an industrial-strength cleaner market segment within the household cleaner total market. A product study was undertaken and the following concept statement written:

A Half-Gallon Container

A super-concentrated liquid cleaner, formulated for industrial use, now is available to homemakers. It's the strongest cleaner ever sold in stores. It will handle extremely difficult cleaning jobs like grease-soaked garage floors, even car engines caked with greasy dirt, as well as those tough cleaning chores inside the home, including wax stripping. Just mix with water as directed. No rinsing necessary. Ideal for preparing surfaces for painting. Gives your detergent a boost when laundry is heavily soiled. Rubber gloves recommended for prolonged use.

A professional independent research firm showed the concept statement to a random sample of one thousand housewives located throughout the United States (see Exhibit 2 for some of the results). Forty-two percent of

EXHIBIT 2

Household Cleaner Usage and Types of Products Used

Household Cleaner Usage

Percentage *Consumers Using*	*Heavy Duty*	*Large Job*	*Small Job*	*Touch Up*
All-purpose Liquids	51	54	53	51
All-purpose Powders	50	44	25	21
Sprays	25	33	48	56
Pine Oils	19	16	16	10
Scouring Powder	20	18	31	20
Aerosol Bathroom	19	16	16	10

Types of Household Cleaning Products Currently Used

Scouring	99%
Liquids	80%
Powders	67%
Pine Oil	59%
Sprays	57%
Bathroom Aerosol	37%

The average consumer used four kinds of cleaning agents in the home.

Source: Independent research firm.

the users of household cleaners expressed interest in purchasing an industrial-strength cleaner; 36 percent of the nonusers indicated buying interest. Among users of Spic-N-Span, the leading powdered cleaner, 41 percent were interested in buying an industrial-strength cleaner (Exhibit 3).

When the concept test results came in, management decided to undertake product "use" testing. Therefore, it had the research agency place the product in 501 homes in five key market areas. Prior to using the item, 49 percent of the housewife respondents had expressed an interest in buying; after using it, 51 percent had buying interest. (See Exhibit 4 for other test results.)

Texize arranged for independent studies of the proposed name and package. Texize already owned the proposed name, Janitor-in-a-Drum, which appeared on an industrial cleaner. Henderson Advertising Agency listed three major reasons for using the Janitor-in-a-Drum name: (1) it reinforced the product image, (2) it was memorable, and (3) it was distinctive. An independent

EXHIBIT 3

Some Concept Test Results[a]

Brand Now Using	Percentage
Spic-N-Span	41
Ajax	35
Mr. Clean	22
Top Job	17
Fantastik	15
409	13
Lestoil	8
Dow	6
Crew	3
Other Brands	13

[a]Percentage of consumers using each brand who were interested in buying Industrial-Strength Cleaner. Random sample of 1,000 housewives.
Source: Independent research firm.

EXHIBIT 4

Usage of Industrial-Strength Cleaner[a]

Use	Percentage
Floors	84
Woodwork	87
Walls	85
Cabinets	92
Grease-soaked Floors	79
Stripping	83
Laundry	78
Bathroom	92
Kitchen	85
Tiles	91

[a]Percentage of consumers who found Industrial-Strength Cleaner effective on specific uses. Sample of 501 housewives. Test cities: New York, Chicago, St. Louis, Dallas, Los Angeles.
Source: Independent research firm.

research organization, one not used for the earlier studies, reported the results of its "name research" (see Exhibit 5). The package, a replica of a 55-gallon drum, according to a study by the same research firm, provided several advantageous features relative to the packaging of competitive products:

1. It reinforced the product strength concept.
2. It contained 32 ounces, whereas major competitive packages contained only 28 ounces.
3. It had a distinctive color and shape.
4. It was easily gripped.
5. It was easy to use.
6. It possessed good stability (the product inside would not easily deteriorate).
7. It had excellent shelf visibility.[1]

EXHIBIT 5

"Janitor-in-a-Drum" Name Research[a]

Associated With	Percentage of Respondents
Heavy-duty liquid cleaner	23
Powdered floor and wall cleaner	22
Liquid drain opener	22
Scouring cleanser	21
Other associations	12
	100

[a]Sample size: 700
Source: Independent research firm.

EXHIBIT 6

Package Research[a]

Attribute	Percentage Indicating
Large job cleaner	68
Cleans quickly	68
Effective	54
Convenient	49
Easy to use	45
Modern	42
Economical	38

[a]Janitor-in-a-Drum name and package tested against four other exclusive designs. Sample size of 240 in Chicago and Atlanta.
Source: Independent research firm.

[1] See Exhibit 6.

Management decided to bypass national test marketing, choosing an area for initial market introduction extending from Maine to Philadelphia. This region had higher per capita household cleaner sales than any other; it contained 22 percent of the United States population and accounted for 29 percent of household cleaner sales. Texize began introducing the product in this area in July 1968, obtaining excellent market acceptance (see Exhibits 7 and 8).

EXHIBIT 7

Janitor-in-a-Drum Consumer Acceptance, Introductory Market Area, October 1968

	Retail Distribution	*(Market Share)* *Nielsen*
Boston	54%	3.2%
Philadelphia	70%	4.5%
New York	63%	4.5%

Average Sales Per Store Stocking

		August	September	October
Boston	Ajax	31.1	33.7	38.0
	Janitor-in-a-Drum	6.1	22.2	40.8
Philadelphia	Ajax	36.6	49.7	44.8
	Janitor-in-a-Drum	2.7	36.0	54.0
New York	Ajax	46.9	53.6	53.5
	Janitor-in-a-Drum	4.6	35.4	71.3

Source: A.C. Nielsen.

EXHIBIT 8

Janitor-in-a-Drum — Attainments vs. Objectives

	Objectives	*Attainment*
Housewife Brand Awareness	60% Year 1	59% — 6 weeks 62% — 14 weeks
Housewife Brand Trial	14% Year 1	11% — 6 months
All Commodity Distribution (Food Stores)	75% Year 1	83% — 6 months

Sources: Company records, A.C. Nielsen, and independent research firm.

During the initial market introduction, Texize sent eight thousand sample bottles to retail grocers and food brokers. It also furnished both types of middlemen with comparison sheets showing consumer cost per application, profitability per unit, and lineal shelf space occupied by Janitor-in-a-Drum and its two major competitors (Exhibit 9). Retailers were urged to stress average cost per application to potential users.

EXHIBIT 9

Consumer Cost/Application

	28 oz. *Leading* *Liquid*	*33 oz.* *Leading* *Powder*	*32 oz.* *Janitor-in-a-Drum*
Average Retail Price	$0.692	$0.590	$0.890
Consumer Cost/Ounce	$0.0247	$0.0179	$0.0278
Ounces/Use	2.0	3.7	2.0
Number Uses/Package	14	9	16
Average Cost/Application	$0.0494	$0.0656	$0.0556
Profitability Unit Sale			
Profit Margin	17.4%	16.7%	25.4%
Profit/Sale	$0.1201	$0.0985	$0.2261
Lineal Shelf Feet			
Single Facing Width	4.0 in.	4.9 in.	4.2 in.
Facing/Shelf Foot	3.00	2.45	2.86
Profit/Unit	$.1201	$.0985	$.2261
Profit/Shelf Foot	$.3603	$.2413	$.6466

The market introduction of Janitor-in-a-Drum was extended nationally in January 1969. At that time retailers and brokers received forty-two thousand trade samples. In March Texize launched a heavy TV advertising campaign. In April newspaper advertisements for Janitor-in-a-Drum across the country carried "twenty-cents off" coupons.

In June 1969 the 64-ounce size was introduced. An existing container, made for another product, was utilized so as to hasten delivery to retailers. Texize salesmen and brokers immediately experienced difficulty in selling the new size. Although retailers received about the same profit margin as on the 32-ounce size, shelf space for the 64-ounce size proved difficult to obtain. Sales were below expectations, and management considered withdrawing the 64-ounce size from the market.

Questions

1. What additional marketing research information might have been requested by management when it first considered introducing Janitor-in-a-Drum?

2. What should texize management have done about the half-gallon (64-ounce) container?

3. How, if at all, could Texize have improved its approaches to product development and market introduction?

7-3

LIGHTING SPECIALISTS, INC.

Electrical Manufacturer—
Developing a Marketing Information System

Lighting Specialists, Inc., of Syracuse, New York, manufactured cast electrical conduit fittings, industrial and residential floodlights, airport and aviation lighting equipment, and a variety of vehicular traffic control systems. Founded as a small partnership in 1897, it expanded to more than 3,200 employees by 1967. Increased competition, changing market conditions, and development of overseas customers brought home to management the importance of marketing information for decision making. Although each of the company's selling divisions conducted marketing research, no central program existed. Management believed that a real need existed to formalize the marketing research activity and to give it organizational recognition.

Lighting Specialists' product offerings consisted of over fourteen thousand items of electrical materials used by industry; forty-two different families of lighting fixtures for uses varying from athletic fields and swimming pools to shopping centers; airport and aviation lighting devices; and traffic control systems, such as detectors, computers, and traffic signals. The company sold its products nationwide through a wholesale distribution network, made up of three large wholesale distributors operating branches throughout the entire country, and numerous independent distributors. For overseas distribution, the company had distributors in fifty-seven foreign countries.

Total company sales amounted to over $35 million in 1966. International operations accounted for 22 percent of these, with Canada the largest foreign market. Total sales in 1966 had increased by 10 percent over the preceding year, most of the increase tracing to the recent acquisition of Turnbull Electric, Ltd., of Montreal, Canada. Management expected sales of approximately $45 million by 1970.

Prior to 1967 the company conducted marketing research on an informal basis within each of its selling divisions. Salesmen were used to collect desired items of information in the course of their various contacts with customers. Sales executives then analyzed the resulting information as time permitted.

The president, V. D. Cover, and other top executives decided to organize a corporate marketing research department and to develop a centralized marketing information system. Changing market conditions and increasing competition emphasized the need for formalizing the entire marketing research activity. Cover outlined the benefits that would flow from this move: (1) better understanding of customer needs, (2) improved sales forecasting, (3) aid in evaluation of all present marketing methods, (4) aid in development of new products, and (5) prevention of competitive surprise in the marketplace.

Cover called in a management consultant, Ralph Murphy, who concurred with management's decision to formalize marketing research. He suggested three steps: (1) development of a job description for the marketing research director, (2) placement of marketing research in the corporate organization, and (3) development of an MIS.[1]

Murphy compiled the job description (Exhibit 1) mainly from a booklet, *Marketing Research Organization and Operation.*[2] Since the description was not accompanied by detailed job specifications, Cover asked Murphy to interview and to recommend one of three individuals to fill the new position. Since management insisted on promotion from within, it identified three of its present employees as the job candidates. (Exhibit 2.)

Murphy interviewed the three candidates, checked their company performance in company files, and recommended W. W. Tone for the job. Management accepted Murphy's recommendation and appointed Tone to the new position. Immediately, Tone began helping in the planning of the new organizational unit of the MIS.

Next, the planning group considered the placement of the function

---

[1] MIS means Marketing Information System.

[2] R. D. Crisp, *Marketing Research Organization and Operation* (New York: American Management Association, Inc., 1958), Research Studies No. 35, p. 40.

E X H I B I T   1

General Job Description for Marketing Research Director

Marketing Research is by definition a "service" function. Its primary responsibility is to provide accurate, timely information on market conditions for the use of all persons concerned, so that considered decisions can be made at operating levels. The service provided can be classified under six major headings:

A. Sales Forecasting:
   1. Economic and trend forecasting
   2. Industry forecasting
   3. Company forecasting

B. Market Research:
   1. Analysis of competitors' position and operations
   2. Market segment analysis
   3. Market share analysis
   4. Trading area analysis
   5. Evaluation of the advertising message

C. Product Analysis:
   1. Attitude studies
   2. Motivational studies
   3. New product consideration
   4. Profitability studies
   5. New uses for present products
   6. New products of competitors

D. Internal Policy Analysis:
   1. Distribution system analysis
   2. Manpower requirements
   3. Pricing policy analysis

E. Maintenance of Data Sources:
   1. Historical reports
   2. Comparative reports
   3. File of information and data
   4. Statistical information

F. Liaison with Subsidiaries:
   1. Generic product grouping consistency
   2. Goal consistency
   3. Open: to be developed as requirements arise

Candidates for the Job

A.P. Jones: Twenty-nine, single, graduated from small midwestern college.

Four years with Lighting Specialists, Inc., as a salesman.

Served two years in the marines, honorably discharged.

Is honest, gives good impression, above-average intelligence.

R.L. Green: Twenty-eight, married with one dependent, graduated from the state university.

Two years with Lighting Specialists, Inc., as a salesman, no previous experience.

Energetic, vivacious personality.

No service background, 4F draft classification.

W.W. Tone: Age thirty-two, married with two dependents.

Received college degree, after completing his service obligation in the army, on a part-time basis while at work.

Seven years experience with Lighting Specialists, Inc., as assistant production manager.

Intelligence well above average.

Thorough understanding of company policies and products.

within Lighting Specialists' organization. Murphy and Tone urged that the marketing research department be set up as a staff function reporting to W. R. Gross, the vice-president of sales. Management concurred with this recommendation. (Exhibit 3.)

The third step proved more difficult as management lacked understanding both of the purpose of a marketing information system and of how to develop such a system. Murphy emphasized the importance of an MIS as a data base for making appropriate marketing decisions. He suggested that management read some articles on MIS, particularly referring them to one on "How to Build a Marketing Information System."[3] He recommended that a committee be set up, composed of himself, Gross, and Tone, to study further and to make recommendations on development of an MIS. Top management agreed, requesting a full MIS recommendation in twenty days.

[3]D. E. Cox and R. E. Good, "How to Build a Marketing Information System," *Harvard Business Review*, May-June 1967, pp. 145-54.

EXHIBIT 3

Organization Chart, Lighting Specialists, Inc., 1967

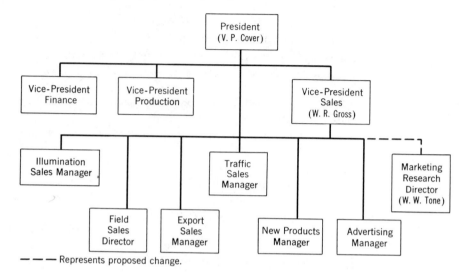

– – – Represents proposed change.

Questions

1. How should this company have gone about developing a marketing information system?

2. Where should management have placed marketing research in the organizational structure?

3. How, if at all, could the job description for the marketing research director have been improved?

GREER INDUSTRIES, INC.

Industrial Products Manufacturer—
Marketing Research Needs

Greer Industries, Inc., a subsidiary of Greer Hydraulics, one of the foremost designers and manufacturers of hydraulic systems and equipment in the United States, was organized in 1955. The subsidiary had been organized to conduct research directed toward improving present products, developing new products, uncovering new product uses, and finding new materials. Any products developed were to constitute the subsidiary's product line and were to be marketed exclusively by it. Greer Industries had no marketing research department, and its management was inexperienced in testing and measuring market acceptance. Its sales manager, however, emphasized that "extensive marketing research will be needed before any new product can be marketed effectively."

One problem facing many manufacturing industries was the lack of a material with any better sealing and wearing properties than those of synthetic or natural rubber. In 1956 Greer developed a new compound, Disowheel, which was a substitute for rubber in industrial tires and wheels. The new compound surpassed natural or synthetic rubbers with respect to tensile strength, abrasion resistance, and aging. It was "as strong as steel" and as resilient as rubber; tires made of Disowheel would outwear synthetic or rubber tires by a ratio of six to one. The material's long-lasting quality made possible savings in maintenance time and inventory costs. Furthermore, Disowheel would not crack concrete or wood block floors, nor would it leave unsightly marks on other floor coverings. Disowheel tires were also rated to carry heavier loads (a four-inch Disowheel tire rated up to a one-ton capacity; the comparable size rubber tire rated only up to four hundred pounds).

Greer's six salesmen sold throughout the United States, calling upon large industrial plants. They received salaries plus a 1 percent commission on sales and were reimbursed for all selling expenses. All reported directly to the sales manager, Rayburn Kitchens, and all worked out of the headquarters in Jamaica, New York. All had formerly worked for the parent company and had both broad technical knowledge and sales experience. Kitchens intended to hire only college graduates when recruiting new men as salesmen.

Although Disowheel was a unique product with no close substitutes, management predicted that competitors would introduce similar products within two years. Since fairly costly raw materials went into the product, management, until it could learn more about the market, initially planned to manufacture it in small lots. The plan was that introductory prices be high compared with prices for either synthetic or natural rubber. Management intended to lower prices later if large-scale production proved feasible.

Greer's management wanted to introduce Disowheel to the market while it still enjoyed a clear competitive advantage. However, there was considerable uncertainty about the extent and the nature of possible market acceptance. While this planning was going on, research and development personnel continued working toward new applications for, and improved formulation of, the compound.

The Greer sales manager met with his assistant and the production manager to discuss the kinds of market information required. They decided that the main information needs were the determination of buyers' attitudes toward the product, the acceptability of a relatively high price, and the comparative advantages and disadvantages of Disowheel as against existing synthetic and rubber products. However, they were at a loss as to where and how to obtain the needed information.

Questions

1. Did Greer's management properly identify all its marketing information needs? What, if any, other information might have been sought?
2. How should Greer have proceeded to obtain the needed items of information?
3. Should the company have introduced Disowheel?

7-5

ONONDAGA POTTERY COMPANY

China Manufacturer—Plate Shape Test

Syracuse China Company, a subsidiary of Onondaga Pottery Company, was the largest United States producer of high-quality decorated chinaware. It employed about twenty-three hundred workers in its two plants in Syracuse, New York, and it marketed roughly eight hundred different designs of chinaware. (See Case 4-6 for a more complete history.) Dr. Jules R. Gulden, director of product development in Syracuse's Dinnerware Division, became concerned with certain marketing implications of impending product design decisions and, upon advice of an industrial design consultant, retained a marketing consultant, Dr. G. B. Angus of Syracuse University's marketing department. The marketing consultant's first assignment was a study of plate shapes. The study design involved making a comparison of consumer preferences for five different shapes of plates. Plates I and II were already in production; III, IV, and V were prototypes.

Dr. Angus set up the research project and then supervised the conduct of a survey in the immediate Syracuse metropolitan area. The questionnaire included comparisons and rankings of plate shapes and respondent classification data (Exhibit 1). At the conclusion of the study, Dr. Angus submitted his report to Dr. Gulden (Exhibit 2).

EXHIBIT 1

Interview No. _____

Census Tract # _____ City _____ Suburb _____

Block # _____ Date _____

Time Started _____

CONSUMER PLATE SHAPE SURVEY

This is a study of consumers' likes and dislikes for different shapes of dinner plates. The plates you will be shown are simply blank, basic molds. No designs or inlays have been placed on them. Assume all are the same whiteness. Any variation in color or weight is due to the fact that these plates are models and not in commercial production.

Answering these questions will take only a few minutes and your response will be most useful and greatly appreciated.

PART I

FIRST COMPARISON (Plates I and II)

Here are two fairly typical shapes of dinner plates. (Show respondent Plates I and II simultaneously.)

1. Which one of these two shapes do you like best?

    _____ Plate I
    _____ Plate II
    _____ Indifferent: forced choice

2. a) What specifically do you *like* about the *shape* of the plate you have selected?

    Comments: _____

    _____

    b) Does the shape of this plate suggest anything else to you other than what you have just mentioned?

    _____Yes   _____No

Comments: _____

_____

3. Why did you *not* choose the other plate?

Comments: _____

_____

4. Additional comments concerning either plate shape:

_____

SECOND COMPARISON (Plates III and IV)

(Show respondent Plates III and IV simultaneously.)

1. Which one of these two shapes do you like best?

_____ Plate III _____ Plate IV _____ Indifferent:
(forced choice)

2. a) What specifically do you like about the shape of the plate you have selected?

Comments: _____

_____

b) Does the shape of this plate suggest anything else to you other than what you have just mentioned? _____ Yes _____ No

Comments: _____

_____

3. Why did you *not* choose the other plate?

Comments: _____

_____

4. Additional comments concerning either plate shape:

_____

_____

NOTE: If Plate III selected: Proceed to THIRD COMPARISON

If Plate IV selected: Proceed to FOURTH COMPARISON

THIRD COMPARISON (Plates III and V)

(Show respondent Plates III and V simultaneously.)

1. Which one of these two plates do you like best?

    _____ Plate III
    _____ Plate V
    _____ Indifferent: forced choice

2. *Why* did you select this plate?

    Comments: _____

    _____

3. Why did you *not* choose the other plate?

    Comments: _____

    _____

4. Additional comments concerning either plate shape:

    _____

    _____

If respondent selects Plate III proceed to FIFTH COMPARISON

If respondent selects Plate V proceed to SIXTH COMPARISON

FOURTH COMPARISON (Plates IV and V)

(Show respondent Plates IV and V simultaneously.)

1. Which one of these two plates do you like best?

    _____ Plate IV
    _____ Plate V
    _____ Indifferent: forced choice

2. *Why* did you select this plate?

      Comments: _____

_____

3. *Why* did you *not* choose the other plate?

      Comments: _____

_____

4. Additional comments concerning either plate shape: _____

_____

      If respondent selects Plate IV proceed to FIFTH COMPARISON

      If respondent selects Plate V proceed to SIXTH COMPARISON

FIFTH COMPARISON (Plate III or Plate IV with Plate I)

(Strike out number not applying.)

(Show respondent her choice of Plate III or IV with Plate I.)

1. Which one of these two shapes do you like best?

      _____ Plate III
      _____ Plate IV
      _____ Plate I

2. Now that you have seen all the shapes do you have any further comments as to why you selected Plate _____ over Plate _____ ?

      _____ Yes   _____ No   _____ Don't know

Comments: _____

_____

Proceed to Questions in Part II

SIXTH COMPARISON (Plate V with Plate II)

(Show respondent Plate V with Plate II.)

1. Which one of these two shapes do you like best?

        _____ Plate V
        _____ Plate II

2. Now that you have seen all the shapes, do you have any further comments
   as to why you selected Plate _____ over Plate_____ ?

        _____ Yes   _____ No   _____ Don't know

   Comments: _____

   _____

Proceed to Questions in Part II

PART II

1. Now let us look at all five plates again for just one moment. Please rank them
   in the order of your choice from "like best" to "like least."

Rank	Plate No.	Mood of Response		
		Empha-tic	Moder-ate	Indif-ferent
1. Liked best	___	___	___	___
2. Liked 2nd best	___	___	___	___
3. Liked 3rd best	___	___	___	___
4. Liked 4th best	___	___	___	___
5. Liked least	___	___	___	___

2. If you will recall all of the times you have shopped for china, would you say
   that most of these times have been for the purchase of china:

        _____ for personal (or home) use
        _____ for use as gifts for someone else
        _____ other reply _____

Comments: _____

_____

3. If you were going to shop for a new set of chinaware now, which *2* of the
   following pieces would be *most important* in determining the *shape* of the set
   you would select?

Mark   _____ dinner plate   _____ cream pitcher
1 & 2   _____ cup   _____ beverage pot
 in   _____ saucer   _____ platter
rank   _____ sugar bowl   _____ other _____
order

    Comments: _____

_____

_____

CLASSIFICATION
DATA

1. Married: _____ Yes   _____ No

   If married: Children   _____ Yes   _____ No

   Number of children _____

   If married: Occupation of husband _____

   _____ Owner, Exec.   _____ Office, Clerical
   _____ Professional   _____ Shop
   _____ Salesman   _____ Retired
   _____ Supt., Foreman   _____ Student

2. Occupation of respondent: _____ Housewife
   _____ Other, if employed _____

3. Education of respondent:

	Yes	No	Graduate Yes	No	Still attend Yes	No
1. some high school	___	___	___	___	___	___
2. some vocation or bus. school	___	___	___	___	___	___

3. some college   ___ ___ ___ ___ ___ ___

4. some graduate
   work   ___ ___ ___ ___ ___ ___

4. Do you own your home?   _____Yes _____No   (pay rent)

4a If you were going to sell your house, what do you think it would sell for at today's prices? $_____

5. How long have you lived in Syracuse or its vicinity (i.e., Central New York)? _____years

6. How long have you lived at this address?   _____years

7. Would you mind looking at this card and selecting the letter representing your approximate total yearly income? (Hand income card to respondent)

   ____A ____B ____C ____D ____No reply.

THANK YOU, YOU HAVE BEEN MOST HELPFUL!
Time interview terminated_____

Address of Interview   _____

_____

Age of respondent:

_____ Teen-ager   (under 18 years)

_____ Young adult   (18-29 years)

_____ Adult   (30-39 years)

_____ Adult   (40-49 years)

_____ Adult   (50 and over)

EXHIBIT 2

Dr. Angus's Report

A. OBJECTIVE

The primary purpose of this study was to determine preference for different plate shapes. Secondary objectives included: (1) reason for shopping for china, and (2) china piece which was considered most influential in determining the shape of the set.

B. SAMPLE

Forty-two respondents were chosen from among 13 different geographic locations, 10 within the city proper and 3 outside (Liverpool, DeWitt, Geddes). No two respondents lived on the same block, and interviewers were instructed to choose houses on predetermined blocks but only to interview people who lived in houses valued at approximately $16,000 or more – the purpose of this instruction was to assure that only respondents likely to be prospects for china would be interviewed. The sample was so designed that it could be used as part of a larger sample should this sample size be found too small. Interviewers obtained respondents' telephone numbers, and the supervisor checked 12 of these at random to verify the fact that interviews had actually been made. No instances of interviewer cheating were found.

C. FINDINGS

Outlined below are the findings and tentative conclusions drawn on the basis of the 42 consumer interviews completed. Because 42 is a small sample, it would not be meaningful to break these results down by age groups, educational attainment, or other classification bases. Blank copies of the questionnaire are attached; please note that Part I is made up of six comparison questions – but an individual respondent makes only four such comparisons; Part II contains other types of questions with question 1 being a check question. Classification data are assembled at the last of the questionnaire.

The key comparison was the "first," i.e., between Plates I and II. Thirty-six of the 42 respondents preferred II over I. This is fairly conclusive evidence that II is the shape with the strongest consumer appeal.

Of the 36 respondents selecting II on the first comparison, 11 chose III and 25 chose IV in the second comparison, better than a two to one vote for IV over III. Those choosing III in the second comparison cast their votes 6 to 5 favoring III over V, while those choosing IV in the second comparison voted 14 to 11 favoring

IV over V. From this we can conclude that IV enjoys stronger consumer appeal than III.

Only 6 respondents selected I in the first comparison, an extremely small sample, so small as to be meaningless in terms of drawing conclusions. Of these 6 respondents, 5 chose III and 1 chose IV on the second comparison — a reversal of what happened in the case of those respondents selecting II on the first comparison. Of the 5 choosing III on the second comparison, 2 still chose III on the third comparison and 3 chose V. The lone respondent, who both chose I on the first comparison and IV on the second comparison, switched to V on the fourth comparison.

In the fifth (or sixth) comparison, individual respondents were asked to choose between their choices of I or II and their choices of III, IV, or V. Of the 36 initially choosing II; 27 again chose II on this last go-around, 3 chose IV, 4 chose V, and 2 were unable to make up their minds. Of the 6 respondents initially preferring I, 3 still preferred I on the last comparison and 3 chose V. This indicates that the group initially choosing II was more open-minded and willing to consider other designs that the group that initially preferred I.

In question 1 of Part II, respondents were asked again to express their preferences. The group initially preferring II were consistent and voted as follows: 27 for II, 3 for IV, 5 for V, and 1 "don't know." The smaller group, i.e., those initially liking I better than II, voted 2 for I, 1 for II, and 3 for V. Both groups, then, were consistent in their answers to this question and in their answers to the fifth and sixth comparison-type questions.

Question 2 (Part II)
Respondents answered this question as follows:
21 buy mainly for personal (or home) use.
16 buy mainly for gift use
2 buy both for personal and gift use
2 don't know
1 never buys china
—
42

Question 3 (Part II)
Summarized below are the results of consumers' answers to this particular question:

	First Choice	*Second Choice*	*Total*
Dinner Plate	24	12	36
Cup	15	16	31
Saucer	2	11	13
Sugar Bowl	1	—	1
Platter	—	2	2
Serving Dish	—	1	1

We can say fairly definitely, then, that these respondents consider both dinner plates and cups of almost equal importance in influencing their choice as to shape design. It is significant, in my opinion, that 36 of the 42 respondents thought of dinner plates as being either the most important or second most important piece in influencing shape choice.

From Classification Data

Age of Respondents:

Respondents were divided by age as follows:

18 or under	0
18-29	5
30-39	16
40-49	11
50 & over	10
	42

I hope, Dr. Gulden, that these comments will prove helpful to you and your associates. It certainly appears that Plate II is the overwhelming preference of consumers, and I feel you are quite correct in the decision to go ahead now with other modifications of this Coupe Shape. When these prototypes are ready, we should again run a consumer test of them against II and probably III and IV, too. Probably this test should be on the scale we originally contemplated for phase two — something over 240-250 interviews in the total sample. A sample of this size will enable us to draw meaningful conclusions of the effect of such factors as income, age, education, etc., on the selection of a shape design.

s/G. B. Angus
T/Dr. G. B. Angus
Associate Professor

Questions

1. Evaluate the appropriateness of the research methodology used for this study.

2. What conclusions should have been drawn by Dr. Gulden on the basis of the research report?

7-6

ASSOCIATED SPRING CORPORATION

Spring Manufacturer—
Data Evaluation and Use

Marketing management at Associated Spring Corporation met to hear a report on, and to discuss, corporate marketing research activities. More specifically, they asked R. C. Morrell, director of marketing research, to review the nature of the company's statistical information and its relation to, and use, in decision making. The group realized that one manifestation of the marketing concept was management's increased use of marketing research in decision making. The group wanted to see if the company's information needs were being satisfied and if the information generated was being used.

Associated Spring Corporation, the world's largest manufacturer of mechanical springs, was located in Bristol, Connecticut. It had fifteen manufacturing divisions in the United States and Canada and working agreements with British, Argentine, and Mexican spring companies. Each manufacturing division was autonomous from a profit standpoint but relied on the corporate office for major policy and capital investment decisions.

Morrell organized marketing research at Associated when he was appointed to a staff position occupying a reporting relationship to the director of marketing. Prior to that time, the various divisional sales managers and sales supervisors performed some token marketing research. The new staff position had no line authority relative to sales departments in the divisions but did have responsibility for transmitting data to each division for market analysis. Divisional accounting departments collected input data and sent it to corporate headquarters. The Electronic Data Processing department (EDP) processed the data from all manufacturing divisions and returned it to each, showing the entire company's efforts from both a sales and a cost-of-sales standpoint. In addition to assuming the expenses involved in data collection, the marketing research unit also budgeted for EDP equipment and machine time. Morrell was responsible for determining the type of data needed and the method of collecting and processing it.

Data, received from the divisions on a quarterly basis, included customers by name and SIC number,[1] total shipments of the preceding year versus cost of shipments, amount of orders received for each quarter and year to date, and amount of shipments versus cost for the quarter and year to date. When the divisional sales departments supplied additional input, evaluation data were provided on individual salesmen; these included the salesmen's major accounts (i.e., one-thousand-dollar potential and over), number of calls made versus budgeted calls, and actual sales versus forecast sales. For reporting convenience, statistics were broken down into a "Sales and Call Planning Program" (see Exhibit 1) and a "Sales Reporting Program" (see Exhibit 2). Divisional sales managers or sales supervisors reviewed these data, condensed them, and passed them on to general management.

The company coded all incoming orders. Each order was coded for customers' ASC number,[2] SIC number, purchase point and shipping point numbers, type of spring, and dollar sales value. From the invoices, which contained the same coding data, came the value of the shipment. Primary data from the main accounting department furnished the cost of manufacture for each shipment. The EDP department keypunched the data for company files.

The full ASC statistical sales report relied on every division's input, as many customers ordered products in one state and had them shipped to another. This explained the rather long time consumed in processing and transmitting information. The system depended upon each division accountant's speed in collecting and delivering required information. A time delay of one and one-half months was not uncommon. To speed up the process, management incorporated a program whereby orders placed within a sales territory were fed

---

[1] SIC (Standard Industrial Code) numbers are two-, three-, and four-digit numbers which are assigned to all industries. They are coded according to major products of the company or division of the company. All reports, surveys, and statistics from the Department of Commerce are accumulated by these SIC numbers, and they have become the basis of numerous industrial market analysis systems.

[2] Associated Spring Corporation.

back to EDP within the first ten days of the following month. The actual times, however, varied according to work loads and priorities placed on the EDP center by other divisions and by the marketing research staff. Management had once considered buying or leasing EDP equipment for each division but dropped the idea.

Associated Spring's situation approximated that described in an article in *Sales Management* magazine in October 1964. The article said, in part: "In effect, marketing information must take second place where computer time is concerned. Right now, implemented at the instigation of other department heads, computer programs are primarily aimed at maximizing efficiency of internal procedures ... Product sales statistics, e.g., are broken out as an afterthought to pre-billing and stock status updating, and often in a form more suitable for use by a bookkeeper than the average sales analyst."[3]

The company used certain statistical data for sales forecasting: company-generated past sales data. Economic data series published by the Federal Reserve Board, specific to each SIC classification, were also used for this purpose. Management modified resultant figures with known economic and customer data, giving a more sophisticated forecast. This constituted a giant step forward when compared with the previous forecasting method, "blue-skying." Forecasting evolved into a blending of statistical data and educated guesses by averaging expert opinion and general account knowledge, for which management relied heavily on the salesmen.

Associated also depended on statistical data to aid in planning cash flow, in determining manpower needs, and in measuring the attainment of corporate objectives. As Morrell put it:

> From this data can unfold innumerable fields of analysis and research and provide a scientific working tool upon which we can justify the recommendation of facility expansion; diversification through new equipment and new products; new plants and their location; materials processes; product research and many other fields.

In July 1964 management realized that one primary fault was lack of understanding of data supplied at division level. Visitations with the director of marketing research, reading on the subject, and complete review of input and output data brought management to a better understanding of research objectives and corporate goals. Management corrected some inaccuracies in the input data, as it became evident that the quality of EDP output data only equaled that of input data. Inaccurate SIC numbers, misidentified purchase points and shipping points, typographical errors, poor field reporting, and wrong accreditation of accounts to specific salesmen were some of the problems

---

[3] *Sales Management,* October 1964, p. 76.

corrected. Prior to this, statistical data had meant little to either management or salesmen because of such inaccuracies. As changes took effect, the data became more meaningful. As a salesman, for example, saw his planning figure or forecast for a specific account come alive statistically, he showed new enthusiasm. Rather than the figures merely being "report cards," they became "road maps."

Management also initiated a new program called *target accounts.* These accounts, the company's largest customers, were reported on a monthly basis to salesmen. Based on incoming orders only (rather than on shipments or cost of shipments which caused data delay), the program proved effective. By up-to-date reporting, management noted monthly fluctuations in buying habits of target account customers.

Management also initiated another new reporting program that was aimed at comparing estimated manufacturing cost with actual manufacturing cost versus sales price by account. This report not only showed how well or how poorly the salesman had priced the account but also gave management an overall appraisal of manufacturing performance against predetermined standards. Information of this nature showed management many hitherto hidden features: SIC competitive prices, relation to profit margin, lucrative SICs, automation needed to increase profit margins as related to dollar volume, and market penetration resulting from improved methods on particular lines.

As many of Associated's customers began to "buy by computer," the importance of marketing research statistics increased. Consequently, management thought it necessary to realign the company's method of estimating potential and profit in certain SICs. In some of the more competitive classifications, management lowered burden rates; in more lucrative classifications, rates were increased. To reiterate, these statistics were viewed at one time as unwieldy, if not impossible, to use. However, it now appeared as though management had begun to value and make use of the research information. Morrell, therefore, seemed satisfied with the company's current research effort.

EXHIBIT 1

Sales and Call Planning Program

This program was developed as a sales tool to provide a complete communication system from customer to sales accomplishment. It provides for corporate and division quotas, the arranging of information for effective utilization of a salesman's time and a "management by exception" control of accomplishment. The following documents make up the information-gathering instruments for this program:

1. *Annual Customer Survey Form*
   Designed to record information pertinent to buying influences,

potential appraisal, quota and call strategy (effective time-cost-return).

2. *Salesman's Yearly Sales and Call Plan*

Arrays the customer information from the survey by potential size for quota and planned sales. Totals are accumulated.

3. *Yearly Sales and Call Plan Summary*

(a) Arrays the pertinent material of calls, potentials, and corporate and division quotas, both by year and quarters, for each salesman by sales management responsibility.

(b) This same form is used to collect the summaries by sales responsibility areas for the total corporate planning. It is, in effect, a complete budget survey.

4. *Salesman's Account Potential Summary (Annual)*

This is designed as a ledger account indicating the number of accounts for each salesman according to potential sizes under "Total Territory Accounts." This report gives the sales manager an aid whereby he can determine the account risk concentration by salesman.

This same form is used to divisionally accumulate the salesman's summary information for each sales management's responsibilities for a total corporate report.

5. *Salesman's Planned Itinerary*

This is designed as a weekly planning tool for the salesman and to communicate these plans to his sales management.

6. *Salesman's Weekly Call Report*

This provides a simple weekly report sheet of the salesman's activities on each customer. The black-lined section is data for TAB and supplies approved call plan credit for the call quota on *Salesman's Report*.

7. *Special Call Report*

This provides for the necessary communication of special or important information to sales management and any other interested persons.

8. *Summary of Salesman's Weekly Call Reports*

This report gives sales management a quick inspection of the weekly sales activity of each of his men. It provides him with an appraisal of the effective use of time by his men.

9. *Salesman's Report*

This is a quarterly report by salesman, by customer, of his plans, calls, quotas, and accomplishment. The sales plan variance section provides, by quick inspection, variances from plan that can be discussed for strategy.

EXHIBIT 2

Sales Reporting Program

The entire Sales Reporting Program was developed around a single form for use in data processing. The single form use — with the data arrayed for different purposes, by customer — provides a continuing similarity of report reading on these various Customer Account Reports. Thus, it provides identical customer data, by plant, for all reports for division and corporate use.

      The entire Sales Reporting Program — from corporate through territory, division, plant, and salesman's responsibility — provides an important management tool for effective profitable sales planning as complementary to the Sales and Call Planning Program. The following numbers refer to the numbers on the attached facsimile pack.

Customer Account Report
1. The entire business of the corporation is listed alphabetically by customer, by plant, to make a composite corporate report.
2. This same information is listed alphabetically by customer, by sales area or territory.
3. The same information is listed alphabetically by customer by plant.
4. To show each plant's sales into various sales territories, its sales are arranged alphabetically by customer, by plant, by territory. Each sales management has copies of all sales into and from its sales territories.
5. Summary data by manufacturing plant is recorded for the corporate report summary.
6. The summary by sales territory is likewise recorded.
7. Within each sales territory the summary information by manufacturing plant is recorded.

Product Coding Report
8. Certain classifications of product codes are tabulated by plant and summarized to give the corporate total. This report is printed out by EDP as a corporate report and also by plant and by territory.

Questions

1. Appraise the appropriateness of Associated's data collection system.

2. Was ASC using the data available to the best advantage?

SECTION 8

LEGISLATION

8-1

POPEIL BROTHERS, INC.

Manufacturer of Food Cutters—
Deceptive Advertising Charge

In January 1971 the Federal Trade Commission announced a proposed complaint against Popeil Brothers, Inc. The Complaint alleged that Popeil was making deceptively inconsistent claims in advertising its food cutter, the Veg-O-Matic. The FTC said that in TV commercials, the company represented that its cutter would slice raw carrots, ripe tomatoes, and other hard-to-slice items, but the Veg-O-Matic package carried instructions cautioning buyers not to slice raw carrots, lemons, and ripe tomatoes. Further, the FTC charged Popeil with making inconsistent guarantee claims regarding the Veg-O-Matic.

In commenting upon the FTC's proposed complaint, Samuel J. Popeil, chairman of the company, asserted that it involved only one of the company's many products. He said, too, that it was limited to possible ambiguities in advertising statements about the products. Mr. Popeil concluded by saying, "There is no issue as to the ability of the Veg-O-Matic to perform as shown on its television commercials."

Questions

1. Was the FTC justified in charging Popeil Brothers with deceptive advertising?
2. What steps should management have taken to prevent further charges of this sort?

8-2

STANDARD OIL COMPANY OF CALIFORNIA

Petroleum Marketer—Deceptive Advertising

In late 1970 the Federal Trade Commission charged that Standard Oil Company of California had used deceptive and fraudulent advertising in its promotion of F-310, a gasoline additive. F-310 had been developed by the company's research unit, Chevron Research, in 1968; it was a gummy substance that appeared to possess an unusual ability to dissolve or prevent deposits that clog carburetors, intake systems, and certain automotive valves. After tests by an outside research organization, the company introduced "Chevron with F-310" in late 1969 with a series of advertisements carrying such headlines as "Dramatic Proof: Chevron Gasolines with New F-310 Turn Dirty Exhaust into Good, Clean Mileage." The FTC not only questioned the effectiveness of F-310 but asserted that a demonstration featuring astronaut Scott Carpenter was rigged. The FTC said that, contrary to the Chevron advertisements, "F-310 is not the most long-awaited gasoline development in history, will not diminish emission of hydrocarbons or carbon monoxide, and will not produce cleaner air." In its proposed order against Standard of California, the FTC specified that "Standard is not to run advertising for Chevron gasoline or any other gasoline for one year unless it is clearly and conspicuously disclosed in such ads that FTC has found previous Chevron with F-310 advertising to be false, and that the products were not effective in reducing air pollution."

Television commercials for Chevron with F-310 carried a "before" and an "after" demonstration with a commentary by astronaut Carpenter. In the "before" phase of the demonstration, a plastic bag attached to a car's exhaust pipe filled with black smoke "before using F-310." In the "after" phase, the car's gasoline tank was filled six times with Chevron with F-310, and the plastic bag appeared clear and transparent. Essentially the same format was used in print advertising for Chevron with F-310. The FTC charged that special gas was used in the first car to produce soot and charged further that the "clear" bag was not actually pollutant free, since it contained hydrocarbons and other invisible pollutants. The FTC also said that a building appearing in the commercial labeled "Standard Oil Co. of California Chevron Research Center" was really the Riverside County (California) Court House.

Various company executives issued statements to counter the FTC's charges. A report in *The Wall Street Journal* quoted the chairman of the board as describing F-310 as "an exceptional breakthrough in gasoline technology" and "an outstanding success in the market."[1] In a company house organ, *Marketing News*, the advertising manager described F-310 as "so unique that it literally is an advertising man's dream come true. It represents a great technological innovation, provides great social benefit and improves gas mileage."[2] The assistant advertising manager said, "We don't think the public is misled by F-310 advertising. In our professional judgment, we think the public understands no product is a cure-all for everything. Obviously no one really thinks the guy using a certain advertised deodorant is going to get all those pretty girls because of the deodorant."[3]

Questions

1. Was the company's promotion of Chevron with F-310 "deceptive and fraudulent," as charged by the FTC, or simply harmless trade puffery, as suggested by the assistant advertising manager?

2. Assuming that "Chevron with F-310" was as great a technological innovation as described by the advertising manager, how should it have been promoted?

[1] *The Wall Street Journal*, January 7, 1971, p. 1.

[2] Reported in *Advertising Age*, May 18, 1970, p. 34.

[3] *The Wall Street Journal*, January 7, 1971, p. 10.

8-3

E. I. DU PONT DE NEMOURS AND COMPANY

Multi-product Firm—False Advertising

In late 1970 the Federal Trade Commission announced a proposed complaint against the Du Pont Company and its advertising agency, BBDO,[1] charging that they used false advertising in the promotion of Zerex antifreeze. The Commission indicated that the "can-stabbing" ad, which depicted the alleged antileak qualities of Zerex, was false, since demonstration conditions varied widely from actual operating conditions. Further, the FTC indicated that Du Pont was aware of possible cooling-system damage traceable to Zerex.

The FTC, in challenging the commercial, said that both pressure and rate of circulation within the can differed substantially from that found in car radiators (4 psi versus 12-15 psi, and 1 gpm versus 35 gpm). No statement was made concerning temperature. The FTC further pointed out that most cooling-system leaks occurred in places where the liquid surged against or around an opening, whereas in the demonstration the liquid flowed past the openings.

In reference to the possibility of damaging properties within Zerex,

[1] Batten, Barton, Durstine and Osborn, Inc., of New York.

the commission appeared ready to invoke the "death sentence" if necessary. Action of this nature would involve a cease and desist order which, once issued, would prohibit Du Pont from marketing Zerex unless it could prove that the product was safe or unless it warned users of the possible danger.

Du Pont executives responded to the charges, saying, "Although we haven't seen a copy of the FTC complaint, based on available information we're convinced that it is totally unjustified . . . The script of our national television commercial and technical data on the can-stabbing demonstration were submitted to the FTC prior to production in 1969. The script was modified in accordance with FTC suggestions. The finished commercial was submitted to the FTC in August 1969 and they made no complaint."[2] Executives also said that "the product was test-marketed in tens of thousands of vehicles. There were no reports of radiator damage . . . Zerex is sold under an unconditional consumer guarantee (and) damage complaints have run at a rate of only 1/100 of 1%."[3]

Questions

1. Was Du Pont guilty of using false advertising?
2. Why was the company unsuccessful in avoiding the charges?

[2] *The Wall Street Journal*, November 27, 1970, p. 5.
[3] *Ibid.* Also *Advertising Age,* November 30, 1970.

CAMPBELL SOUP COMPANY

Food Processor—Misleading Advertising

In March 1969 the Federal Trade Commission issued a complaint against Campbell Soup Company charging it and its advertising agency (Batten, Barton, Durstine and Osborn) with misleading advertising. The offending advertisement, a television commercial, was alleged to exaggerate the abundance of "solids" in a can of Campbell's soup. Specifically, the FTC charged Campbell with violating Section 5 of the FTC act that pertained to unfair competitive methods and deceptive practices.

The Cambell Soup Company, incorporated in New Jersey in 1922, was the world's largest manufacturer of canned soups. The company was also an important manufacturer of spaghetti, macaroni, blended vegetable juices, frozen precooked dinners, and other food products. Sales expanded from $516.2 million in 1960 to $884.5 million in 1969 – a rise of over 70 percent. Campbell distributed its lines through wholesalers and retailers, and direct to large chains, retailer cooperatives, institutional and industrial accounts, and governmental units.

The TV commercial showed a bowl of Campbell's soup in a "ready-to-eat" situation. Several clear glass marbles were placed in the bowl, preventing the solid ingredients from sinking to the bottom, thereby giving the impression of more solid ingredients (garnish) than actually existed. The nature of this "mock-up" was not revealed to viewers. The FTC asserted that this demonstration both exaggerated and misrepresented the quantity or abundance of solid ingredients in Campbell's soup; it charged that the commercial was false, misleading, and deceptive.

Questions

1. Was Campbell Soup guilty of using false and misleading advertising?
2. Is it possible to use "mock-ups" in TV commercials without somehow misleading the consumer?

AAMCO AUTOMATIC TRANSMISSIONS

Franchise Marketer—
Deceptive Price Advertising by Franchisees

In 1970 Aamco Automatic Transmission of Bridgeport, Pennsylvania, a franchise marketer, entered into a consent agreement with the Federal Trade Commission. Under the terms of the agreement, Aamco was required to police its franchisees to eliminate deception in the advertising and the selling of auto transmission repairs. Aamco agreed not to provide franchisees with advertising or promotional materials that listed particular prices, except in cases where the franchisees had previously and independently determined the prices. The consent agreement specifically prohibited representations that franchisees would make minor repairs for $4.50 to $28.00, that they would perform inspections for $23.00, or that they would provide towing or any other services free.

The consent agreement grew out of FTC charges that a great deal of Aamco price advertising was directed solely to the obtaining of leads to prospective customers. Contrary to Aamco's advertising, the franchised Aamco transmission shops, the FTC charged, did not regularly repair many automatic transmissions with a simple $4.50 "adjustment," with the $13.75 "safeguard" service, or with its $23.00 "removal and inspection" service.

The consent agreement also made Aamco responsible for investigating complaints against its franchisees and for maintaining surveillance over them to see that they complied with the consent agreement. Aamco was to be held accountable for a franchisee's violations when the violations were uncovered by its surveillance operation and if "reasonably diligent steps" were not taken to correct the siutation. While Aamco was expected to investigate any complaint, receipt of individual complaints would not be considered "knowledge" of an abuse unless Aamco failed to investigate a franchisee against whom there were eighteen or more customer complaints in a particular year.

Questions

1. Should Aamco have been held responsible for its franchisees' failure to honor Aamco's advertised prices?
2. To what extent did the consent agreement protect the interests of consumers?

GENERAL ELECTRIC COMPANY

Appliance Marketer—
Suit Charging Illegal Price Discrimination

In late 1970 Fulford, Inc., of Austin, Texas, an appliance retailer, filed a suit in the United States Federal District Court in Austin against the General Electric Company. The civil suit charged that General Electric had violated federal price discrimination prohibitions. George Fulford, owner of the appliance store, alleged that GE's practice of selling appliances to home builders at lower prices than to retailers violated the Robinson-Patman Act. He asked for unspecified damages and a permanent injunction against GE's continuing this pricing practice.

Announcement that the suit had been filed came at a news conference in Chicago, sponsored by the National Association of Radio, Television and Appliance Dealers. The trade association had previously campaigned long and hard to end alleged dual pricing, which it asserted was a widespread industry practice. Previously, it had complained to the Federal Trade Commission that many appliance makers were violating the Robinson-Patman Act, which prohibited selling the same product to the same class of buyers at different prices. However, the FTC had rejected this earlier complaint, ruling that builders and retail dealers were different classes of customers.

In early 1971 GE and Fulford announced that the suit had been settled. The announcement said that "as a result of serious discussions, all misunderstandings have been resolved, and a mutually satisfactory basis for continuing to do business together has been determined." Exact details of the settlement were not revealed, but the statement did say that Fulford, whose GE franchise had been suspended, would retain its dealer franchise.

Questions

1. Was Fulford, Inc., justified in filing a price discrimination suit against GE?
2. Under what conditions is it appropriate and lawful for a marketer to use dual pricing?

8-7

AMALGAMATED SUGAR COMPANY AND UTAH–IDAHO SUGAR COMPANY

Beet Sugar Producers— Alleged Price-Fixing through Basing—Point Pricing

In a civil antitrust suit filed in Federal District Court in Salt Lake City by three large sugar buyers in early 1971, Amalgamated Sugar Company and Utah-Idaho Sugar Company were accused of conspiring to fix the price of sugar and to sustain and fix artificial freight charges, in violation of the Sherman Antitrust Act. The three large sugar buyers (Albertson's, Inc., a supermarket chain: Spudnuts Industries, Inc., a doughnut marketer; and Fisher Baking Company) further alleged that the two beet sugar producers discriminated against buyers in sixteen western states by charging phantom freight on sugar shipments.[1] The complaint charged that the defendants used a multiple basing point system, whereby a buyer in Salt Lake City, for instance, paid a prespecified freight charge regardless of where the shipment actually originated. The plaintiffs asked for an award based on assertedly inflated costs due to the alleged phantom freight and price conspiracy, and they also asked for an injunction against the alleged practices.

---

[1] *Phantom freight* is a freight charge that is in excess of the actual shipping costs.

Questions

1. Under what conditions is it illegal to charge phantom freight?

2. How should the two sugar producers have priced their output?

8-8

ADOLPH COORS COMPANY

Brewer—Alleged Price-Fixing and Imposition of Illegal Sales Restraints on Middlemen

In early 1971 the Federal Trade Commission announced that it planned to issue a complaint against Adolph Coors Company of Golden, Colorado, which marketed beer in eleven western states. The company was the nation's fifth largest brewer and had annual sales of over $200 million. The FTC charged that Coors set the wholesale prices its distributors charged for Coors beer and provided the distributors with suggested retail prices for the beer. Then, the FTC contended, Coors threatened the retailers with limiting stocks of Coors beer if they did not sell at the suggested price. The FTC's proposed complaint also charged that Coors prohibited its distributors from selling its beer outside their assigned territories and required them to prohibit retailers of Coors draft beer from selling any other brand of draft beer.

In reacting to the FTC's announcement, Coors management said: "We are distressed by the implication that we are guilty of some kind of wrongdoing. Our company isn't doing anything different today than what we have been doing ever since Prohibition ended in 1933. The trade practices employed by Adolph Coors Company are standard trade practices."

Management also accused the FTC of questioning what amounted to standard operating procedures in the brewing industry. "Distributorships with territorial limitations, for example, are the established pattern in both the brewing and soft-drink industries and in other industries as well. We are confused and puzzled by the FTC action over practices which Coors and many other companies have followed for nearly four decades. It appears that Adolph Coors is being questioned about industry practices which have existed for a long time and which are in standard use in American industry today."

As for the FTC's allegation that Coors fixed prices, management maintained that in a major part of the company's market, state law required pricing standards. Citing California as an example, a state in which Coors sold roughly half its output, one executive noted that California required the posting of wholesale and retail prices by brewers and wholesalers.

Questions

1. Should Coors have been prohibited from setting wholesale prices for its distributors and providing them with suggested retail prices?
2. Should the company have been restrained from confining its distributors to making sales in assigned territories?

8-9

UNITED BISCUIT COMPANY OF AMERICA

Baker—Price Discrimination

In 1959 the Federal Trade Commission began an investigation into alleged discriminating pricing practices by the Sawyer Division of the United Biscuit Company of America[1] in the sale of its products to retail grocery store customers. The Sawyer Division was one of the company's eight operating divisions, covering an area comprising Illinois and portions of Indiana, Iowa, Wisconsin, Michigan, Kentucky, and Missouri. The commission's case with respect to the actual operation of the company's discount practices was based on purchases made and discounts earned during two separate periods of 1959 by thirteen independent stores and by a few chain store outlets located in portions of three communities served by the Sawyer Division – Gary, Indiana; South Bend, Indiana; and Burlington, Wisconsin. As a result of its findings the FTC

[1] Renamed the Keebler Company on June 8, 1966.

found Keebler Company guilty of violating section 2 (a) of the Clayton Act, as amended by the Robinson-Patman Act, 15 U.S.C.A. 13(a).[2]

The Keebler Company, incorporated in Delaware in 1927 as the United Biscuit Company of America, was one of the largest domestic sellers of crackers, cookies, and biscuits. It had baking plants in such cities as Macon, Georgia; Grand Rapids, Michigan; Chicago; Cincinnati; and Denver. In 1968 sales amounted to over $151.5 million, and total income was just under $6 million.

The company's retail customers were divided into two major groups: (1) *independents*, those owning and operating only one grocery store, and (2) *chains*, those owning and operating more than one store. The latter included major corporate chains such as the Great Atlantic and Pacific Tea Company, the Kroger Company, and National Food Stores, as well as smaller corporate chains. Independents included Better Foods, Inc., Gene's Supermarket, and Wally's Fifth Avenue Mart, all of Gary, Indiana.

The FTC's complaint charged that the company's Sawyer Division used graduated monthly schedules to discriminate in price between its customers; that these schedules allowed for discounts up to 6 percent and were based on the dollar volume of purchases made by each store; and that if a purchaser had more than one store, such as a corporate chain, its discount was calculated on the basis of the aggregated purchases of the stores operated by that purchaser. As a result, it was alleged, individual outlets of the chains as well as supermarkets (large independents) were enabled to get larger discounts than competing smaller independents. (See Exhibits 1 and 2.) As the volume of a customer's purchases grew, the percentage of his discount increased, resulting in the opportunity either to realize a greater margin of profit per package or to reduce retail prices in relation to competitors. The commission found that, as a result of differences in volume discounts, United charged some customers a higher price for like goods than it charged competing customers. This, it contended, constituted a price discrimination and tended "substantially to lessen competition."

United contended that evidence did not support the findings that its discount practices resulted in price discrimination that might substantially lessen competition. The company argued that the discounts were, under any view, insubstantial. It maintained that the small dollar amounts earned by those customers granted discounts were minimal even when they reached the maximum of 6 percent. Consequently, United argued, the discounts, particularly when translated into dollar amounts, were incapable of producing any anticompetitive effects.

---

[2] Section 2(a) provides in part: It shall be unlawful for any person engaged in commerce ... to discriminate in price between different purchases of commodities of like grade and quality ... where the effect of such discrimination may be substantially to lessen competition or tend to create a monopoly in any line of commerce or to injure, destroy or prevent competition ....

EXHIBIT 1

Gary, Indiana
January - March 1959

Store	$ Monthly Purchase			Percentage Discount			$ Discount Payable			$ Additional Amount Payable at 6%		
	Jan.	Feb.	Mar.	Jan.	Feb.	Mar.	Jan.	Feb.	Mar.	Jan.	Feb.	Mar.
Independents:												
Better Foods, Inc.	11.67	18.82	41.68	0	0	3	0.00	0.00	1.25	.70	1.13	1.25
Gene's Supermarket	117.16	116.38	130.95	5	5	6	5.86	5.82	7.86	1.17	1.16	—
Tobe's Supermarket	319.42	333.97	439.88	6	6	6	19.17	20.04	26.34	—	—	—
Wally's Fifth Avenue Mart	45.37	43.21	33.19	4	3	2	1.81	1.30	0.66	.91	1.29	1.33
Chains:												
A & P	82.61	62.79	83.13	6	6	6	4.96	3.77	4.99	—	—	—
Kroger Store (No. 628)	43.42	47.28	103.94	6	6	6	2.61	2.84	6.24	—	—	—

EXHIBIT 2

Gary, Indiana
October - December 1959

Store	Monthly Purchase $			Percentage Discount			Discount Payable $			Additional Amount Payable at 6% $		
	Oct.	Nov.	Dec.	Oct.	Nov.	Dec.	Oct.	Nov.	Dec.	Oct.	Nov.	Dec.
Independents:												
Better Foods, Inc.	28.35	25.02	21.86	1½	1½	0	.42	.38	0.00	1.28	1.12	1.31
Gene's Supermarket	66.63	138.92	106.05	2½	5	3½	1.67	6.95	3.71	2.23	1.39	2.65
Tobe's Supermarket	170.71	99.93	0.00	6	3½	0	10.24	3.50	0.00	—	2.50	—
Wally's Fifth Avenue Mart	24.78	26.64	58.30	0	1½	2	0.00	.40	1.17	1.49	1.20	2.33
Chains:												
A & P	26.28	50.60	57.33	6	6	6	1.58	3.04	3.44	—	—	—
Kroger Store (No. 628)	123.27	.56	14.86	6	6	6	7.40	0.03	0.89	—	—	—

In addition, United filed a motion for certain compliance reports filed with the FTC by National Biscuit Company and Sunshine Biscuits, Inc., its two major competitors. United alleged that National and Sunshine were granting quantity discounts on biscuit products to their retail grocery customers despite the existence of certain outstanding cease and desist orders against them and that issuance of an order against United banning all discounts would place the company at a competitive disadvantage. The commission denied the request for disclosure, stating that the reports had not been acted upon by it and that, in any event, there had been an insufficient showing that the orders in the other cases were relevant to this case, since "each matter before the Commission must be considered on its own merits."

Questions

1. Did the FTC's action, "protecting" small retailers, prevent chain stores from gaining the economies of bulk buying?
2. Did Keebler's pricing practices adversely affect competition?
3. Was the FTC's order against the Keebler Company justified?

8-10

THE BORDEN COMPANY

Food, Dairy, and Chemical Products Company—
Price Discrimination—
Brand versus
Private Label

The Borden Company engaged in the manufacture, processing, and marketing of food, dairy, and chemical products. Since 1938 it had sold both Borden brand and private-label evaporated milk. The company priced private-label milk lower than its Borden brand, an action leading to a Federal Trade Commission price discrimination complaint in 1958.

The FTC charged Borden with selling milk of "like grade and quality" at lower prices to some purchasers. Further, the commission charged that Borden's intent was "to lessen, injure, or prevent competition." Borden's management argued that price differences were due to cost differences. It also argued, although admitting that the milk was chemically identical, that consumers preferred the "brand name," thereby reflecting a "market difference in grade and quality."

Case adapted from Morris L. Mayer, J. B. Mason, and E. A. Orbech, "The Borden Case—A Legal Basis for Private Brand Price Discrimination," *MSU Business Topics,* Winter 1970, pp. 56-63.

The hearing examiner accepted Borden's cost analysis as a justification for price differences. He further stated that there was insufficient evidence to show competitive injury. However, he did indicate that he considered the products to be of like grade and quality. The parties appealed, Borden challenging the examiner's findings on like grade and quality and the FCC challenging cost justification and failure to prove injury. The commission reversed the examiner's decision, rejecting Borden's cost analysis and finding potential injury to competition.

In 1962 it ordered Borden to cease and desist from discriminating in price between competing purchasers of food products of like grade and quality. Borden petitioned the United States Court of Appeals to set aside the order.

The court of appeals ruled that consumer preference for the Borden's brand constituted a difference in grade and quality. The court was of the opinion that market value was important in establishing grade and quality. Therefore it ruled on December 4, 1964, that the Borden brand and the private-label brand were different in grade and quality. The court did not consider cost or injury to competition.

The FTC appealed to the Supreme Court, and in March 1966 the Court reversed the decision of the court of appeals, remanding the case back to that court for determination of cost justification and competitive injury. The court of appeals handed down its second opinion in July 1967, holding that there was insufficient evidence to support the FTC's price discrimination charges.

The 1967 decision was based upon the court of appeals' belief that competition had not been injured and that certain customers had not been favored. The court also stated: "We are of the firm view that where a price differential between a premium and non-premium brand reflects no more than a consumer preference for the premium brand, the price difference creates no competitive advantage to the recipient of the cheaper private brand product on which injury could be predicted. Rather it represents merely a rough equivalent of the benefit by way of the seller's national advertising and promotion which the purchaser of the more expensive branded product enjoys."[1]

Questions

1. Does the FTC have further grounds for appealing the 1967 decision?
2. Could Borden have avoided the long (1958-67) legal proceedings?

[1] The Borden Company v. FTC, 381 F.2d 175 (5th Cir. 1967).

8-11

BULOVA WATCH COMPANY

Watch Manufacturer—Resale Price Fixing

In January 1971 the Federal Trade Commission announced a proposed consent order against Bulova Watch Company. Bulova, a large firm, sold watches and clocks nationally, achieving sales of approximately $100 million in 1968. Its brands, Bulova, Caravelle, and Accutron, were well recognized. The order was directed at prohibiting Bulova from fixing resale prices on its products. The order also indicated that the company had used other methods to suppress competition.

The FTC alleged that the company fixed prices by suggesting resale prices to retailers and by affixing these to products. Furthermore, the commission charged that Bulova frowned upon dealers who cut prices from suggested levels. As a policy, Bulova had also tried to prevent discounters from handling its brands. Bulova management did not view the consent agreement as an admission of a law's violation. It argued strenuously that its fair-trade policy was legal and emphasized that it would continue to enforce fair trade where

Adapted from *The Wall Street Journal*, January 5, 1971, p. 16.

permitted by state law. Company management said that only 14 states and the District of Columbia did not have fair trade legislation. Final FTC action was pending.

Question

Should Bulova have been prohibited from establishing "suggested retail prices"?

8-12

MERLE NORMAN COSMETICS

Cosmetic Marketer—Trademark Violation Charge

Merle Norman Cosmetics marketed a complete cosmetic line through approximately two thousand "studios" throughout the United States. The company also sold such items as jewelry and hosiery. In 1961, after having applied for trademark registration, having been granted an application, and having been issued a registration certificate, the company introduced Ladybug Red, a new lipstick.

Villager Industries filed an appeal with the Trademark Trial and Appeal Board of the United States Patent Office requesting cancellation of Merle Norman's certificate, although the trademarks were not identical and were awarded in different product areas. Villager claimed a prior (1958) registration of the Ladybug trademark for its women's apparel and accessories. The company sold its apparel line in over fifteen hundred department stores and specialty stores and advertised it in such prominent magazines as *Harper's Bazaar, Glamour,* and *The New Yorker.*

Adapted from *Advertising Age*, May 4, 1970, p. 66.

Merle Norman's management pointed to the differences in products and in marketing channels. It also argued that its trademark possessed a unique color characteristic. Further, it asserted that consumers were not confused by the similarity of the trademarks.

Questions

1. Was Villager justified in filing its petition against Merle Norman?
2. Were Merle Norman's arguments sound in defending its use of Ladybug Red as a trademark?

8-13

CHEMWAY CORPORATION

Toothbrush Manufacturer—
Dangerous Product and Misleading Claims

In 1970 The Federal Trade Commission charged Chemway Corporation with selling toothbrushes containing matter potentially hazardous to users' health. The charge indicated that the Chemway Dr. West's Germ Fighter toothbrush was treated with phenylmercuric acetate (a mercury solution), a potentially dangerous substance if swallowed. The complaint also accused Chemway of misrepresenting the antibacterial characteristics of the toothbrushes in its advertising.

In issuing the proposed complaint, the FTC hoped to obtain a consent agreement with Chemway which would provide for a discontinuance of the alleged practices. The proposal barred Chemway from selling toothbrushes containing the acetate unless it could establish proof that the products were safe. The FTC also wanted to prohibit Chemway from making misleading claims about the medical value of the toothbrush.

Case adapted from *The Wall Street Journal,* December 7, 1970, p. 18, and *Advertising Age,* December 7, 1970, p. 1.

A typical ad made such claims as "Citizens, throw away your toothbrushes. They're crawling with germs . . . buy the Germ Fighter toothbrush by Dr. West. It's treated with a compound that inhibits the growth of germs at least four months."

Company officials expressed bewilderment at the FTC's proposal. "We discontinued the use of mercury and dropped all advertising on this feature in early 1969," said one company officer. "In 15 years of marketing Dr. West's, we have never experienced an incident or indication of health hazards."

Questions

1. Was the FTC justified in its charges against Chemway?

2. Were company officials justified in their bewilderment at the "late" charges?

SECTION 9

INTERNATIONAL MARKETING

OSAKA FIBER COMPANY

Textile Manufacturer—
Use of Trading Companies as Agents

In 1969 Tokyo Textile Company, a large Japanese manufacturer, established Osaka Fiber Company to produce a new fiber which had been developed by the American Textile Company (U.S.A.). Under the licensing agreement, American Textile provided the required production and processing know-how and assisted in sales and marketing of Osaka's output to the Japanese market. Tom Yamada, with fifteen years sales experience at Tokyo Textile, was made sales manager of Osaka Fiber. American Textile sent George Williams, who had over twenty years of United States fiber sales experience, to Japan to serve Osaka Fiber as sales consultant. One of the initial marketing decisions that Yamada faced involved determining the advisability of using the traditional "trading companies" as sales agents.[1]

---

[1] Traditionally, Japanese businessmen emphasized industrial technology, allowing wholesalers to dominate the marketing channels. When Japan was opened to Western trade, the largest wholesalers horizontally and vertically integrated into the Zaibatsu organizations, which have since dominated Japanese production and marketing. Zaibatsu descendants formed large, highly integrated general wholesale organizations known as *trading companies*. In 1959 about twenty of these controlled basic distribution in Japan, acquiring some, if not all, of manufacturers' output in many industries. See Lawrence P. Dowd, "Wholesale Marketing in Japan," *Journal of Marketing*, Vol. 23, January 1959.

The new fiber, called Flexible, was a synthetic, unique in that it had high elasticity. When blended with other synthetic or natural fibers, the resulting fabric also became elastic. Thus, it was an ideal material to use in making swim wear, ski pants, socks, and underwear. Osaka varied its content between 10 and 20 percent of the total finished fabric, depending upon the fabric type and its end use. Mainly because of its limited number of uses, Flexible sold at a high price per pound. Since it was a new material concept to the textile industry, its use by a clothing maker required special technology in knitting, weaving, and other processing operations. Several other fiber manufacturers were known to be planning to produce a similar fiber, and considerable competition was expected at an early date.

In August 1969 Yamada and Williams discussed possible marketing channels for Osaka Fiber. Yamada believed the company should follow traditional Japanese custom and sell through the trading companies, but Williams favored circumventing them and selling directly to textile manufacturers. The Japanese trading companies distributed the product of different manufacturers but refrained from handling competitive items (See Exhibit 1). Japanese manufacturers traditionally depended upon them for wholesale distribution. They provided most manufacturers with a much larger domestic and foreign sales force than they could otherwise individually afford. For example, one trading company had more than ten thousand salesmen covering the Japanese market and roughly two thousand working in areas outside Japan.

Yamada argued that Flexible fiber should be sold through the trading companies. His main argument was that the parent company, Tokyo Textile, sold its fibers, with which Flexible would be blended, through the trading companies, and if Osaka sold direct to users, then Tokyo would have trouble in getting the trading companies to continue handling the blended fibers. He also argued that the trading companies could be helpful in furnishing information on the market, ideas for new product uses, and suggestions as to new users. In addition, the trading companies assumed the risk of uncollectable accounts, helped finance their customers by extending credit, and helped customers plan advertising and sales promotion.

Manufacturers, in an effort to maintain stable prices, usually controlled both list prices to trading companies and resale prices to their customers, the actual users. Trading companies customarily maintained resale prices set by manufacturers, and instances of price-cutting were rare. Trading companies were paid commissions ranging from 2 to 5 percent.

Williams advanced the following arguments favoring direct sale to users: (1) Flexible fiber required special treatment in knitting, weaving, and other processing operations; therefore, sales and technical service were important. (2) Flexible's very high quality strongly encouraged its use; consequently, users could easily sell their outputs with or without the trading companies' help. (3) Because of the limited number of uses for Flexible there were only a small

Channels for Fiber Marketing in Japan

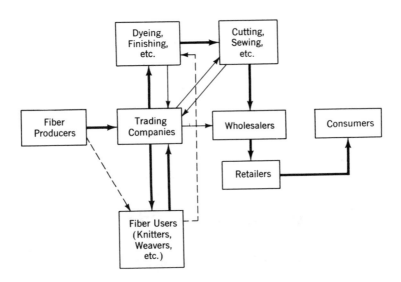

number of potential users, thus making it easy for Osaka to obtain market coverage. (4) Trading company salesmen lacked technical know-how and therefore were not well-equipped to help in the development of new end uses. (5) Leakage of secret know-how to competitors would be easier to control if trading companies were not used.

Trading companies were quick to detect any movement by any of their principals toward selling direct. Thus, Osaka management regarded a market test of direct selling as being clearly out of the question. Nevertheless, a decision on marketing channels had to be made soon.

Question

Should Flexible have been sold through the trading companies or direct to users?

9-2

CROMWELL MANUFACTURING COMPANY

Electrical Products Manufacturer — Planning and Researching International Marketing Operations

Cromwell Manufacturing Company, located in upstate New York, made and sold electrical construction materials, outdoor lighting equipment (including airport lighting systems), and traffic signals. Its annual sales approximated $60 million, the electrical construction materials accounting for 55 percent of the total. In the United States the company sold its products through wholesale distributors to industrial users, institutional buyers, and various governmental units and agencies. All customers were required to buy through the wholesalers, so Cromwell salesmen worked mainly with the distributors, rarely calling on final buyers. For many years Cromwell had routinely turned all buying inquiries from abroad over to the distributors for processing, and although the company set up an International Division in 1968, the distributors were still selling to foreign accounts two years later. This put them in direct competition with three Cromwell foreign affiliates, a source of considerable annoyance on the part of executives of the International Division. As part of a long-range program to "make more sense out of Cromwell's international marketing," the division's marketing manager, Charles Williams, began an investigation of world markets, hoping to arrive at better answers to the question, Who should handle sales in what markets?

Cromwell of Canada, the oldest affiliate, and wholly owned, had achieved a fairly strong market position in the Dominion. However, it had only a limited manufacturing operation, producing only those Cromwell products for which substantial Canadian demand existed. Orders for other Cromwell products not so much in demand were forwarded to the parent company where specialized personnel analyzed each such Canadian order, determined whether it was profitable to pay the Canadian import duty, and, if so, saw to it that the order was shipped and billed to the Canadian buyer. Since Cromwell of Canada had its own management and sales force, the sole administrative link between it and the parent company was the reporting relationship between its president and the president of Cromwell Manufacturing Company.

An affiliate in Mexico operated along much the same lines as Cromwell of Canada. With its headquarters and manufacturing plant located in Mexico City, it had started as a joint venture of the parent company and a small group of Mexican businessmen. In 1967 Cromwell acquired 100 percent ownership of the Mexican affiliate. As late as 1970 this affiliate confined its selling activities solely to Mexico, making no effort to cultivate sales throughout the rest of Latin America or in the West Indies.

The third affiliate was the European one based in Milan, Italy. It was the newest member of the Cromwell family of companies, having been started as a joint venture with several Italian industrialists in early 1970. Cromwell management had decided to enter into this joint venture after having analyzed a research report focusing on the sales potentials of its product lines in the European Common Market. Although manufacturing operations had yet to start up, the plan was that this affiliate make and sell all the Cromwell lines to buyers in Italy, France, West Germany, Belgium, Luxembourg, and the Netherlands.

Williams, the International Division's marketing manager, reported to the division head, C. C. Lucido, who was also the vice-president of international operations. Williams's main responsibility was to research and develop new international markets. He was assisted in this work by two area representatives who had rather comprehensive duties and responsibilities; in fact, more so than any other Cromwell marketing personnel. Not only did the area representatives plan and perform market studies of various kinds on an international basis but they were active in such projects as making credit arrangements for foreign buyers and staging sales meetings in cooperation with the managements of the affiliates. Both men were highly knowledgeable concerning international marketing procedures, and both knew a great deal about different socioeconomic and cultural factors influencing marketing abroad.

Early in 1970 Williams and the two area representatives began a systematic investigation of world markets. Their first step was to divide most of the world, except for the United States and Canada, into three major geographical areas: (1) Latin America (excluding Mexico) and the West Indies, (2) the Far East, India, Pakistan, Iran, the Persian Gulf countries, and Africa (excluding those parts of Africa and the Near East bordering on the Mediterranean), and (3) Europe and those non-European countries fronting on the Mediterranean. At this point, the decision was tentatively made to assign the sole responsibility for marketing operations in the third area to the Italian affiliate.

Determining "who should have the responsibility" for marketing operations in the other two areas proved considerably more difficult. With respect to the second geographical area, further analysis was postponed until surveys of markets in the first geographical area could be completed and analyzed, and until a decision could be made for that area. In the meantime, existing customers were to continue to be served under present arrangements, most of them buying from United States wholesalers of Cromwell's product lines.

Thus, the research team's effort focused mainly on finding good answers to the question, "Who should supply customers in Latin America (excluding Mexico) and in the West Indies?" Because of its proximity to these markets and because Spanish was the main trading language throughout most of this area, the Mexican affiliate would have seemed to be the logical answer. However, investigation soon showed that shipping costs out of Mexican ports were very high and shipping service was rather irregularly scheduled. Furthermore, land carriers, both rail and truck, from Mexico City to Gulf and Pacific Coast ports did not appear capable of providing the special handling that many Cromwell products required. Coupled with these things, of course, was the fact that the Mexican affiliate did not manufacture all the items in the three product lines. Thus, it was deemed infeasible to service Latin America and the West Indies from the Mexican affiliate.

The procedures used in carrying out the survey of the Venezuelan market were representative of those carried out in other Latin American and West Indian markets. The first step was a presurvey involving the collection and analysis of various statistical indicators and the compilation of a roster of Venezuelan business contacts. Three main information sources were tapped: (1) United States Department of Commerce publications and listings of Venezuelan firms, (2) previous buyers of Cromwell products with operations in Venezuela, and (3) the Venezuelan consulate in New York City, which proved the most fruitful source of needed data. The research team concluded, in fact, that the United States government information on Venezuela tended to convey a somewhat distorted view. "To investigate any foreign market realistically and effectively," Williams said, "you've got to go to the particular country and draw your own conclusions, because you must see what the potential is in the country for your own particular product line."

The next step involved an actual visit to Venezuela by the research team. They had two purposes in mind: (1) to make an on-the-spot market survey and (2) to make preliminary arrangements for local distributors to handle Cromwell's lines at a later date when the decision was finally made as to how they would be supplied. The team made contacts with the United States and the British embassies, the Venezuelan Ministry of Public Works, and various utilities and construction companies; these contacts had the purpose of obtaining data on sales potential and on marketing possibilities. In seeking candidates for possible distributorships, the research team looked for Venezuelan businessmen operating businesses covering all important areas of the country, but they were also careful to investigate each prospective distributor with respect to his relationships with other manufacturers, his government contacts, his financial resources, his technical capability to market the Cromwell lines, and his capabilities with respect to stocking and servicing the lines.

At first the research team concluded that by selling through several Venezuelan distributors, perhaps four or five, it should be possible for Cromwell to attain a Venezuelan sales volume of roughly two hundred thousand dollars annually. Some further investigation, however, revealed that certain local firms could probably design and turn out competing items in a period of two or three years. Locally based competitors, too, would undoubtedly be successful in getting the government to erect trade barriers to imports; thereby hindering if not altogether stopping the flow of Cromwell products into the country. The team thus revised its earlier conclusion and decided to establish a joint venture with an existing Venezuelan manufacturer, if this proved feasible. Further study indicated that the market was large enough to support a joint venture, and Cromwell launched a search for a Venezuelan partner. Not finding a local manufacturer both equipped and interested in such a venture, Cromwell finally joined one of the firms it had previously investigated as a possible distributor, and a local manufacturing operation was thereby organized, scheduled to go "on stream" in early 1971.

Questions

1. How might Cromwell have improved its approach to international marketing?
2. As Cromwell extends the scope of its international operations, what problems should it have anticipated in its relationships with its domestic distributors? How should these problems have been handled?

9-3

CONTINENTAL FOOTWEAR COMPANY

Shoe Manufacturer—Foreign Source of Supply

Continental Footwear Company manufactured and marketed women's straw shoes and slippers throughout the United States. Sales to large chains such as National Shoe, Miles Shoe Company, and A. S. Beck accounted for more than 80 percent of the company's total sales of $1.7 million. The remainder went to independent jobbers who bought rejects and cancellations. Fourteen full-time salesmen, averaging eight years' service, sold to the chain store buyers. Continental also had sales representatives, in nine market areas, who sold primarily to "job lotters" of rejects and cancellations. Continental's sales declined during 1970 by 15 percent compared with 1969, and management was alarmed because many chain store buyers were buying more and more foreign-made shoes.[1]

       Continental shoes, marketed under each chain's brand name, retailed from $2.98 to $5.98 per pair. Competitive foreign-made shoes retailed from $2.69 to $4.98 per pair. In addition to their price advantage, imported shoes,

[1] See Appendix A.

according to chain buyers, had more original styling, higher quality, and better craftsmanship.

In January 1971 Continental's top executives met to discuss ever-increasing competition from abroad. Charles Stone, the general manager, proposed the following solution:

> Our sales to the chains have dropped off due to the influx of foreign shoes. We must do something to counter the increased sales of Asiatic shoes, but because we cannot match the original styling and lower production costs which exist in foreign countries, we cannot make a competitive shoe in America. Marketing research shows the Asiatic-styled shoe is growing in popularity. I propose that Continental set up a subsidiary company, which we will call Intercontinental Shoe, to import the vamps, patterns, and lasts from the Hamas Company of Hong Kong. They will make arrangements with us whereby they will export the desired product to our Intercontinental Company. The shoes can be finished in our present plant and made ready for sale. The facilities there are more than adequate and since the straw patterns have already been woven and designed, the finishing of the shoes at our plant will be relatively simple.
>
> It will take about 40 days to ship the shoe components from Hong Kong to New York. Continental would be vulnerable to cancellations if the shoes are late but, if we add a safety margin to our production and shipping schedules, we shouldn't run into trouble. We might have to face the problem of a rise in tariff rates, but these rates would apply to all imported shoes including our competitors.
>
> Instead of distributing our foreign shoes to chain stores, why not market them to large department stores such as Sears? For years we have only sold to chain stores, never to department stores. With these foreign shoes, we have the right goods to break into the department stores. Someday we may be able to sell them our domestic shoes if we get a foothold through our foreign shoes sales. I would like to put our own brand name on the imports. Perhaps we could call them "Flickies." With our own brand name and a good advertising campaign, our sales will surely rise.
>
> By selling these shoes to department stores we will be opening a new market, plus eliminating any intra-competition that would occur if the shoes were sold to the chains already buying Continental's domestic line.

Questions

1. Should the semifinished shoes have been imported by Continental?
2. If Continental had decided to market imported shoes, should it have sold them under its own brand name?

Appendix A

Continental Footwear Company

Shoe manufacturers . . . insist that imports are responsible for their plight and demand some type of quota arrangment to protect them from the rising flow of overseas merchandise. So far Congress and the White House have been impervious to their pleas, but the shouts are getting louder and more desperate every day.

"It's an economic problem — we just can't compete against countries where labor is anywhere from one-tenth to one-quarter of ours," says Warren M. Weitzman, treasurer of Seymour Shoes, Inc. . . . "We don't want anything different from what the Europeans are doing for their shoe industries."

Twenty-seven of the 221 footwear manufacturing units in New England — where shoes represent the largest employer in the non-durable field — with 6,795 men and women — discontinued operations last year. United States production of leather and vinyl shoes declined to 592 million pairs in

Some excerpts from a report in *The New York Times,* February 1, 1970, Sec. 3, pp. 1 and 13.

1969 from a record of 656 million pairs in 1968, while imports, primarily of women's footwear, rose to 200 million pairs from 175 million pairs. In 1955, imports totaled just 8 million pairs.

The average wage rate, which accounts for 30 to 40 percent of the cost of shoes in the domestic industry, of $2.62 an hour, is substantially above that of other footwear manufacturing countries. For example, in Italy the hourly rate is $1.04, in Japan, 58 cents, and in Spain, 56 cents. Taiwan and Portugal have even lower rates.

Importers and many retailers attracted by the higher-profit margin of imported footwear claim that these shoes have better styling and cost the customer less money. They believe that a large percentage of these imports, moreover, are made by subsidiaries of American manufacturers, who are plagued in the United States by obsolete facilities and an aging work force.

SECTION 10

DOMESTIC MARKETING OVERSEAS

COLOMBIAN COMPANY OF SHOE LASTS, LTD. (HORMAS)

Small Manufacturer—
Appraising the Marketing Function

Hormas, located in Bogotá, Colombia, produced wooden lasts used in shoe manufacturing. Although a small company, it was the industry's largest in Colombia, and management estimated its 1965 market share at 27 percent.[1] Hormas sold its products nationally through distributors in the major cities to industrial and craftsman shoemakers. It sold direct from the factory to the large shoe manufacturers in Bogotá. Normally, customers either sought out distributors or went direct to manufacturers, placed their orders, and deposited 50 percent of the invoice price.[2] Most last manufacturers promised one-month delivery, but orders from smaller shoemakers sometimes had lower priority and took longer. Market information was poor and the marketing process within Hormas was unwieldy, and the three owners sought improvements.

In January 1965 a change in management occurred when Carlos Fernández, nephew of one of the owners, was hired as general manager. It was agreed that he would also continue his association with Bogotá, Ltd., a large

---

[1] No industry data were available from either private or governmental sources.

[2] In effect, customers partially financed the manufacturers' operations.

Colombian company in which he was a partner. Because of Hormas's small size and lack of clerical problems, the owners believed that Fernández could handle the general manager's position on a part-time basis. Therefore, he reported daily at 5:00 P.M. and worked until about 6:30 P.M. Monday through Friday.

Two executives assisted Fernández — Juan Castillo, office manager, and Pedro Mosto, another partner in Bogotá, Ltd., who had earlier agreed to act as a part-time management consultant. Mosto recommended accounting procedures; performed studies in production planning, organization, and control; analyzed records; and prepared financial operating statements. His main responsibility, however, involved conducting market studies and recommending marketing policies. For instance, he studied company sales trends, estimated market potential, collected information about the industry's structure, and prepared the sales forecast. He also recommended prices, product changes, and promotional policies to Fernández. One other key executive, J. D. Izaza, manufacturing supervisor, had left in mid-1965 to take a marketing manager's position with one of Hormas's competitors; his old position had not yet been filled (Exhibit 1).

EXHIBIT 1

Hormas Organization Chart—1965

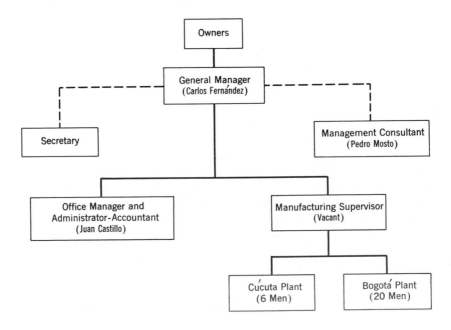

Hormas had been founded in Cúcuta, a city of over one hundred thousand population about four hundred kilometers to the northeast of Bogotá; it retained its drying and cutting plant at Cúcuta but had moved the actual last-manufacturing operation to a larger plant in Bogotá, Colombia's shoe-manufacturing capital. Also located in Bogotá were competitors: Luz and Dural, both of which started operations during the 1950s; El Mazo and Prohormas, both starting in the early 1960s; and three very small shoe last makers, all of which had been organized during 1965. Thus the shoe last industry was heavily concentrated in Bogotá, as was nearly all the shoemaking industry. Shoemakers ranged in size from factories ordering more than one thousand pairs of lasts annually down to what were essentially shoe repair shops that bought no more than ten pairs of lasts per year.

Shoe lasts made in Colombia were priced lower than those imported from Europe and elsewhere in Latin America. The Colombian government protected the last-making industry against foreign competition, setting 1965 import duties at two and one-half times the price of domestic lasts. Consequently, foreign competition was virtually nonexistent.

In shoe manufacturing, the lasts determine shoe length, width, and style. Therefore, each shoe size and style require a different last. When a shoe style "went out," manufacturers generally discarded the lasts; but some smaller shoemakers cut down last tips and affixed other tips more nearly like the shoe style then in fashion.

Some Colombian shoe manufacturers had almost totally mechanized production lines, whereas others relied solely on hand craftsmanship. Shoe lasts made for industrial use came with two small additional accessories which enabled them to fit shoemaking machinery. Smaller shoe last manufacturers sold almost exclusively to craftsmen, but the three largest firms — Hormas, Luz, and Prohormas — concentrated on the mechanized market segment. Hormas sold the greatest number of lasts to the largest mechanized manufacturers, but Luz and Prohormas both had increased in importance as competitors for the business of this segment (Exhibit 2).

Hormas was the industry's price leader, and the other last makers generally altered their prices in the direction of Hormas's changes. However, most of them sold their outputs at slightly lower prices; Prohormas was the only competitor charging higher prices. Hormas's management set prices for shoe lasts bought by mechanized customers at a level about 5 percent higher than for those paid by customers who were craftsmen. Prices varied according to last length and style; therefore, average price per pair of lasts changed from year to year, depending upon the particular mixture of last types ordered by the customers as a whole.

Hormas was the only company that had national distribution. All the competitors confined their distribution to areas near their factories. Hormas sold through "distributor-stores"; these carried not only shoe lasts but shoe

EXHIBIT 2

Columbian Makers of Shoe Lasts
and Estimated Unit Sales for 1965

Shoe Last Maker	Location	Market Coverage	(Pairs of Shoe Lasts)			Percentage of Industry Sales
			Industrial	Crafts	Total	
Hormas	Bogotá	National	17,500	12,500	30,000	27
El Mazo	Bogotá	Bogotá	—	17,500	17,500	16
Luz	Bogotá	Santander	2,000	13,000	15,000	13
Dural	Bogotá	Bogotá	—	12,500	12,500	11
Prohormas	Bogotá	Bogotá	2,000	4,250	6,250	6
Estuatua	Bogotá	Bogotá	—	5,000	5,000	4
La Patria	Bogotá	Bogotá	—	5,000	5,000	4
Concietro	Bogotá	Bogotá	—	1,250	1,250	1
Others (Bogotá)	Bogotá	Bogotá	—	7,500	7,500	7
Others (outside Bogotá)		?	—	12,500	12,500	11
Total			21,500	91,000	112,500	100%

Note: Estimates by Pedro Mosto for his 1964 market and sales forecast. Actual 1965 sales for Hormas amounted to 26,993 pairs.

findings such as leathers, tips, glue, and gum. Hormas granted its ten distributors exclusive distribution rights except in Bogotá where it sold direct to large "house accounts." Nevertheless, many old customers in outlying cities, most of them small accounts, also ordered direct from the factory. Distributors received a discount of 15 percent off list prices. In 1965 Hormas had ten distributors and 135 direct accounts.

Shoemakers, large and small, ordered lasts for existing styles or provided last manufacturers with prototype lasts for new styles. The country's largest shoe manufacturer usually made its own prototype lasts, frequently copying popular European styles. Shoe last manufacturers merely built from the prototype lasts provided by customers or from those already on hand. Some shoe styles retained popularity for several years, others for only a single season. Each last style was built in different lengths, with widths proportional to the width of the prototype. In Colombia, manufacturers did not "size" shoes by width. If a particular style did not fit a customer's foot because it was too wide or too narrow, he had to search for a proper fit in another style.

Fernández made two major marketing moves. First, he raised prices by 20 percent, increasing Hormas's average price per pair of lasts from 27.50 to 33.00 Colombian pesos. After this price increase, which made the company's prices as high as those of Prohormas, Hormas suffered a sales loss estimated at three thousand pairs. Second, he and Mosto undertook a comprehensive study of the Colombian market for shoe lasts, seeking to learn more about customers' needs, market and sales potentials, and competitors' operations. They also analyzed company records, finding a high turnover rate for customers buying direct. However, the records were not in sufficient detail as to specific customers buying through particular distributors.

Late in 1965 Fernández and Mosto met to discuss Hormas's performance for the year and to outline plans for 1966 and beyond. Fernández asked Mosto to submit major recommendations for improving future marketing operations. In late December Mosto put forth the following recommendations:

1. That we hold the price line in 1966, since we have been able to lower production costs and obtain a satisfactory margin. We do not want to price ourselves out of the craftsman market segment.
2. That we reduce minimum order size from 30 to 15 pairs. Many of our craftsmen customers do not need 30 pairs in one order, and we can break-even on 10-pair orders; therefore, a 15-pair order is profitable.
3. That we offer different widths in each style. This will give us a clear advantage over competitors.
4. That we launch an advertising campaign, particularly promoting our modern drying process which has eliminated shrinking problems.
5. That we identify all shoemakers, establish a direct contact with them, explaining the advantages offered by us.
6. That we establish personal contact with all distributors. Company officials have not personally met any distributor except the one here in Bogotá. We have no control and know nothing of their inventory situation.
7. That we hire another man and place him in charge of all marketing activities.
8. That we get a replacement for Izaza as soon as possible.

Questions

1. What action, if any, should Fernández have taken on each of Mosto's recommendations?
2. What other factors should have been considered in improving this company's marketing performance?

10-2

SPRINGBOK VOLUNTARY WHOLESALERS, LTD.

Voluntary Chain—
Securing Increased Cooperation from Members

Springbok Voluntary Wholesalers, Ltd., with central offices in Cape Town, Republic of South Africa, was the only voluntary grocery chain in an area one-sixth the size of the United States (five hundred thousand square miles). Its six hundred members had retail sales of approximately 84 million rand in 1965 (about 15 percent of the total market).[1] However, members bought only about 16 million rand through Springbok's nine wholesale locations; they secured their remaining merchandise requirements from Springbok's wholesale competitors and direct from manufacturers.

Springbok's keenest competition at the wholesale level came from large manufacturers who sold direct, even to the smallest retailers, and at the identical prices they charged to Springbok. Furthermore, manufacturers' merchandising teams built store displays and assisted retailers in stock control

[1] A South African rand was the equivalent of 1.40 U.S. dollars.

and ordering. They also advertised extensively; consequently, their brands were well known throughout the country.

Springbok's retail members met intense competition from three large chains. Two were department store groups, the third operated both department stores and supermarkets. In South Africa most department stores featured grocery departments. These three competitors transacted approximately 19 percent of the retail grocery business in the country. Springbok retailers also met local competition from nonaffiliated independent stores which accounted for 66 percent of the country's retail grocery sales. Springbok members, therefore, had a 15 percent share of the market.

Springbok retail outlets varied in size from forty to two thousand square meters; it was estimated that 75 percent had under two hundred square meters. Management had considered promoting standardization in store size because it was difficult for consumers to build up a "proper Springbok image" if they compared a large modern supermarket with a smaller traditional type of forty square meters a few kilometers away. Although store size standardization was considered important in building a more favorable consumer image, Springbok had thus far failed to emphasize this aspect.

Springbok retailers handled diverse merchandise lines. Sales of "grocery-store" products accounted for most of their volume. However, most of the retailers, many situated more than eighty kilometers from the nearest large city, carried numerous other types of merchandise, including even such lines as fishing tackle and light farming equipment. The customary practice was for them to purchase nonfood lines not from Springbok (which did not handle most such lines) but from independent wholesalers.

Springbok's house brands (private brands) included food items and such household products as tissues and wax paper. Springbok imposed stringent specification control over the manufacture of its house brands. Periodically, management had each such brand chemically analyzed and compared with company specifications. Most relationships with suppliers of house brands had been satisfactory and long term.

Springbok's headquarters staff included an executive director, a marketing manager, a development manager, and a publications editor. The executive director, Dick Jones, a dynamic individual with an extensive sales background, managed the overall operation. The marketing manager, P. T. Wendt, negotiated with manufacturers for special offers to use as month-end promotions, developed new house brands, did quality checks on existing brands, and coordinated all promotional activities with the advertising agency. The development manager, J. D. Eakin, was responsible for training Springbok's members; he had studied operating methods of United States voluntary chains prior to joining Springbok, had considerable sales experience, and spent much of his time traveling the market area and leading training seminars for wholesale and member personnel. At times he served as a management consultant for the retailer-members. The publications editor, J. E. Leverette, edited two magazines: one, a house organ for the six hundred retailer-members; the other, a small monthly, distributed free to store customers.

Central office management dealt mainly through Springbok's nine wholesale branches. Each branch sold to retail members through a force of three fieldmen who reported to a local sales manager. Fieldmen acted as general consultants to the retailers, helped retailers present a good image, made recommendations for recruitment of new members, and sold and promoted Springbok's products, especially the house brands.

Few fieldmen had university training and few had formal company training, but most had experience in food retailing. They were paid straight salaries but were eligible for annual bonuses. Generally, they were poor planners, and the sales manager had little real control over their activities.

Springbok's prices to its members were competitive except on lines where the manufacturers sold direct to retailers at wholesale prices. Retailer committees, meeting monthly, set members' resale prices on house brands and month-end specials. Nine such committees, one for each wholesale branch, set resale prices for all members in their respective zones. Management regarded decentralized pricing as necessary because of the large differentials in transportation costs existing among the various zones. These committees also had the power to admit new stores and to request members' resignation. Prices charged by Springbok retailers in the different zones on non-house brands varied with the intensity of local competition.

Retail members paid an entrance fee of 40 rand plus weekly dues ranging from 4.5 to 7 rand, depending upon the number of month-end leaflets and point-of-purchase posters requested. In addition, retailers were asked from time to time to contribute to zonal promotion funds, but the amounts involved were inconsequential. Members received from Springbok: (1) the right to use the chain's name, (2) uniform store signs, (3) house brands, (4) centralized buying, and (5) promotional assistance and materials.

During early 1966 the executive director wrote each retail member, listing "acceptable" manufacturers with whom they should cooperate. He further asked that the products of nonlisted manufacturers be displayed only on the retailers' bottom shelves and that the salesmen involved be refused permission to do in-store merchandising. With this tactic he hoped to force manufacturers selling direct to Springbok retailers to change their policies and to negotiate through Springbok's central office. The *letter*, as it was subsequently called, was not altogether successful because many retailers refused to act as had been requested. Furthermore, member retailers were generally lethargic about trying to increase sales of house brands (on which they averaged a markup of about 21 percent). Many times, too, they failed to support month-end promotions (leaflets went undistributed and point-of-purchase materials were not utilized).

Questions

1. What else, if anything, might have been done by Springbok to increase the cooperation of its members?
2. Should additional house brands have been introduced by Springbok?

SECTION 11

MARKETING STRATEGY

PARMAKER, INC.

Small Manufacturer—
Proposals to Change Marketing Methods

Parmaker, Inc., of Atlanta, Georgia, manufactured a full line of golf clubs (woods, irons, and putters) and sold them throughout the United States. Jerry Dugan founded the company in 1966 to specialize in making putters but expanded to a full line in 1968. Parmaker sold both professional and nonprofessional golf-club lines, achieving good initial success, especially in the southeastern United States. However, in 1971 pro-line sales fell off, causing management to consider certain corrective measures.

Dugan, an outstanding touring professional and the designer of Hammerhead, the leading putter on the market, commanded the respect of knowledgeable golfers. Thus Parmaker achieved large initial sales on both of its lines, particularly the pro-line models. However, pro-line sales had recently dropped off as the company experienced some degeneration in its product life cycle and faced stiffening competition from more mature manufacturers, such as Spalding, Wilson, and First Flight. Meanwhile, the non-pro line continued to do well, accounting for 65 percent of the $1.5 million sales in 1970.

A five-man sales force sold the non-pro line to major retailers and sporting goods wholesalers. They sold Parmaker's "signature models" and negotiated with a few major retailers for private-brand orders; Parmaker's own brands accounted for 90 percent of its non-pro sales, since most middlemen desired to take advantage of Parmaker's name. Signature models retailed at prices 25 percent below pro clubs, although they were of only slightly lower quality.

Parmaker's fifteen-man "pro-line" sales force sold exclusively to pro shops. Salesmen called on club professionals, showed new models, and wrote orders for the next season. They were paid a salary plus a commission on sales, their total compensation being comparable to that of salesmen for the major competitors.

Parmaker, like other manufacturers, advertised in trade magazines such as *Golf Pro* and *Golf Digest*. In 1969 and 1970 the company had used point-of-purchase posters, but management had recently concluded that P.O.P. materials were ineffective.

All pro-line clubs were sold exclusively through professional outlets to golfers from the pro's "in-house" inventory or by special order from the factory. As a newcomer to the golf industry, Parmaker met its major resistance in this traditional channel. Although its quality and prices were comparable and although a group of leading PGA[1] players had endorsed its products, Parmaker found it difficult to achieve adequate distribution in the face of well-entrenched competitors. Numerous club professionals were affiliated with major competitors as advisers or as players and received free personal golf equipment, season-end discounts, and attentive repair and delivery service.

Additional resistance traced to traditional marketing methods used in the pro-line market segment. For example: (1) *Pro shops sold largely from inventory* rather than by special order. Clubs made up a large portion of the total inventory investment in the pro shops, for example, ten sets of clubs represented approximately three thousand dollars of retail value. Club pros were reluctant to tie up greater-than-normal amounts in inventory because they might face substantial losses, particularly since club models changed annually. The usual practice was to stock a limited number of club sets in standard weights and lengths, and golfers wanting heavier, lighter, shorter, or longer clubs were required to have the pro "special order" from the manufacturer. Clubs ordered in this manner took from six to eight weeks for delivery. The limited inventory policy of pro shops plus the rather long waiting time involved for delivery of special orders aided in the growth of companies manufacturing custom-made clubs. (2) *Only rarely did pros allow prospects to hit golf shots with new clubs.* This created a dilemma for customers, on the one hand, as they wanted to try out the equipment before buying, and for the pro, on the other hand, as he

[1] Professional Golfers' Association.

could not afford to absorb the depreciation (sometimes as much as 25 percent) when new clubs became scratched or marred. (3) *Innovations, though usually promoted nationally, were inadequately demonstrated in pro shops.* Manufacturers stressed technical improvements leading to "better feel," "greater distance with less effort," or "less error," but few succeeded in explaining the technical reasons behind changes, at least to the satisfaction of customers.[2] Most pro-line golfers talked of swing weights and other technical factors, and most pro shops owned equipment for measuring swing weight; however, little was actually known or published about the role played by swing weight in the execution of a golf shot. Innovations in clubs were generally accompanied by higher prices.

Dugan discussed the pro-line market segment with his marketing manager. He said: "We face a growing market for golf clubs as more people take up the game but, at the same time, club pros resist stocking larger inventories, our own non-pro lines compete with our pro clubs, and we see club pros becoming affiliated with more than one manufacturer. We see a unique situation here and I want your recommendations on ways in which we can increase our effectiveness in marketing to this segment." Although the marketing manager expressed some offhand opinions at the time, he did not make firm proposals until the next week's executive meeting at which he made four suggestions:

1. That we begin a program of research on golf clubs, so as to determine the effect of such factors as swing weight, overall weight, club length, shaft flex, grip, etc., on the execution of a golf shot.
2. That we provide demonstration clubs of varying specifications as a "floating inventory" in pro shops. That our salesmen give demonstrations with this equipment, playing practice rounds with club pros and prospects, allowing prospects to use demonstration clubs and to compare them with old clubs. That a reporting system be set up on prospects as well as the recording of "research" results. We could give away some golf balls as a part of promotion-demonstration.
3. That we sell standard models as before on a limited basis but that we emphasize the personalized approach and back this up with "quick" delivery – a maximum of two weeks after receipt of order – out of our factory or regional warehouses. As we progress with this system we will be better able to forecast requirements and, therefore, cut delivery time.
4. That prices be raised 10 percent once this program is underway. We will experience increased selling costs but we will also be able to command a higher price if the proper service is provided.

[2]Some criticized golf club manufacturers for this apparent lack of customer interest or for departure from the marketing concept, as happened, for example, in the introduction of aluminum shafts.

Questions

1. Should the marketing manager's recommendations have been accepted?
2. What other alternatives should have been explored?

JAY AND ELLSWORTH MACHINE COMPANY

Machine Manufacturer—
Marketing Changes after Acquisition
by Conglomerate

In the fall of 1967 the management of Jay and Ellsworth Machine Company of Lexington, Massachusetts, attempted to evaluate progress achieved since the organization's acquisition three years before by Arkho, Incorporated. Some executives speculated, at the time of acquisition, that Arkho's dynamic and forward-looking management might prove too fast moving for a conservative old New England firm. The acquisition had brought about some fundamental changes in basic management policy. All segments of the business felt the changes, but none were affected as directly as the sales division in both structure and operation.

Jay and Ellsworth started operation in 1835, producing hand-operated water pumps for all types of wells. It soon branched into small arms manufacturing and, by 1850, produced guns for military purposes. Between 1850 and 1890 the company made various machines for New England's flourishing lumber industry, including steam boilers and saw riggings.

In 1889 John A. Hotchkiss, a superintendent at Jay and Ellsworth, revolutionized the making of screws, nails, bolts, and pins through his invention of a new lathe based on an entirely new turning principle which operated at a finer tolerance and therefore produced higher-quality products. A single Hotchkiss lathe was capable of producing three or four times the output of a standard lathe. Hotchkiss's new machine tool contributed significantly to country-wide standardization of screw threads.

Not long afterward, recognizing industry's need for a device to inspect screw threads, Jay and Ellsworth responded by perfecting an optical comparator. This device, through a complex system of lenses and mirrors, projected an image on a large screen. Later, in addition to its use in screw inspection, other applications for the comparator were found in measurement and quality control of such products as razor blades, electrical components, transistors, and recording equipment.

Further demands of industrial firms led Jay and Ellsworth to develop thread grinders, automatic die headers, and various automatic lathes. These, along with turret lathes and comparators, constituted the company's product line in 1967. Products within these five basic categories served the industrial equipment needs not only of such large companies as General Electric, Raytheon, and Gillette but of numerous smaller manufacturers.

Sales in 1965 approximated $20 million. As most of the products represented significant customer outlays, company sales fluctuated with overall business conditions. A boom year for the economy meant a busy year for machine tool companies, whereas a recession depressed sales drastically.

Jay and Ellsworth maintained strong customer ties. Customers expressed confidence in the company's policies and its high-quality products. Jay and Ellsworth continually worked on the development of new processes, introduced frequent innovations, and generally helped set the pace in the machine tool industry's technological development. Since customers regarded its products as highly reliable, Jay and Ellsworth was able to set its prices above those of competitors. Customers also regarded Jay and Ellsworth's service as superior. These aspects of the company's reputation enabled it not only to survive but to excel in a highly competitive industry.

Jay and Ellsworth operated ten district sales offices in the major United States cities. Before the acquisition, the sales manager's duties had included both product development and customer sales. After Arkho took control, seven product sales managers were appointed to handle all marketing activities except direct sales. Similarly, each of ten new district sales managers supervised two to six salesmen. Arkho replaced Jay and Ellsworth's manufacturers' agents with salesmen from its Thompson-Robin Division, into which Jay and Ellsworth had been integrated. (Exhibits 1 and 2 show the organization before and after the acquisition.)

Arkho management also modernized the district offices. These became centers for machine tool design, sales, physical distribution, and service. Arkho management encouraged coordination and cooperation in product

EXHIBIT 1

Jay and Ellsworth Marketing Division (Before Acquisition)

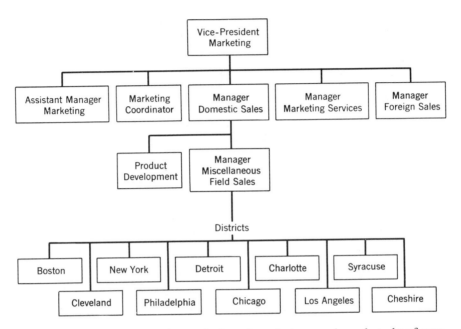

planning, computer use in sales analysis and market research, and study of new distribution systems.

The company recruited salesmen who possessed a mechanical or engineering bent, since selling the complex machines in the Jay and Ellsworth line required extensive technical knowledge. Salesmen also handled service problems, and technical troubleshooting skills proved invaluable. The usual selling situation was one in which the salesman worked to adapt the products to a client's specifications; in most instances, the salesman understood the customer's service needs better than the customer himself. Thus a Jay and Ellsworth salesman was a knowledgeable engineer as well as a salesman.

Upon acquisition by Arkho, Jay and Ellsworth's sales approach changed appreciably. As employees of the Thompson-Robin Division of Arkho's Metal Products Group, Jay and Ellsworth salesmen found themselves selling the entire Thompson-Robin line as well as the familiar product line. This placed additional strain on salesmen and raised important questions concerning sales training.

Gary Couch, Thompson-Robin vice-president and a long-time executive with the Jay and Ellsworth organization, indicated the change in training philosophy:

EXHIBIT 2

Jay and Ellsworth Marketing Division (After Acquisition)

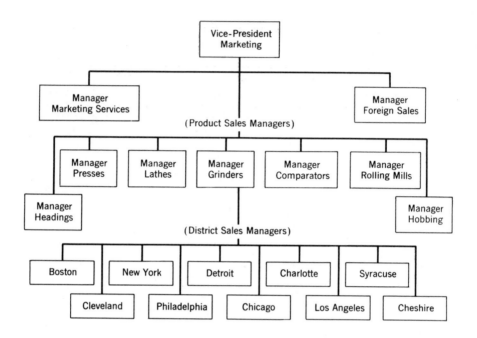

Our sales training program is now quite formal whereas in the past it was rather "hit or miss." We now have a Director of Training who plans all sales training. Some programs last for one or two years, depending upon job complexity and the man's adaptability. However, we have been unable to train for some positions and have gone outside to hire advanced sales and marketing personnel.

Jay and Ellsworth salesmen willingly participated in formal corporate training. Still, much of the training was O.J.T. conducted by teams of two or three trainers in decentralized locations and lasting for shorter periods than formal centralized training.[1]

Consolidation of the sales force also brought a new sales compensation system. Under the old compensation plan salesmen had received base salaries plus commissions tied to a merit-rating system. Men were ranked

[1] O.J.T. means on-the-job training.

according to seniority, productivity, and sales management's appraisal. Management pooled yearly commissions and then divided them according to the rating scale. For example, older or more-productive salesmen might have received .0025 percent of the pool, whereas younger or less-productive salesmen might have received only .0012 percent. Because seniority was weighted heavily, the system favored older salesmen.

The commission-sharing feature tended to equalize compensation among regions, the main reason for its introduction. The industry was highly susceptible to economic fluctuations, and a salesman's success in getting orders depended to a great extent on business conditions in his territory. Commission sharing helped to assure salesmen of more steady commission income; however, it created a morale problem, as outstanding salesmen felt that they contributed more to the pool and should receive larger shares.

Arkho's new sales compensation system established a 15 percent higher base salary (on the average) and a fixed commission rate on net sales. Salesmen thus received compensation more closely proportionate to their sales productivity. Older salesmen tended to disapprove of the new plan, as many had accrued a high merit rating and a built-in commission advantage. Most younger salesmen liked Arkho's plan, as they were no longer tied to a merit-rating system based largely on seniority.

Top management set quotas for salesmen after joint conferences with salesmen and district managers. Management also conducted quarterly quota reviews and made revisions if large deviations were apparent. Salesmen and district managers could request review and revision at any time.

Arkho designed an imaginative sales development program which attempted to answer the question: Customer, what can we do for you? Prospects were urged to visit Thompson-Robin's headquarters where a wide variety of the latest machines were in actual operation in a large demonstration room. After determining the precise nature of a prospect's problems, Thompson-Robin engineers showed him solutions to similar problems among the displays in the showroom. In some cases, machines were set up to produce a particular customer's product (usually instances in which a part was used as a subassembly), and demonstrations were run at production-line speeds. Customers reacted favorably to these demonstrations; usually they were strongly convinced that the company could satisfy most of their requirements. Demonstrations were supported with a comprehensive promotional program including movies, slides, product brochures, sales pamphlets, and research reports.

For customers not able to visit the demonstration room, Thompson-Robin provided similar information at each district sales office. Films, slides, and tapes highlighted product demonstrations. Exact scale models supplemented audio-visual presentations and provided prospects with clear ideas of company products and the marketing program.

Questions

1. Appraise the extent to which Arkho had succeeded in integrating Jay and Ellsworth's marketing operations into its organization. What problems remained?

2. Should Arkho have changed the salesmen's compensation plan?

3. Should the product managers have been added?

11-3

BENSON'S, INCORPORATED

Fruit Cake Manufacturer—
Changing the Marketing Program

Benson's, Incorporated, Athens, Georgia, organized initially as a regional bakery, eventually diversified and became a leading producer of fruitcake. Introduced in 1953, the fruitcakes were sold through civic clubs as fund raisers. While the company directed some sales effort toward other market segments, the bulk of its sales and the heart of the business remained the fund-raising market. Sales to this market segment were still increasing, but they had increased at a slower rate since 1967. Since that time, too, selling expenses and turnover of direct sales personnel had also increased. Profit margins had gradually declined, and management sought appropriate corrective measures. In late 1968 management focused its attention on the direct selling effort to civic clubs. Two major changes were planned for the 1969 Thanksgiving and Christmas selling seasons: (1) inauguration of an independent agent plan and (2) establishment of a national telephone selling system.

      The initial idea of catering to the fund-raising market had come from a local Junior Chamber of Commerce fund-raising campaign. This test program was highly successful, as the cakes proved easy to sell. The next year, in 1954, the fruitcake products were distributed through similar fund-raising drives elsewhere in Georgia and in South Carolina. Results continued to be encouraging, so the fruitcake phase of the business was expanded. Benson's Old Home Fruit Cake became a highly profitable item. The company reorganized in 1966 into a Bakery Division and an Old Home Kitchens Division, the latter having total responsibility for the fund-raising market (see Exhibit 1). By 1968 Old Home Kitchens' sales amounted to approximately $5 million.

EXHIBIT 1

Organization Chart: Benson's Old Home Kitchens

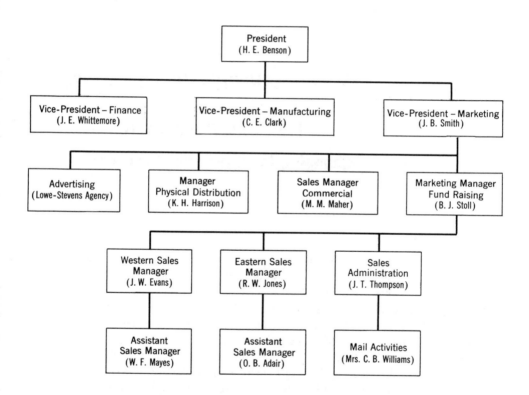

Benson's sold two products exclusively through civic clubs, the Old Home Fruit Cake and the Pecan Buttercake, introduced in 1967. Private-label fruitcakes were distributed by the commercial division through organizations such as grocery chains, large retail stores, and dairies. Old Home Fruit Cake (75 percent choice fruits and nuts and 25 percent pound cake batter) was a rectangular cake and was packaged in three sizes. Pecan Buttercake was a round pound cake with pecans, offered in one size (see Exhibit 2). These two items, comprising the entire product line in the fund-raising department, accounted for approximately 90 percent of the sales of the Old Home Kitchens Division.

EXHIBIT 2

Products

	Suggested Retail Price	*Approximate Price to Clubs*[a]
Old Home Fruit Cake		
Three-pound main seller	$3.50	$2.40
Two-pound cake	2.75	2.00
One-pound cake	2.00	1.40
Pecan Buttercake		
One-pound cake	1.50	1.00

[a]Freight prepaid east of Rockies. Bonus or quantity discount not included.

Distribution to the civic club market was through a field sales organization made up of area college students working during summer vacations. In the summer of 1968 fifty-two salesmen worked the forty-eight contiguous states. They were selected by the assistant sales managers and the marketing manager of the fund-raising division and were given one week of home office training before being assigned to territories. During the summer months they covered their territories, using company-leased cars and calling upon old accounts and new prospects. They submitted orders, weekly call reports, and expense accounts. Direct mail follow-up of calls by the home office was accomplished, and most orders came in during the early fall (since the civic clubs' selling season began in late October and early November). Salesmen received credit for orders if they had called on the accounts involved during the summer; however, commissions and bonuses were not paid until the end of the year.

Claxton Fruit Cake Company of Claxton, Georgia, provided intense fruitcake competition. The company used a similar price structure, had a good quality product, and sold through an agency civic club. Benson's, however, considered its product quality superior, its price more reasonable, and its total program unique. Competition for fund-raising dollars also included club promotions of other tangible products (such as candy, light bulbs, and brooms) and such service club functions as fashion shows and exhibition golf matches. Benson's emphasized value received by ultimate customers and per unit profit to club buyers. It assisted the clubs by providing advertising mats, display posters, sales organization kits, and sample slices of fruitcake.

EXHIBIT 3

Proposed Organization Changes—Fund-Raising Department

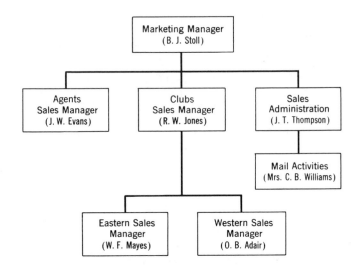

Most of the 1968 promotional budget, which amounted to 6 percent of sales, went to magazines and direct mail. Club magazines, such as *Kiwanian, Lion,* and *Rotarian,* dominated; however, popular magazines, such as *American Home, Family Circle,* and *McCall's,* were also used. Printed materials, brochures, display posters, sales kits, advertising mats, and sample slices accounted for the remaining promotional expenditure.

The changes planned for 1969 did not affect the commercial organization or bakery; they applied only to the fund-raising division. In early 1969 Benson's initiated the agent plan with a goal of establishing forty agents in major metropolitan areas. Agents were to operate, as had the college sales force, selling Benson's fund-raising products to civic organizations. Experienced men, those who had had similar selling jobs, were sought as full-time agents. Agents were to receive commissions on sales and expense allowances for samples and selling tools. They were to report to John Evans, the newly appointed manager, whose responsibility was to include agent selection, training, compensation, and supervision.

The other planned change was referred to as *phone power.* Southern Bell Telephone Company provided the company with a detailed plan, integrating the program into Benson's marketing system. Fifteen part-time employees, former college salesmen, were to call customers and prospects on Wide Area Telephone Service (WATS) lines. Plans specified that 80 percent of the telephone contacts were to be with 1968 customers and "dropouts" (those purchasing previously but not repeating in 1968). The remaining 20 percent would be WATS calls to clubs inquiring about Benson's program. "Cold calls" were not made. Customers and prospects were to be contacted sometime between 8:00 A.M. and 9:00 P.M. in their respective time zones. Management predicted that the cost of phone power would be lower than that of previous contact methods. Some reorganization seemed essential for full-scale implementation of the plan. (See Exhibit 3.)

Questions

1. What "business" was Benson's actually in?

2. Were the planned changes for 1969 in the fruitcake operation improvements?

3. What other improvements might have been considered?

11-4

NATIONAL STUDENT MARKETING SERVICE

Marketing Organization—

Campus Distribution System

National Student Marketing Service, Inc. (NSMS), of Washington, D.C., specialized in marketing to United States college and university campuses. NSMS sold a broad line, including a date-matching service, airline discount cards, magazines, paper dresses, record club memberships, and summer employment guides. Organized in 1964, NSMS's sales reached $1.5 million by the school year 1966-67. The company sold merchandise promoted through display posters on campuses and coupon handouts distributed in student mailboxes, dormitories, and fraternity and sorority houses, by direct mail, and through campus representatives and others. Several problems inherent in NSMS's unique marketing methods confronted management.

The company's early success was due mainly to its president, Cortes Randell. Once an engineer for General Electric, Randell developed the concept when later, as a class project at the University of Virginia's graduate school of business, he put together a summer employment guide. He test marketed the guide in 1963, and results proved so surprisingly successful that he decided to start a full-time business. NSMS was born, and in two and one-half years it became the largest firm of its kind in the country.

Randell decided that as his men traveled to colleges to tack up summer guide posters, they could also place similar posters for other products or services. Initially, he selected posters promoting "Operation Match" (computer dating) and American Airlines discount cards. Randell soon added posters for other products and actual sales of some, and his firm experienced phenomenal growth. One key to NSMS's success was Randell's ability to market the right product at the right time. For example, in 1967 he capitalized fully on the paper dress fad, using his widespread sales force to achieve rapid coverage of the entire college market.

Prior to the academic year 1967–68, NSMS employed a "skimming" strategy, covering only the larger schools. Randell arranged with three independent agents to do all the college posting; these agents hired students as helpers. Agents were paid 30 percent on sales and averaged four hundred to five hundred dollars per week in earned commissions. NSMS exercised very little control over the agents; however, Randell wanted to develop different marketing arrangements as the business grew, ones that would lend themselves to tighter control.

In 1967–68 Randell decided to expand by selling on all mainland United States college campuses. He divided the country into sixteen regions (Exhibit 1), hired sixteen full-time regional men, and placed them under a sales

EXHIBIT 1

Regional Territories

manager, Robert Harris. Territories differed in size according to the relative size of college populations. Management assumed that buying power would not differ significantly among schools; therefore, regional sales would be roughly equal. Regional men were paid a 20 percent commission on their sales up to quota; they were paid a 30 percent commission on *all* sales plus a bonus if they reached quota.

NSMS employed sixteen college students as fieldmen to assist the regional men during the peak selling period (August 21 to September 21). Fieldmen were paid a 20 percent commission on their sales. Regional men were not responsible for supervising the fieldmen but received a 50 percent override on fieldmen's sales. Marty Mackowski supervised the sixteen field salesmen from the central office.

A marketing conference in Washington started each new selling year with regional men and fieldmen in attendance. Here, management presented information about the company, its products, its markets, and its sales techniques. Minimum field training was provided at colleges in the Washington area. Management sought to achieve two training objectives: (1) to acquaint each salesman with his job and (2) to provide a high level of enthusiasm for NSMS's sales effort. Trainees were also taught how to assist in the managing of campus representatives (see Appendix A).

Trainees left Washington highly enthusiastic about their jobs, and market saturation became a key goal. However, by November 1967 sales were running below forecasts, and salesmen in some regions had reached only 20 percent of their quotas. Management put forth five reasons for the disappointing results: (1) forecasts had been based unduly on past experience, (2) as compared with initial posters, additional posters produced only a marginal effect on sales, (3) schools differed in available bulletin board space, (4) some states, for example, California, had passed regulations banning commercial notices on bulletin boards in public institutions, and (5) unrealistic sales quotas had been set.

Regional men, as full-time employees, were affected most by these conditions. They found their jobs lonely, since they lacked personal customer contact. Many considered the job tedious and of low status, and Harris predicted a 50 percent turnover among regional men for 1968–69. Although management began to give advances (drawing accounts) and started to use "fixed price" posters,[1] regional men were still unhappy with the time lag between poster placement and commission receipt.

Management, however, seemed pleased with the program, at least as it applied to the fieldmen. Mackowski planned to expand this phase to twenty men in 1968. Again, however, there were large earnings disparities among regions.

---

[1] Salesmen received a fixed amount of money for each poster placed.

Margo Lee, campus coordinator, managed the network of approximately three hundred representatives. She supervised the campus "reps" through monthly newsletters (see Appendix B). She planned to introduce a sales manual for campus reps during the 1968–69 selling year. Regional men acted as advisers and trainers to college representatives — meeting with them monthly.

Miss Lee used three methods for recruiting representatives: (1) job notices posted by regional men, (2) posters mailed to fraternities and sororities requesting aid in finding campus representation, and (3) volunteer applications from acquaintances of student reps. She screened applications, giving considerable weight to "past work experience," "spare time available," and "auto ownership."

Campus representatives received 20 percent commissions on sales; regional men also received a 50 percent override on sales by campus reps. Performance of campus reps varied greatly from one campus to another. The campus representative was "low man on the NSMS totem pole." He received NSMS materials after regional men and fieldmen had already worked on his campus. Competition developed between campus representatives and regional men and fieldmen; consequently, many representatives quickly became disillusioned with their jobs. In an effort to bolster representatives' morale and sales, Miss Lee designed a sales contest (see Appendix C).

Assuming that these difficulties could be ironed out, NSMS's future prospects appeared bright. Plans existed to expand the product offerings and to increase market coverage. Other plans included adding a chain of college book stores.

Questions

1. What accounted for NSMS's early success?

2. Evaluate NSMS's indoctrination training program for regional men and fieldmen.

3. What problems should NSMS have anticipated facing in the future?

4. What steps should have been taken by Randell to improve this operation?

Appendix A

NSMS College Marketing Conference Manual

TUESDAY, AUGUST 15
    Evening: Men arrive at Sheraton-Park

WEDNESDAY, AUGUST 16
    9:00   Welcome & Introductions
    9:15   History & Goals of NSMS
    10:00   Descriptions of Accounts
    11:00   Coffee Break
    11:15   Job Descriptions & Responsibilities
    12:15   Lunch
    1:30   General Sales Philosophy of NSMS
    2:00   Commissions
    2:30   Mike Michaelson, President—Franklin Square
    3:00   Coffee Break
    3:15   Sales Techniques I
    4:00   Coding, Inventory & EDP Reports
    4:30   Territories & Routing

    7:00-10:00   Territory routing (in rooms)

THURSDAY, AUGUST 17

9:00	Discuss Routings
9:15	Sales Techniques II
10:30	Coffee Break
10:45	Campus Rep Management
11:45	Stan Thomas, Director—College Bureau, Time Inc.
12:15	Lunch
1:15	Instructions for Field Training
1:30	Field Training
8:05	Senators vs. Indians, D.C. Stadium

FRIDAY, AUGUST 18

9:00	Review of Field Training
10:30	Coffee Break
10:45	Poster Display Advertising
11:15	Travel tips, Expenses
12:00	Lunch
1:00	Instructions for Field Training
1:15	Field Training
Evening:	OPEN

SATURDAY, AUGUST 19

10:00	Review of Field Training
11:00	Driving Safety Films
12:00	Lunch
1:00	Procedures; phoning, reporting, advances, problem situations
2:30	Group Discussion

SALES DISTRIBUTION METHODS

There are several distribution methods that must be employed for maximum penetration on a particular campus. The proper use of these methods will virtually guarantee a higher rate of return.

No one distribution method is the best. Each method has its time and place, but on almost every campus all methods can be used. This is called a distribution mix. There is a simple formula to follow:

Largest amount of material + best distribution mix = Most $$

It has been proven time and time again . . . . the man who distributes the most material will make the most money regardless of the territory in which he is working. There has never been a high sales territory; only a high sales representative. The distribution mix will give a good worker a big edge.

POSTERS   When circumstances permit, posters should be placed in every conceivable place that has student traffic on campus (hallways, stairwells, classrooms, near vending machines, bathrooms, lounges, libraries, student union, dining halls, gym, dorms, fraternities, sororities, outdoor bulletin boards, entrance doors to classrooms buildings, and any other places your "genius" may discover).

Placement is important. A poster placed in the center of a board will soon be covered or removed as other people fight for space. Posters should be stapled in the corners or around the edges so that half of the poster is off the edge. Edge hung posters take up less space, and are more visible. The staples can be driven into the wood so that it will be more secure. Be careful about placing posters too high on the board — will students be able to reach the coupons?

Many of the posters have Kleen-stick on the backs. These can be used in places where there are no boards such as stairwells. They can be used along side crowded boards. Don't waste them — use regular posters on bulletin boards.

PERSONAL DISTRIBUTION — HANDOUTS   Handouts get the material into the students' hands. No one can guarantee that a student will walk over to a poster and take one. Do the walking for him and give him one. When he's got it in his hand, the chances that he will buy are greatly improved. You can expect a 3 or 4 percent return as opposed to a 1 percent via posters.

It is best to hand out material to stationary students; those in lines, or seated in cafeterias, student unions, etc. They are more apt to read what you give them. Best items — Columbia/Record Club of America, Time/Newsweek, Franklin Square.

DORMITORIES   In addition to placing posters, material should be placed under dormitory doors. Best items — Columbia/RCOA, Time/Newsweek, Franklin Square. In girls' dorms, you may be able to get a girl to do it for you. If not, try to leave some at the desk.

DESKTOPS   This is one of the most effective methods of distribution. In most schools, classes don't start until 8 or 9 A.M. Get into classroom buildings by 7:30 and put material on every desk — one room Columbia/RCOA, next room Time/Newsweek, next room Franklin Square, and so on. Students welcome any excuse that will take their minds off what's being said by the professor. By the time they leave class, many of them will have filled out the return cards. While in classrooms, don't forget to put up posters.

Posters will stay up longer in classrooms, but don't put up more than 3 in any room — if you crowd the board, the professor may take them down. If there are no boards, put a Columbia or Franklin Square holder on the blackboard chalk tray in the corner near the door.

MAILBOXES   Always   ask   someone   where   the student mailboxes are. Many schools have open boxes which can be stuffed with material. Stay away from U.S. Post Offices — they won't let you in. In school mailrooms, the girls will usually let you stuff boxes — they may even help you. Always try to do it yourself because if you just leave a stack of material, it will usually get thrown away. Leave material at the mailroom only if you can't get in. If mailboxes are in the dorms, make sure you get them all.

CAMPUS REPRESENTATIVE MANAGEMENT

A large, active campus rep system is vital to the growth of NSMS as we move into the areas of marketing research, product testing, consumer surveying, sales promotion, and career employment recruiting.

Your responsibilities for campus reps lie in three major areas:

RECRUITING   Although we have recruited many campus reps, you should shoot for a campus rep on every significant campus (over 2500) in your territory. You will be supplied with recruiting posters and application forms. On large campuses (over 5000), personal recruiting would be time well-spent . . . remember for each $1.00 a rep earns, you get 50 cents . . . and a good rep can earn over $1000!

MOTIVATION   There are so many activities competing for a student's time, that he often puts NSMS pretty low on his priority list. He can't earn money for you or himself if he isn't getting that material out! Remind him that by spending a few extra hours a week he can take his girl out for dinner instead of for a coke. In addition, we will be sponsoring sales contests and incentive programs, offering records, radios, TV's, cash bonuses, and other great prizes!

SUPERVISION   There is only one way to make certain that a rep is covering a campus well . . . and that's by covering the campus yourself! Campus reps are not to be expected to saturate a campus; they are supplemental. They can bring in a lot of additional sales, but don't rely on them alone. There is no substitute for material which you personally distribute. You'll receive weekly sales reports for each rep, so you'll know exactly how well he's doing. You have the right to hire or fire a rep at any time, but we'll want to know why. A campus rep evaluation form must be filled out for each and every rep you visit. Your evaluation of the rep will be extremely important in our planning for marketing research programs.

PROCEDURES

REPORTING   The inventory Pick-Up Report should be filled out each time you visit a warehouse. Indicate the amounts and code numbers of the material you pick up. The report *must* be mailed the same day you pick up the materials.

The material distribution report must be completed for each campus you visit. Commission checks or advances will not be sent unless these are received *without* fail. These reports will provide information which the computer must have for the marketing penetration and marketing analysis reports. Also, these reports will help you to distribute your time more effectively among the various campuses in your territory.

All regional and field representatives should report in once a week by phone. Calls should be collect, station-to-station. Under no conditions will the company accept charges for more than two calls a week.

The Washington address may be used as a mailing address for personal mail; mail will be forwarded to you in the field via General Delivery.

FINANCIAL   NSMS will provide an advance draw of $125 a week. Money will be wired via Western Union when you report in by phone. Under *no* circumstances will a rep be advanced more than $125 a week. A receivables sheet will be kept on each rep who is advanced money. When commissions earned exceeds commissions advanced, rep will begin receiving regular commission checks.

EQUIPMENT

All representatives are supplied with the following items, which if lost will not be replaced by NSMS.

ARROW JT–21 STAPLE GUN   Always keep at least one carton of staples on hand (Arrow JT–21 5/16″ staples) at all times. Running out of staples in a small town can cost several hours of production time.

MATERIAL BAGS   These heavy duty bags will last for a full season. If they start to go, replace them *before* they do.

CLIPBOARDS   The best time to fill out material distribution reports is *immediately after finishing a campus.* A clipboard is easier to write on than a leg.

Appendix B

Excerpts from a Student Representative Newsletter

YOUR REGIONAL MANAGER

Your regional manager is one of sixteen full time road men who canvass all the schools in the country distributing NSMS materials where there is no Campus Representative. If, however, he does visit a campus where there is supposed to be a rep and he finds no materials displayed, he is instructed to cover the campus himself. Otherwise, he simply distributes materials of accounts that are not handled by the Campus Representative.

The regional manager is to serve as your advisor and to help you work out any problems that may arise. He is not in competition with you. You and your regional manager are to work together and be mutually beneficial to one another. He will contact you and meet with you at least once a month. You will find that your regional manager will become one of your very best aids in maximizing your commissions.

A WORD ABOUT COMPETITION

There will be occasions throughout the year in which you will encounter competition between our accounts and other similar operations.

Specifically be on the lookout for the National Directory Service out of Cincinnati, National Employer Directory Service out of San Antonio, Advertisement and Placement Institute out of Brooklyn and University Publications out of Denver.

The New England Subscription Service and Collegiate Advertising Limited handle Time, Record Club of America, Newsweek and Columbia Record Club (on the West Coast only). We do have agreements with them, however, to leave their material alone and, in turn, they will not bother *our* materials. Enclosed is an example of the subscription card. Please become familiar with it, so you will be able to abide by our agreement.

Appendix C

The Greed Game

O.K., Gang, it's time to announce the prizes for the NSMS 1967–68 Greed Game. The game is open to all NSMS Representatives who have demonstrated their inherent talents for making money.

To put it in simple terms, we're running a sales contest. Here's how it works:

We have divided all schools into five classifications based on student enrollment:

A	0-2,500
B	2,500-5,000
C	5,000-10,000
D	10,000-20,000
E	20,000 and above

If you cover more than one school, you are classified according to the total enrollment of all schools covered. There will be prizes in all categories.

For a start, we are awarding five *portable T.V.'s* to the top Rep in each classification. Runners-up will receive an *AM-FM portable radio*. These prizes will go to the Reps with the highest total sales in each classification as of April 30, 1968.

A TRIP FOR THE GREEDIEST OF THEM ALL

We will award a free trip to the top Rep in the country, based on a total sales ratio (total sales vs. number of students covered). We haven't decided where the trip will be yet, but we'll announce it in an upcoming newsletter. (How about a fabulous all expense paid trip to Muncie, Indiana?)

GREED OF THE MONTH CLUB

From now on we'll be running a monthly cash contest. The first contest will be announced shortly.

So, let's get moving! All Reps who have not demonstrated their greed will do so immediately. The more sales that you bring in, the more prizes we'll give out — sort of a profit sharing agreement. If you have any comments and/or ideas concerning the Greed Game, write to the Greed Game Advisor, C/O NSMS. GOOD LUCK!!!

THANK YOU

I want to thank all the Reps who were in Washington this Summer and who stopped by the office to visit. We loved having you and I enjoyed meeting you. I correspond with you all so regularly that it is great getting to know you. I hope that whenever you are in town you will make a point of coming by the office. You are always welcome.

Sincerely,

Margo Lee
Campus Coordinator

11-5

ROBIN AIR SERVICE

Fixed Base Operator—
Organizing and Coordinating Marketing
Activities

Robin Air Service, a fixed base operator located at the Humberg Airport in a large metropolitan city, sold and serviced business and private aircraft. Shortly after acquiring the company in 1965, D. A. Robin changed the name from Humberg Air Service to honor his father, John Robin, a well-known pioneer aviator. The company was almost bankrupt at the time, and its sales growth since had been erratic. Sales reached $950,000 in 1968, the highest on record, but D. A. Robin expressed concern over the inconsistent effort to increase sales and to actively solicit new customers. Chiefly because of a stringent financial situation, management directed its attention to strengthening the internal organization, to improving the quality of work, and to controlling costs.

     The Robin Company offered seven types of services to operators of business and private aircraft:

1. Maintenance and repair
2. Flight instruction and ground schools
3. Charter service and plane rentals

4. Radio equipment sales and service
5. New and used aircraft sales
6. Flight line sales and service: gasoline and oil, parking of aircraft, overnight tie-down space rental
7. Storage: hangar space rental and permanent outside tie-down space

The company was organized along product and service lines (Exhibit 1). It serviced and based planes ranging in size from one-place single-engine craft to large multi-engine converted military craft and business jets. Robin, as a Shell Oil dealer, purchased all its gasoline, kerosene, and oil from the local Shell distributor. It ordered repair parts directly from aircraft manufacturers and wholesalers, as it did not stock parts for resale. However, it did carry a small assortment of radio parts, although major components were procured from manufacturers.

EXHIBIT 1

Robin Air Service Organization Chart

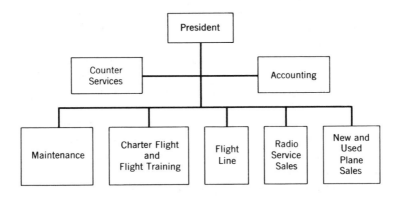

In 1968 the firm was not affiliated as a dealer or distributor for any aircraft maker, but management hoped to acquire a Beech dealership by 1970. Previously, in 1965, a Piper dealership had been dropped, and, in 1967, a Mooney dealership. Robin wanted to obtain the Beech dealership because the entire Beech line of planes related more closely to the business market segment than that of any other plane manufacturer. Planes assigned by Robin to its charter and flight instruction department were also available for sale as used aircraft. In addition, Robin listed for resale planes of other owners, receiving commissions on any resulting sales. As Robin was not currently a dealer or distributor, it had no new-plane inventory.

The company used a cost-plus pricing system, charging the cost of the product or service (including overhead expenses) and adding a fixed percentage for profit. Occasionally, the profit percentage was cut to meet competition, but D. A. Robin wished to compete mainly through superior service and work quality, not on a price basis. He was generally satisfied with the company's costing procedures, which indicated each sale's net margin, since, especially on small sales, using a full-cost or net profit approach could often result in the incurring of losses.

The metropolitan area housed three major airports, all sufficiently large and conveniently enough located to serve most needs of private business aircraft. D. A. Robin considered Humberg the best location, as it was closer to more large businesses, in an area of greater recent industrial expansion, and nearer residential areas where most pilots and aircraft owners resided. In addition, Humberg had special appeal for pilots of smaller aircraft, since all commercial air traffic used the municipal facility.

Each airport in "Metropolitan" housed two fixed base operators, all offering essentially identical services. D. A. Robin considered Executive Flight (also at Humberg) and Flight Service (at Municipal) his chief competitors; both were Cessna Aircraft dealers. Executive Flight's location, adjacent to the runway and visible to incoming pilots, was superior to Robin's.

D. A. Robin personally handled all sales and, in addition to serving as president, acted as new and used plane sales manager and flight line manager. Previously, these had been separate executive positions, but all had been vacant for nearly a year. Although Robin had not set departmental sales goals he believed such goals desirable. He also planned to set up a salesmanship training program for each department, since he believed that all employees should ultimately be involved in selling.

The company received a moderate number of complaints concerning flight line service and maintenance work. On occasion, maintenance work was not completed on schedule, as promised. D. A. Robin personally handled the more serious complaints.

Advertising was limited. In 1968 it consisted mainly of a monthly ad in *Southern Winds,* a magazine for regional, private aircraft owners. In addition, two direct-mail pieces were sent to all business jet and twin-engine owners in the United States. Listings also appeared in the metropolitan telephone directory, an expenditure considered essential because most new contacts traced to this source. D. A. Robin personally directed all advertising.

Question

How should Robin have gone about improving his company's operations, particularly in the marketing area?

BRUMFIELD PUMP WORKS

Pump Manufacturer—
Market Segmentation Strategy

Herbert Brumfield founded the Brumfield Pump Works in Cleveland, Ohio, in the early 1920s. Gear pumps of that era operated on the principle of trapping a liquid between two meshing gears and forcing it out. Brumfield observed this operation, noted the excessive wear, and invented a simpler, more efficient product — the sliding-vane pump. His pump employed a single rotor with a set of sliding vanes arranged so as to slide against the cylinder wall when under centrifugal force, thereby decreasing friction wear and increasing pump life. This innovation gave his company an initial competitive advantage, led to rapid growth, and established Brumfield Pump as an industry leader. Competitors, however, soon followed with their own versions of the sliding-vane pump. In 1966 Brumfield's major problem was that its cast-iron pumps competed increasingly with stainless-steel pumps for business.

Beginning in 1950 stainless-steel pumps made rapid inroads into the market, particularly in applications requiring certain specifications. For instance, the chemical industry wanted pumps capable of handling highly corrosive materials, and the food industry required pumps meeting high sanitary standards. Stainless-steel pumps could meet these specifications, whereas cast-iron pumps could not.

In initiating an effort not only to follow the two main competitors but to participate in what appeared to be a growing market, Brumfield asked all departments to submit plans for the company's entry into the stainless-steel pump field. The vice-president of engineering submitted product parameter requirements, describing competitors' models from an engineering and pricing viewpoint and including estimates on Brumfield's probable development and production costs for the industry's biggest volume product — a three-inch truck pump for liquid fertilizers. The vice-president of sales, noting that his department lacked market information, recommended a thorough study of the market for stainless-steel pumps.

Under its founder, the company had experienced moderate success, showing a loss only in 1932 — a depression year. Jacob Brumfield, the founder's son, became president in 1940, and under his leadership sales had grown steadily, reaching $5.7 million in 1965 and $6.8 million in 1966. Profits reached a new high of $680,000 in 1966.

Brumfield employed 350 workers in its modern plant in Cleveland. It used the latest machinery and production methods, having spent $1.5 million in 1964 for capital equipment and for thirty-five thousand square feet of additional manufacturing and administrative space. Two giant electric furnaces provided a steady supply of high-quality iron for molding and machining.

Although the Brumfield name was synonymous with high-quality rotary pumps, the company's prices on the cast-iron line were competitive. Management estimated that the industry priced stainless-steel pumps, on an average, 10 percent higher than cast-iron models. Brumfield enjoyed a high degree of brand loyalty among its customers, particularly those in the petroleum and chemical industries. Preference studies conducted by McGraw-Hill in 1966 on behalf of *National Petroleum News* showed that 41 percent of the potential users of truck pumps preferred Brumfield over its two major competitors, Squirt and Slushwell.

Brumfield made and marketed four lines of cast-iron pumps:

1. *Power pumps:* These were motor- or engine-driven pumps mounted on stationary bases. They had numerous applications in nearly every major industry handling liquids, ranging from paint and peanut butter to gasoline and glue.
2. *Truck pumps:* These were pumps for mounting on tank trucks, such as gasoline and fuel delivery trucks and large highway transports. Brumfield was the world's largest supplier of rotary truck pumps.
3. *LPG pumps:* Introduced by Brumfield in 1954, these pumps were designed for handling liquified gases such as butane, propane, and

EXHIBIT 1

Brumfield Pump Works: Company and Sales Organization

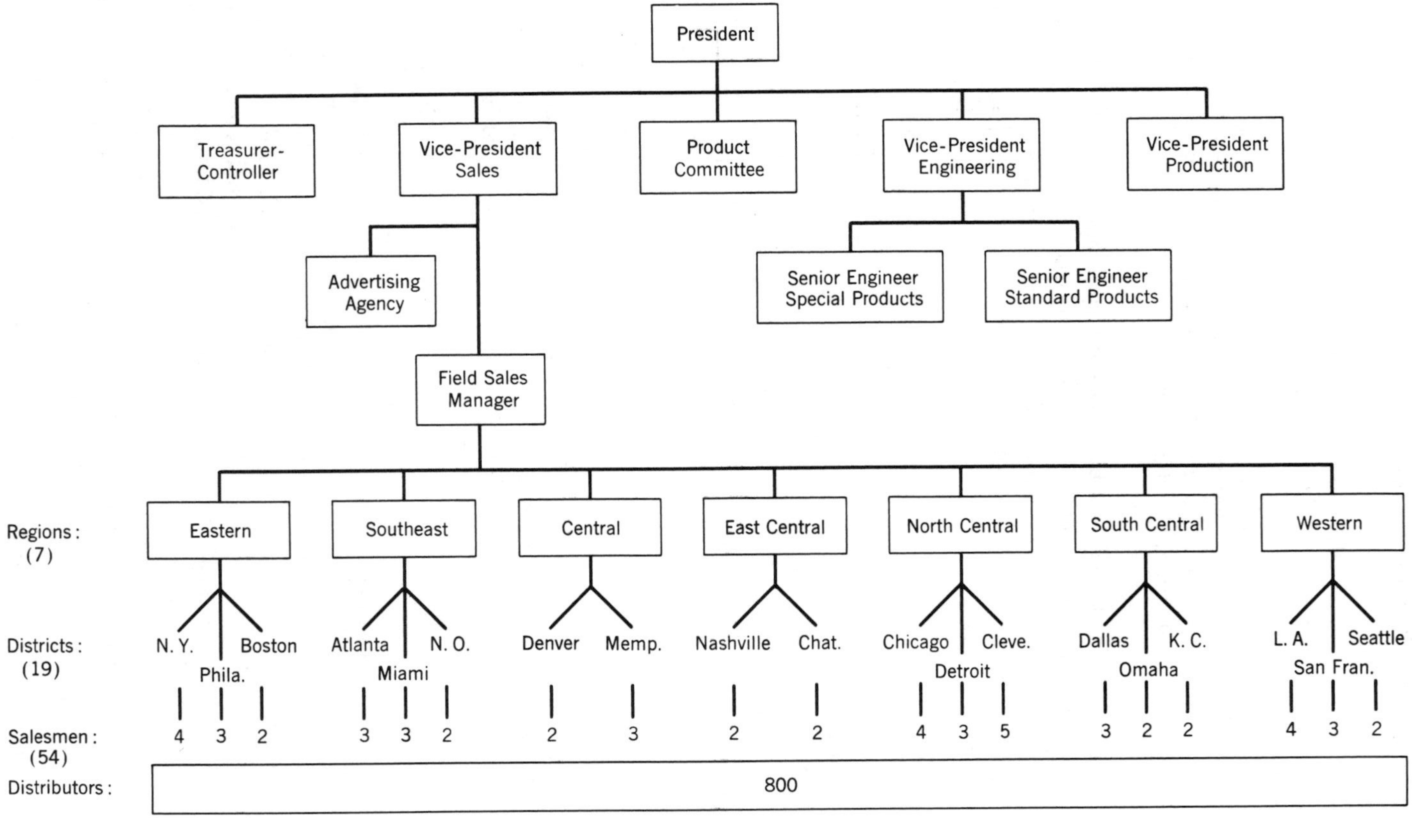

ammonia. This line included pumps for mounting on propane trucks used in residential delivery and for use as transfer pumps at bulk stations.

4. *Hand pumps:* This line consisted of hand-operated, barrel-mounted pumps used by industrial plants, building contractors, and farm operators for transferring small quantities of fuels, lubricants, and other fluids.

An analysis of the company's $6.8 million sales for 1966 revealed that power pumps accounted for 27 percent, truck pumps for 23 percent, hand pumps for 10 percent, LPG pumps for 9 percent, repair parts for 22 percent, and accessories and foundry castings for the remaining 9 percent. Sales by industry were:

	18 months ending 12/31/65	*12 months ending 12/31/66*
Food processing	7.2%	7.0%
Chemical processing	17.8	24.6
Petroleum	19.8	20.5
Nonmanufacturing	19.7	15.8
Machinery	19.2	16.4
Ships and boats	7.5	5.9
Miscellaneous manufacturing	8.8	9.8
	100%	100%

An analysis of 1966 *customers* revealed that 43 percent were in the petroleum industry, 25 percent were in general manufacturing, 16 percent were United States governmental agencies, 9 percent were in the LP gas industry, and 7 percent were foundry operators.

The sales organization, headed by Glen Martin, consisted of fifty-four salesmen who developed sales through more than eight hundred equipment distributors located throughout the country. Salesmen reported to nineteen district managers, who in turn reported to seven regional sales managers. Martin was both vice-president of sales and sales manager for the Central Region. He also coordinated and directed all aspects of Brumfield's overall marketing effort. The field sales force, under Bob Carter, operated in various ways to reach prospective buyers and to maximize sales coverage (see Exhibits 1-5).

Regional sales managers developed and supervised their respective territories, also performing engineering and field services. Regional and district managers received salaries and annual bonuses, which were based on sales over quota. Top management forecast sales, recommended quotas, and budgeted expense items. Controllable expenses became a base for further compensation; if

EXHIBIT 2

Brumfield Pump Works: Distribution System for Power Pumps

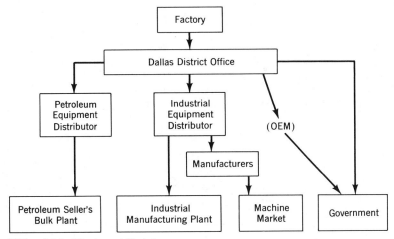

OEM = Original Equipment Market

EXHIBIT 3

Brumfield Pump Works: Distribution System for Truck Pumps

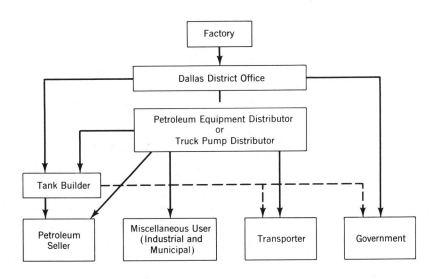

EXHIBIT 4

Brumfield Pump Works: Distribution System for LPG Pumps

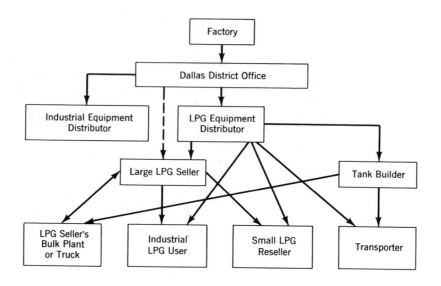

EXHIBIT 5

Brumfield Pump Works: Distribution System for Hand Pumps

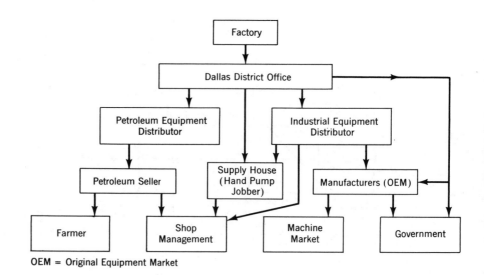

OEM = Original Equipment Market

a manager held such expenses under the budgeted amount, he received 50 percent of the saving. Conversely, if he exceeded the budget, 50 percent of the overage was deducted from his bonus.

Field salesmen received salaries and commissions. Commissions averaged 8 percent of sales. Salesmen paid their own expenses and submitted expense vouchers, and Brumfield reimbursed them monthly.

Salesmen submitted weekly call and expense reports. Reports of contact, "pink sheets," were submitted when salesmen uncovered unusual sales opportunities. "Blue sheets" represented requests for pump types not in the Brumfield line, but which salesmen felt would be logical additions. Each blue sheet named the customer and the desired pump specifications. Such specifications included size of pipes in the system, capacity of pumps (expressed in gallons per minute), differential pressure in the system, viscosities of the materials handled, and other properties of the liquid to be pumped. When blue sheets indicated a sufficient demand for a particular type of pump, Martin forwarded a report to the product committee and to Jacob Brumfield.

Authorized Brumfield distributors carried representative stocks and parts and employed crews trained in making pump installations. Distributors purchased the pumps for resale, not on consignment. Each distributor sold certain product types in an assigned area, usually specializing in one of the four pump lines.

A Cleveland advertising agency handled Brumfield's advertising and sales promotion. The company confined its advertising to trade publications and direct mail. Prime prospects for direct mail promotion were all contacts reported on pink sheets. The agency also performed some advertising research, but its efforts mainly reflected the results of published recognition and brand preference studies.

After 1957 the number of blue sheets and product requests from customers arriving at the home office multiplied greatly. More and more salesmen and factory-based engineers returned from the field with requests for items that the company did not make. The advertising agency reported that a 1963 study by McGraw-Hill for *Chemical Engineering* magazine indicated that over 50 percent of the rotary pumps being used in manufacturing plants were made of stainless steel. One chemical producer, with a pump maintenance budget of $.75 million, told Bob Carter, "in 1956, 85 percent of my pumps were cast iron, whereas in 1966, 50 percent are stainless steel." Two more major competitors had introduced stainless-steel pumps during 1966, and Jacob Brumfield appeared worried as he dictated a letter calling for a top management meeting to discuss market segmentation strategy.

Questions

1. Should Brumfield have introduced a line of stainless-steel pumps? Why? If so, as a part of which line(s)?

2. How might Brumfield have improved its marketing information system?

3. What recommendations would you have made to Brumfield concerning its market segmentation strategy?

LEARNING FOUNDATIONS INTERNATIONAL

Electronic Learning Centers—
Franchise Marketing

Learning Foundations International, an Athens, Georgia, firm founded in 1967, offered electronic learning for students and adults through a nationwide group of franchised electronic-learning centers. Management believed that its learning centers were not directly competitive with those of any other organization. By 1969 a total of twenty-one franchises had been granted, but Learning Foundations' advertising program, designed to bring in center business, was not producing desired results. Of the franchised centers, fourteen were operating profitably, and three of the other seven had not been open long enough to be in the black.

      Learning Foundations was established by Gary L. Pleger, an Athens attorney and business executive. An individual tutoring service, the program consisted of two parts: (1) initial testing of school age students, and (2) prescription of courses either for academic enrichment or for overcoming deficiencies in particular subject areas. The courses, all in programmed-instruction form, were presented through use of learning instruments. Pleger devised this instructional scheme in response to what he regarded as one of the nation's most pressing needs: the need for educational assistance, as a supplement to regular schooling, on an individual, self-paced basis at a cost most families could afford. Learning Foundations' catalog of courses contained over one hundred learning programs, embracing a fully integrated curriculum of basic school subjects, as well as career and industrial skills courses, such as foreign languages, typing, stenography, and executive development.

Pleger had recognized that in order to tap the widest possible market, tuition rates have to be considerably lower than those for traditional private tutoring. Although courses varied in length and, accordingly, varied in price, the average instructional rate was four dollars per hour. Management viewed this rate as considerably more attractive to prospective users than the six to fourteen dollars per hour rates it knew were being charged by conventional tutors. Executives stated that the instructional efficiency and effectiveness made possible by Learning Foundations' program cut the total cost to the student to about one-fourth the average cost of conventional tutoring.

In the Learning Foundations centers, each enrollee studied his course in a private, electronically equipped booth. Because of the intense concentration required, a maximum of two hours in any one day was the recommended learning period. Enrollees selected whatever time of day or night that best suited them. There were no formal classes; each student progressed individually, according to his ability.

The Learning Foundations standard for comprehension of course material was 90/90 (90 percent of the students would have to achieve 90 percent comprehension of each course's content). The courses were so constructed and pretested as to achieve this standard. Learning Foundations guaranteed to each student, at no additional cost, continuing study of the prescribed courses until the desired level of proficiency was attained.

The company had incorporated in its system a philanthropic policy, helping disadvantaged families and individuals to meet their educational needs. As a part of this policy, the company required all licensees to devote a minimum of 10 percent of their annual total hours of instruction to providing free scholarships to the disadvantaged. Thus, by providing electronic learning to the disadvantaged through free scholarships while administering the program for profit to those able to pay the usual rate, Learning Foundations combined philanthropy with profit making.

Learning Foundations had centers in eleven states, from Massachusetts to Washington, and in cities ranging from twenty-five thousand to over one million in population. All but four company-owned centers (in Atlanta and Athens, Georgia) were owned by licensees (franchisees). Initial licensees in cities that could accommodate more than one center were eligible to obtain the "distributorship" right to develop additional centers in their immediate areas. Center licensees could also secure distributorship rights for larger areas (such as for several counties); in such cases, they became responsible for establishing additional learning centers in their areas at a growth rate specified by Learning Foundations.

Pleger had chosen to develop the youth and family market segments first, although he also recognized promising market segments both in industry and in government. Although some centers were located in downtown or suburban office buildings, Learning Foundations favored shopping center locations. Most centers were near middle- or upper-income residential areas, since families living in such areas represented the market segments that, experience had shown, could most easily be developed.

Prior to April 1969 the consumer marketing program had been conducted on a trial-and-error basis without benefit of formal market research. Management had felt that the educational crisis in the schools was so widely recognized that a market survey was not as important as a strong franchise sales thrust and an aggressive advertising program. The franchise advertising campaign, in such media as *The Wall Street Journal, Business Week*, and *The National Observer*, had enabled the organization to grow to twenty-one centers by early 1969. The sales effort directed at securing licensees was considered satisfactory, and the company met its goal of "at least five new licensees a month."

The company's first mass media advertising was aimed at segmenting the potential market. The potential market included almost the entire population, since it included everything from preschool to adult education and offered career courses, industrial skills training, executive development programs, recreational skills courses, current events, and many others. In fact, this wide diversity of offerings was considered the company's major obstacle in building a strong advertising program.

Because the curriculum was so wide and varied, the first newspaper ads were aimed at such specialized market segments as those who wanted to learn typing, stenography, computer programming, and foreign languages, as well as at parents whose children needed to improve school grades. Separate ads were designed for each market segment. Response to these ads was disappointing, and the expense of running a wide variety of different ads in major metropolitan daily newspapers was so high that finally the many ads were consolidated into one ad featuring the skills and language courses. Although the new ad incorporated a coupon, prospect response was still discouraging.

Various other newspaper advertisements emphasizing a shift in product emphasis were also tried. The importance of the career programs — typing, shorthand, languages — was de-emphasized. More promotional effort was directed to the school-family market segment. One ad was designed to appeal to parents who had school-age children with "poor grades," this approach attracting somewhat greater response than other ads. Management, however, regarded the "poor grades" appeal as a negative approach, one that might create the image that Learning Foundations was a place where "losers" went to boost their grades.

The image Learning Foundations wanted to project was that the centers devoted their major resources to the development of superior minds. Several feature ads following the "superior mind" theme were prepared. These drew favorable comments from educators and others, but no new business could be traced to them. The "superior mind" ads were then offered to the licensees for experimental use in their areas.

To dramatize Learning Foundations as a resource for further development and intellectual enrichment of student "winners," management retained football star Fran Tarkenton as a national spokesman for the company. During his college career, Tarkenton had been named to the All-American team, as well as to the gridiron All-American team, a rare accomplishment. As a professional, he had distinguished himself as an outstanding player and had also been prominent in the development of VISTA (Volunteers in Service to America), the domestic version of the Peace Corps. He personified the young, clean-cut, "winners" image that Learning Foundations wanted to project.

Next, a series of ads and other promotional materials was produced around Tarkenton. Such headlines as "For Your Child Every Second Counts . . . says Fran Tarkenton, football great," were developed. Coupons were used, and larger-sized ads were placed in major metropolitan newspapers. These included photos of Tarkenton in action on the football field or working out at a Learning Foundations auto-tutor and a coupon for the reader's inquiry. Response improved, but management still did not regard it as satisfactory. Most business at the Atlanta and Athens centers as well as licensed centers around the country still came from personal contact work by the director or the licensee — speaking to civic and business organizations and to PTAs and other groups, and developing interest through promotion of the scholarship program.

Testimonial ads for print media and radio were then put together, using information from the success stories that were accumulating in company files. Newspaper ads featured pictures of individuals who had achieved success through Learning Foundations courses along with brief testimonials. Compared with earlier ads, without testimonials, these ads proved two to three times more effective in terms of producing responses in the test market — Atlanta. This improved response to the advertising encouraged management considerably.

Although management believed that the advertising phase of the marketing program had not been as productive as it could have been, most licensees had experienced profitable growth, were expanding their operations, and were aggressively promoting their business. Some licensees, however, who were not aggressively making personal contacts with business leaders, educational administrators, and other "influentials," had experienced poor sales and were pessimistic about the future.

Learning Foundations' prospects for growth were viewed as good by both its own executives and outside financial analysts. In early 1969 management budgeted seventy thousand dollars a year to provide additional supervision for licensees' operations. This meant that the initial investment for research and development would not be recouped as soon as had been anticipated.

Management negotiated for additional capital to strengthen the marketing program. Key points in the new marketing program included buying back those centers that were not performing satisfactorily, opening up company-owned centers in several major cities, and launching an extensive public relations program. Most of the new funds would be used to buy back "failures" and to open new company-owned centers.

The public relations director wanted market information that would be useful but inexpensive to collect. He drew up an extensive list of needed market information, preparing a proposal that would provide the data most essential to planning the next year's operations. He estimated that the market survey, if performed by an outside public relations or advertising agency, would cost from twenty-five thousand to thirty thousand dollars.

Questions

1. Appraise the overall marketing strategy of Learning Foundations and suggest how, if at all, it might have been improved.
2. What types of marketing information might have been useful to Learning Foundations? How and where could such information have been obtained?

11-8

THE COCA-COLA COMPANY

Soft Drink Marketer—Market Segmentation: A Systems Approach

An Atlanta, Georgia, pharmacist, John Pemberton, founded the Coca-Cola Company in 1886. Asa Candler bought the company in 1888 for twenty-three hundred dollars; eighty years later, in 1968, Coca-Cola employed 26,422 people and had assets of over $802 million. In mid-1969, Kelvin Wall, a Coca-Cola executive who had formerly been with *Ebony* magazine, proposed that the company concentrate on greater penetration of specific market segments to supplement its long-standing practice of blanket market coverage. He felt that the company especially needed to improve its effectiveness in marketing to low-income market segments. Using marketing research findings, Wall proposed a "systems approach" as a base for marketing to low-income neighborhoods.

BACKGROUND INFORMATION ON COMPANY MARKETING

Coca-Cola served the vast soft drink beverage market – a convenience goods market. Past marketing strategy was that of blanket saturation, emphasizing product availability and familiarity as motivating factors aimed at promoting impulse and habitual buying. Although the firm operated primarily in the soft drink market, it had acquired Minute Maid Corporation in 1960 and Duncan Food Company in 1964, merging them both into its Coca-Cola Company Foods Division.

The company made and sold syrups and concentrates for soft drink beverages and, through its food division, processed coffee, tea, and citrus products. Soft drinks were sold under the registered trademarks Coca-Cola and Coke, brand names Fresca, Sprite, and Tab, and a line of flavors called Fanta. Offerings in the food division included Maryland Club and Butternut ground and instant coffees, teas under private labels for food chains, and Minute Maid citrus products. In 1961 Coca-Cola, U.S.A., had offered 18 different products in one hundred different packages. By 1969 its divisions were marketing a total of 250 different products in five hundred different package sizes.

Company sales rose from $.55 billion in 1962 to $1.2 billion in 1968 (see Exhibit 1). Foreign operations accounted for about 45 percent of this volume. Bottlers and jobbers distributed soft drink syrup, with about 70 percent of domestic syrup sales going through some eleven hundred bottlers who prepared and sold soft drinks in exclusive territories. Bottlers reached the final consumer through sales forces totaling ten thousand men calling on more than 1.7 million retail outlets. The remaining syrup was sold through thirty-four

EXHIBIT 1

The Coca-Cola Company Sales, 1962-1968

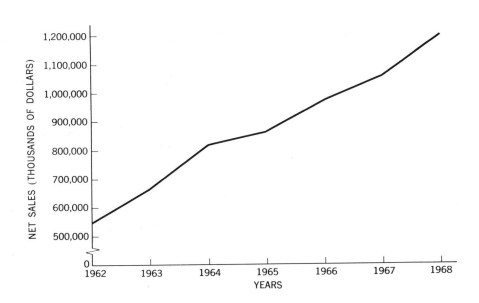

hundred jobbers and through thirteen thousand jobber salesmen who called on 175,000 retailers, primarily soda fountains (see Exhibit 2).

EXHIBIT 2

The Coca-Cola Company Distribution System

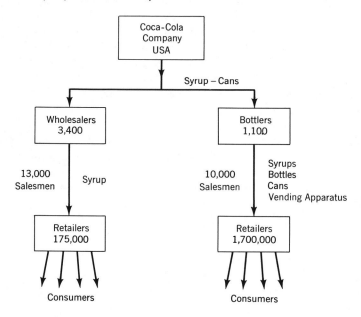

The bottlers' salesmen served as a base for plotting each succeeding year's marketing campaign. These men constantly checked merchandising conditions in the outlets they contacted. They received brief training, primarily of the on-the-job type, and afterward were assigned to routes. Bottler salesmen received straight commissions, a pay plan that management believed facilitated control. Bottler management watched the routes' sales, compared performance with past sales, coordinated promotion efforts, and otherwise maintained tight control. Corporate sales executives coordinated sales between the company, wholesalers, and bottlers.

Four major producers provided Coca-Cola with its soft drink competition: (1) Pepsi-Cola, (2) Dr. Pepper, (3) Royal Crown Cola, and (4) Canada Dry. Other soft drink competition came from private brands in food stores. Food manufacturers provided competition for Coca-Cola's food division. Price changes were infrequent; however, when made, they were substantial with regard to percentage, and all industry members tended to follow quickly.

The company spent large sums on advertising to maintain constant consumer contact and to encourage repeat sales. Its advertising saturated the environment and was a part of the life-style of most Americans. The advertising budget averaged from 5 to 8 percent of company net sales.

Coca-Cola's sales promotion department coordinated bottlers' local advertising and prepared their copy. The company's ad agency, McCann-Erickson, Inc., also assisted bottlers in formulating local sales strategy. The company paid a percentage of the costs of cooperative local advertising efforts. Bottlers paid a small portion of the cost of national advertising.

In its perception of the market, Coca-Cola's management attempted to "be all things to all people." The homogeneous market concept was evident from statements made by top management.

> Economists struggle with the shifting boundaries of class markets and mass markets, but for Coke there has always been just one market — the market, people everywhere.

> Thirsty humanity is the market today. Everywhere people are is an outlet for Coca-Cola.

> People of every race, creed, color, and economic status enjoy 'the pause that refreshes with ice cold Coke.'[1]

KELVIN WALL'S PROPOSAL

Kelvin Wall's proposal to management constituted a significant change in marketing strategy. Wall stated that "the synergistic effects of various marketing programs to low income consumers call not only for a different marketing mix but for a systems approach."[2] Low-income families were defined as those earning less than five thousand dollars annually. He estimated that 7 million white and 2 million black families made up this segment.

Wall noted that buying patterns of low-income families, although influenced by neighborhoods, also exhibited individualized influences. He considered life-styles an important marketing consideration and prepared a list of factors which he believed encouraged use of a systems approach (see Exhibit 3).[3] Patterns indicated in Exhibit 3, when interrelated with consumer behavior, were believed linked to several marketing activities including (1) distribution, (2)

---

[1] *The Refresher*, 75th Anniversary Edition (Atlanta: The Coca-Cola Company, 1961).

[2] Kelvin Wall, "Marketing to Low Income Neighborhoods: A Systems Approach" (paper presented to the American Marketing Association, Atlanta, Georgia, June 18, 1969).

[3] Ibid., p. 2.

merchandising, (3) product mix, (4) sales policies, (5) packaging mix, (6) advertising program, and (7) dealers relations activities. (See Exhibits 4 and 5.)

EXHIBIT 3

Factors Encouraging Use of a Systems Approach

1. Increased central city low-income population.
2. Low-income groups have experienced a greater increase in income than in their cost of living.
3. Their neighborhood stores primarily consist of small outlets. Consumers purchase frequently and in smaller units.
4. Life style of consumers is need-oriented, peer-directed, income-limited, mobility-inhibited, and isolated from the rest of the city.
5. Community organization exerts pressure for faster economic and social changes.
6. Low-income families are heavily concentrated by region and within the cities.
7. There is a unique communications network within the community or neighborhood.

EXHIBIT 4

A Systems View of Marketing in Low-Income Neighborhoods

Sociological-Economic Characteristics	*Marketing Implication*	*Marketing Function or Function Affecting Marketing*
Increase center city low-income population as middle-class out-migration continues.	Low-income segment more important to most major consumer goods marketers and in-city retailers.	Distribution/physical. Sales coverage. Advertising coverage. Product & package mix. Package size mix. Wholesaler/jobbers.
Greater increase in income of low-income group than cost of living.	This part of the total market will exercise more influence because of increased income and rapid population growth. Competition for their dollars will intensify.	New products. New outlets. Sales coverage. Distribution/physical. Product, package, package size mix. Advertising coverage.
Neighborhoods have small outlets. Consumers purchase smaller units.	Maximizing sales or profits requires different marketing and sales strategy because of different outlet mix and purchasing patterns.	Distribution/physical. Sales coverage. Dealer promotions. Product, package, package size mix. Sales promotion. Retail store audits.

Sociological-Economic Characteristics	Marketing Implication	Marketing Function or Function Affecting Marketing
Community organization. Pressure for social and faster economic changes.	Mass urban marketers, both retailers and manufacturers, will either respond to these pressures voluntarily or be forced to respond through direct economic action against them.	Product or service quality. Existing outlets. New outlets. Employment practices. Personnel training. Advertising content. Advertising media. Public relations. Sales promotions. Joint ventures. New distributors.
Life Style. Need-oriented. Peer-directed. Mobility-inhibited. Income-limited. Isolated from rest of city.	Both retailers and other marketers faced with wider differences in consumer motivations, and behavioral patterns between low-income consumers than with any other combination of income groups.	New products. Merchandising policies. Outlets – old and new. Copy platforms. Sales promotion. Fashion/styling/colors. Music. Advertising media. Retail store audit. Market research. Public relations. Distribution.
Low-income families. Heavily concentrated by region and within cities. — density increase with low-income — low-income whites — low-income blacks (Both important factors.)	The problems and the needs of low-income people are more similar than unique or distinct among subgroups. The amount of money they have to spend and their relationship with the total community are, in general, their two most important problems.	Sales promotion. Point-of-sales. Advertising media. Copy platform. Music. Package size. Product mix.
Communications. — neighborhood outlet — parts of communications network — conversation topics limited — how said as important as what is said — metaphoric and anecdotical — peer group network	Conventional media can and do bring messages into the low-income areas. But, these are considered messages from the "outside" and the impact is questionable since their form and language is not the group's own.	New media. New copy. Sales promotion. Point-of-sales. Music. Public relations. Outlets.

EXHIBIT 5

Residential Patterns for Whites and Blacks

| | Whites | | Blacks | |
	1960	*1970 (est.)*	*1960*	*1970 (est.)*
Central cities	48,800,000	46,800,000	9,800,000	12,100,000
Suburbs	55,700,000	74,400,000	2,900,000	4,400,000
Small towns and other nonfarm areas	42,500,000	49,400,000	4,600,000	5,100,000
Farms	11,800,000	7,800,000	1,500,000	1,100,000
TOTAL U.S.	158,800,000	178,400,000	18,800,000	22,700,000

Note: White Americans increased by 19.6 million, or 12.3%, in the 1960's, while Black Americans increased by 3.9 million, or 20.7%. Central cities lost an estimated 2 million whites and gained about 2.3 million blacks.
Source: For 1960, U.S. Census Bureau. For 1970, projections by *U.S. News & World Report* Economic Unit, based on census data.

As the low-income individual was immobile, he made small, frequent purchases. Wall suggested the importance of product delivery and of consumer acceptance of small retailers in low-income neighborhoods. Wall, a black himself, suggested that the black was particularly influenced in buying by company employment policies toward minority groups. He implied that advertising directed to low-income groups was more effective when oriented toward demonstration rather than verbalization. He believed that blacks responded more favorably to advertisements featuring blacks.

Wall ended his proposal to top management by reiterating the need for a systems approach for marketing to low-income segments by saying:

> Cultural and credibility gaps exist in low-income neighborhoods. Residents think in terms of "we" and "them," therefore successful marketers must translate this image. More marketing research should be directed to this segment, as many marketing executives do not understand the life styles of those in a class completely different from their own. Sound community relations, employment practices, and marketing programs are interrelated. Marketing success depends upon our understanding of this segment and upon the strength of small neighborhood retailers — particularly in the cities.[4]

[4] Ibid., Items i, ii, and iii.

Questions

1. Evaluate Wall's proposal for a systems approach for marketing Coke's soft drinks to the low-income market segment.

2. Income level appears to have been Wall's main criterion for market segmentation. Is income more important than social class membership in explaining consumer expenditures? Why?